DOUBLE VISIONS,
DOUBLE FICTIONS

Double Visions, Double Fictions

The Doppelgänger in
Japanese Film and Literature

BARYON TENSOR POSADAS

UNIVERSITY OF MINNESOTA PRESS

MINNEAPOLIS • LONDON

The University of Minnesota Press gratefully acknowledges the generous assistance provided for the publication of this book by the Asian Languages and Literatures, a department of the College of Liberal Arts at the University of Minnesota.

Portions of chapters 1 and 4 were previously published as "Rampo's Repetitions: The Doppelgänger in Edogawa Rampo and Tsukamoto Shin'ya," *Japan Forum* 21, no. 2 (2010): 161–82; available at http://www.tandfonline.com/doi/abs/ 10.1080/09555801003679074. An earlier version of chapter 5 was published as "Fantasies of the End of the World: The Politics of Repetition in the Films of Kurosawa Kiyoshi," *positions: asia critique* 22, no. 2 (2014): 429–60; reprinted by permission of the publisher, Duke University Press.

Published by the University of Minnesota Press
111 Third Avenue South, Suite 290
Minneapolis, MN 55401-2520
http://www.upress.umn.edu

ISBN 978-1-5179-0262-9 (hc)
ISBN 978-1-5179-0263-6 (pb)

A Cataloging-in-Publication record for this book is available from the Library of Congress.

CONTENTS

A Strange Mirror

The Doppelgänger in Japan

Recurrences of the Doppelgänger

The myriad manifestations of the motif of a haunting encounter with one's own double, which often foretells one's doom—the motif of seeing one's so-called doppelgänger, in other words—have made appearances in a wide range of literary and cinematic traditions. Subsumed under its name is a constellation of interlinked images—everything from look-alikes, psychological projections, evil twins, alter egos, genetic clones, perfect disguises, disembodied souls and shadows, and others—all of which involve the idea of an interplay between identity and difference. These repeated recurrences of the figure have led to its being variously understood as an illustration of psychoanalytic concepts like narcissism or the uncanny, as modernist expressions of the fragmentation of the subject engendered by the historical experience of rapid modernization and cultural transformation, or as an embodiment of a fantastic or monstrous alterity.

The earliest known use of the word "Doppelgänger" (lit. double-walker) is usually credited to German Romantic author Jean Paul (born Johann Paul Friedrich Richter, 1763–1825), who refers to the concept in his novel *Siebenkäs* (1796–97). The novel tells the story of two friends—Siebenkäs and Liebgeber—so identical in appearance that they are able to switch identities, fake deaths, and take over one another's lives.[1] Tellingly, when the writer first introduces the term, he glosses it in a footnote that defines *Doppelgänger* with the words "so people who see themselves are called" [*So heissen Leute, die sich selbst sehen*], indicating the concept's novelty to readers at the time. Since then, the motif of doubling has become familiar through its recurrence in all manner of other texts, exhibiting an imaginative mutability that has allowed it to traverse easily the territories of different genres, cultures, and media. From its beginnings in German Romanticism, the doppelgänger returns in the Gothic tradition, manifesting as the repeated hauntings of a murdered count whose identity is stolen in E. T. A. Hoffmann's (1776–1822) *Die Elixiere des Teufels* (*The Devil's Elixirs*, 1815), or the titular rival with the same name as the protagonist in Edgar Allan Poe's (1809–1849) "William Wilson" (1839), or the murderous alter-ego in Robert Louis Stevenson's (1850–1894) *The Strange Case of Dr. Jekyll and Mr. Hyde* (1886), along with many other examples. From there, its travels continue, making further appearances in countless other writings in such genres as metaphysical detective fiction, science fiction, and body horror.

The doppelgänger has also crossed cultural and historical boundaries, making its presence felt not only in Euro-American films and fictions, but also in the Japanese literary and cinematic landscape in the form of translations of works from elsewhere, as well as the writings of Japanese authors themselves. Its arrival in Japan traces back to the year 1902, which saw the publication of Mori Ōgai's (1862–1922) Japanese translation of Heinrich Heine's poem "Der Doppelgänger" (The doppelgänger, 1827) in the magazine *Geibun*.[2] Heine's poem itself is not particularly remarkable within the context of the larger corpus of works about the doppelgänger, simply depicting its protagonist's brief encounter with his double before a lover's old house. However, the significance of Ōgai's translation can be located in his rendering of the poem's title as "bunshin" (lit. split-body), which may very well be one of the earliest examples of the use of the term *bunshin* as the Japanese rendering of the German *Doppelgänger*. In the ensuing decades since this initial appearance of the term, "bunshin" would become the standard translation in Japan to refer to the popular literary motif of an encounter with one's identical double or second self.[3] Ōgai thus introduced not only one of the earliest examples of European doppelgänger stories to appear in translation in Japan, but also the very language and terminology to articulate the concept.

Subsequent to his translation of Heine's "Der Doppelgänger," Ōgai revisited the figure in one of his own works of fiction. His "Fushigi na kagami" (A strange mirror, 1912) tells the story of a man who splits into two distinct entities. The short yet meandering story begins with scenes of a married couple arguing about their household finances. In the midst of one of their discussions, the husband experiences a strange sensation of seemingly detaching from his body. Describing the feeling as something "akin to iron being drawn by a magnet" [*tatoeba jishaku ni tetsu ga suiyoseraru yō ni*], the narrator finds his soul separated from his body.[4] While his body remains seated at the table mumbling responses to his wife, like an invisible shadow his soul stands apart and observes with bemusement. The story then takes a further turn to the absurd when the narrator's soul is yet again drawn by the same magnetic force, which pulls him across the city, until he ends up being absorbed into a large mirror standing in the middle of a stage inside a mansion.

Although few would consider "A Strange Mirror" itself a major work within Ōgai's oeuvre, it is nonetheless noteworthy for other reasons, namely, for prefiguring and preparing the ground for an unprecedented storm of fictions of the doppelgänger that would burst upon the Japanese literary landscape at the beginning of the Taisho period (1912–1926). Tellingly, the term *bunshin* does not at any point appear in the body text of Ōgai's short story. Instead, the author opts for more generic terms such as "soul" [*tamashii*] or "shadow" [*kage*] to describe the narrator's double. Yet, the theme of doubling was more explicitly named when the story was republished as a part of a collection of Ōgai's short fiction titled *Sōmatō/bunshin* (Revolving lantern and doubles, 1914). One possible explanation for this explicit naming of the motif in its reprinting is the appearance of several Japanese translations of doppelgänger fictions in the intervening years, among which were Edgar Allan Poe's "William Wilson" (1839) and Oscar Wilde's *The Picture of Dorian Gray* (1890) in 1913, not to mention the release of an early doppelgänger film, Stellan Rye and Hanns Heinz Ewers's *Der Student von Prag* (*The Student of Prague*, 1913) in 1914, among many others.[5] Put simply, the beginning of the Taisho period marked the moment of the popularization of the concept of the doppelgänger, leading to the retroactive identification of Ōgai's work with this theme.

In the wake of Ōgai's early experiments with the figure of the doppelgänger, numerous doppelgänger fictions by Japanese authors soon followed, proliferating especially during the 1920s and 1930s.[6] Against the
backdrop of a pervading sense of crisis and dislocation brought about by
rapid urbanization, imperial consolidation, and the restructuring of all
aspects of everyday life by a burgeoning image-commodity system, a generation of authors would repeatedly make use of the motif in their fictions.
Edogawa Rampo (1894–1965) and Kozakai Fuboku (1890–1929) both employed the figure's embodiment of multiple identities as tricks and plot
devices in their detective stories several times; Akutagawa Ryūnosuke
(1892–1927), Satō Haruo (1892–1964), and Kajii Motojirō (1901–1932) all
made use of the motif in their respective writings for the purpose of representing psychical fragmentation and breakdown; Tanizaki Jun'ichirō
(1886–1965) depicted images of the doubling or splitting of the self to
articulate anxieties vis-à-vis the construction of racial and colonial identities. Indeed, the doppelgänger's recurrent appearances during this historical period were sufficiently notable that a number of critics have
identified the motif (and the theme of the fragmented self in crisis, more
generally) as one of the defining features of the literature of the 1920s and
1930s in Japan.[7]

However, the story of the doppelgänger's repeated returns does not
end here. Several decades after the publication of Ōgai's short story and
the ensuing popularization of the figure during the 1920s and 1930s,
another wave of interest in the doppelgänger appeared in more recent
years as well. Since the 1980s and into the present, the motif again proliferates in as wide a range of texts as, for example, various anthologies of
doppelgänger fictions; the surreal and fantastic novels of authors such as
Abe Kōbō (1924–1993), Murakami Haruki (b. 1948), Shimada Masahiko
(b. 1961), and Tsutsui Yasutaka (b. 1934); films that include Suzuki Seijun's
(b. 1923) avant-garde neo-erotic-grotesque "Taisho Trilogy" of *Tsigoineru-*
waizen (*Zigeunerweisen*, 1980), *Kagero-za* (*Heat-Haze Theater*, 1981), and
Yumeji (1991), Iwai Shunji's (b. 1963) more romantic treatment in *Love*
Letter (1995), Kurosawa Kiyoshi's (b. 1955) genre-crossing *Dopperugengā*
(*Doppelgänger*, 2003) and *Sakebi* (*Retribution*, 2006), or Kitano Takeshi's
self-referential doubling in *Takeshis'* (2005). Further examples of appearances of the doppelgänger or other related motifs such as clones, magical

twins, and dolls abound in other popular cultural forms like anime and manga, not to mention the multiple film and other media adaptations of prewar doppelgänger fictions by authors such as Edogawa Rampo. Indeed, I would argue that much like the earlier flourishing of the 1920s, there is again a veritable proliferation of the doppelgänger in the literary and cultural discourses at the end of the twentieth century, all of which form a part of what Marilyn Ivy has discussed as a neo-nostalgic retro-boom of interest in the historical period prior to the Second World War in Japan, commodifying and repackaging the aesthetics of the mass culture of the 1920s and 1930s not just in literature or film, but in other areas including tourism, theater, and cultural studies more broadly.[8]

Double Visions, Double Fictions examines the material and social conditions instrumental for the recurrence of the figure of the doppelgänger in Japanese literary and cinematic texts at these two particular historical conjunctures. It is premised on understanding that the doppelgänger's significance lies not only in its function as a literary device, but more importantly, in its capacity to open up a critical practice of concepts, an optic for the examination of the assemblage of technologies and discourses that the figure's historical emergence brings to attention. As the following pages will show, what is most significant about the doppelgänger's manifestations in Japanese films and fictions is how it occupies the point of intersection of several topics that have received substantial scholarly attention within the field of Japanese studies in recent years, namely the historical impact of the dissemination of psychoanalytic theory, the emergence of the genre of detective fiction, the development of early cinematic technologies, and the expansion of Japan's colonial empire. A sustained attention to the figure therefore allows for working across these subjects, thus opening up the field of analysis informed by critical theory, popular culture, visual studies, and postcolonial discourse, not as separate domains, but instead as interlinked areas of concern.

Psychoanalysis, History, and the Doppelgänger

What, precisely, is the doppelgänger? Although the study of the doppelgänger as a literary motif is not unprecedented, perhaps as a consequence of its mutability and multiple appearances, fixing a definition to the doppelgänger beyond a broad description of its characteristics has been a

notoriously difficult and much contested endeavor. A number of critics—
C. F. Keppler and Tony Fonseca, for instance—have lamented the em-
barrassing murkiness of the concept. Fonseca wonders if "perhaps the
doppelgänger was destined to vagueness, given the number and variety
of Romantic authors, German, Russian, and American, who took Jean
Paul's simple phrase and created their own versions."[9] Likewise, Keppler
even goes so far as to write that "[I] did not really know what I meant by
'Double,'" that he has been "sliding about haphazardly between notions
that were far from identical with one another."[10] Yet, despite this purported vagueness to the concept, there has certainly been no lack in efforts
to fix a definition to the doppelgänger. As the existence of the several
previous studies of the motif attest, numerous attempts have been made
to discern the double and seek the origins of its appearances. For example, Ralph Tymms describes the figure as "a figment of the mind, to which
one attributes the promptings of the unconscious self, now dissociated
from the conscious personality."[11] In a similar vein, Robert Rogers presents the doppelgänger as a representation of unconscious drives and as
the embodiment of "essentially intrapsychic or endopsychic" struggles.[12]
More recently, John Herdman has suggested that "the Doppelgänger is a
second self, or *alter ego*, which appears as a distinct and separate being . . .
but exists in a dependent relation to the original."[13]

Specific differences in the details of these definitions aside, one notable common thread in much of existing scholarship on the doppelgänger
is that, for the most part, studies of the figure make use of a decidedly
psychoanalytic frame of analysis. Indeed, the impact of psychoanalysis
on the discourse about the doppelgänger motif is difficult to overstate,
with Clifford Hallam going so far as to assert that "any Double figure in
prose fiction which can be explained by anthropology (including folklore), spurious scientific theories, philosophy, or some other system, can
in most cases be understood more fully, more clearly, and, in crucial ways,
more convincingly by depth psychology."[14] Given how the figure of the
double makes itself readily readable in terms of a range of psychoanalytic
concepts—be it narcissism, or the mirror stage, or split subjectivity or
the uncanny, or the compulsion to repeat, or projection, et cetera—this
is perhaps not all that surprising. After all, psychoanalytic approaches to
the doppelgänger go back to some of its earliest critical articulation in the

early twentieth century. In his famous discussion of E. T. A. Hoffmann's "Der Sandmann" ("The Sandman," 1816), Sigmund Freud references the doppelgänger as an emblematic figure for his influential concept of "the uncanny" (*unheimlich*—literally, unhomelike). The uncanny describes the experience wherein something encountered is simultaneously hauntingly beautiful and terrifying, that is, at once familiar and alien. For Freud, this is an effect that is produced when that "which is familiar and old-established in the mind and which has become alienated from it only through the process of repression" subsequently returns to disturb the present.[15] The doppelgänger can be understood as enacting the return of a repressed childhood narcissism, "a regression to a time when the ego had not yet marked itself off sharply from the external world and from other people."[16]

Freud, though, was not the first to take up the doppelgänger as a psychoanalytic object of inquiry. Credit for this must go to a one-time colleague of Freud's, Otto Rank, whose book *Der Doppelgänger* (*The Double*, 1925, trans. 1971) is widely regarded as the pioneering examination of the figure.[17] In several respects, *The Double* set the stage for the subsequent research. In fact, Rank's characterization of the figure as emblematic of the concept of narcissism—or more accurately as a kind of defensive response against narcissism—is precisely what Freud elaborates upon in his discussion of the uncanny. In Rank's analysis, if narcissism can be understood as a form of "pathological self-love," then what the doppelgänger represents is not an original childhood narcissism itself, but rather its excess, which returns from its repression in an inverted "defensive form of the pathological fear of one's self, often leading to paranoid insanity and appearing personified in the pursuing shadow, mirror-image, or double" in an attempt to discharge or disavow it.[18] It is thus perceived as uncanny not in spite of but precisely because of its similitude to the image of oneself.

Strictly speaking, Rank's project is not a literary study of the doppelgänger. Although he does take up literary texts and authors as case studies for the doppelgänger's manifestations, the psychoanalytic frame he deploys is unconcerned with questions of literature per se. Instead, the doppelgängers that appear in the literary texts that he examines are in large part utilized as evidence of his assertion that the authors he discusses were subject to "psychic disturbances or neurological and mental illnesses and during their lifetime they demonstrated a marked eccentricity in behavior."[19] Rank does not end his discussion on this point, however. He further builds upon literary examples by delving into representations of the doppelgänger in myth and folklore so as to show "the common psychological basis of the superstitious and artistic representations of these impulses."[20] Put differently, Rank uses literature as a starting point, only to delve into the figure's earlier manifestations in so-called "primitive" culture as a point of contrast to its ostensibly modern psychological form. He then suggests that the latter (and its association with foretelling imminent death) is an inversion of an earlier understanding of the double as representing an immortal soul or a ward *against* death. With this move, Rank extends the understanding of the doppelgänger as a manifestation of a return of the repressed to give it a historical dimension as well. Just as the doppelgänger's uncanny effect is the product of the familiar returning in alien form, its modern form is the primitive double turned alien and threatening. As such, despite its employment of discredited approaches such as armchair anthropology and the psychoanalytic diagnoses of absent authors, Rank's study is nonetheless noteworthy for its recognition that the key feature that differentiates the double from other literary motifs rooted in the supernatural is its underpinnings within a modern conception of subjectivity.

Despite this existing critical context, to simply adopt a psychoanalytic framework in reading the doppelgänger runs the risk of privileging psychoanalysis as a metalanguage or an ahistorical interpretative scheme. Reading the doppelgänger as a figuration of psychoanalytic concepts presupposes the a priori existence of a category that is both stable and ahistorical, outside of its literary or discursive representations. Instead, I believe that a more productive exercise would be to track down the discursive work of psychoanalysis in constructing the doppelgänger as an object of knowledge. If the incessant attempts at defining the doppelgänger noted above are any indication, they illustrate precisely how the figure of the doppelgänger is under discursive contestation, regularly defined and redefined yet at once persistently resisting and exceeding attempts at its definition. Privileging the psychoanalytic model of the doppelgänger obfuscates these contestations and the recognition of how, in the words of Michel Foucault, discourses do not merely designate pre-existing objects, but are instead "practices that systematically form the objects of which they speak."[21] Psychoanalysis is not merely an interpretative scheme that provides a means through which the figure of the doppelgänger in literary texts can be examined and apprehended. Rather, such a schema produces the doppelgänger as a legible figure within particular discursive regimes. In other words, psychoanalysis does not so much provide a means of illuminating the doppelgänger as contain the doppelgänger within a specifically modern logic of subject formation, as even Rank himself appears to recognize when he distinguishes between mythic and modern versions of the doppelgänger. Thus, without dismissing the potential theoretical insights of psychoanalytic categories of analysis, I believe that the challenge here is to map out the *historical* unconscious of the doppelgänger—or, as Jameson once put it, "radically to historicize Freudianism itself, and to reach a reflexive vantage point from which the historical and social conditions of possibility both of Freudian method and of its objects of study came into view."[22]

In this effort, I pick up from a brief observation about the doppelgänger that Tzvetan Todorov makes in his discussion of the genre of the fantastic. Pointing to Rank's study of the doppelgänger motif as a key example, he suggests that the doppelgänger serves as an example of how "psychoanalysis has replaced (and thereby made useless) the literature of the fantastic."[23] What Todorov highlights here is a coincidence in the themes of the literary fantastic (in which he includes fictions of the doppelgänger) and psychoanalytic objects of analysis, indeed suggesting that the functions of the literary fantastic and psychoanalysis—which is the opening up of a discursive space to articulate social taboos—are largely identical. Of course, Todorov may very well overstate his claim here. As a case in point, Andrew Webber has rightly pointed to the continued proliferation of literary representations of the doppelgänger since the coming into being of psychoanalysis as a counterpoint to Todorov's contention, writing that "the literary double is a stubborn revenant and duly returns after the event of Rank's essay, where it arguably eludes the exorcism of comprehensive analysis anyhow."[24] However accurate Webber's point about the prematurity of Todorov's proclamation of the death or obsolescence of the fantastic, there is another implication that can be drawn from his analysis. In positing the argument that psychoanalysis takes over the themes of fantastic literature, Todorov refuses to privilege psychoanalysis as a metalanguage. Instead, he places it side by side with the literature of the fantastic as a coequal discourse that similarly exhibits an obsession with seamless causality and a pattern of equilibrium to disequilibrium and back to equilibrium in its narrative structure.[25]

With this in mind, in place of employing psychoanalytic approaches in an attempt to trace the figure's origins and to fix, to distill, to literally de-fine (to set finite boundaries to) the doppelgänger into an ahistorical essence whose origins lie in the depths of the psyche, I locate the significance of psychoanalytic theorizations of the doppelgänger in their role in proliferating the figure by way of its consolidation into what Lawrence Grossberg has called "a cultural formation."[26] It is not through the identification of some essential point of origin that the figure of the doppelgänger becomes meaningful, but precisely through its recurrence, for only in its repetition does the doppelgänger emerge as a motif that signifies, only in its repetition do individual texts form a relation to a broader set of texts whose members bear resemblance with one another. Insofar as one accepts that there is a *perceived* relation among the disparate texts from disparate locations in which the motif appears, it is arguably through these psychoanalytic approaches to the doppelgänger that these texts have been placed into relation with one another, forming out of them a coherent object of discourse, which is then referenced by subsequent texts that appear, thus further consolidating the concept and its associated narrative devices and motifs. Put differently, psychoanalysis plays a crucial part in the initial constitution of the doppelgänger as a body of intertextual exchange, as something akin to a genre of film and fiction.

In calling the doppelgänger a genre (however narrowly and informally constituted), my approach here is indebted to Mizuno Rei's meta-analysis of the existing discourses on the doppelgänger. She notes that despite multiple distinct manifestations—not to mention the often conflicting and contradictory definitions of the figure offered—certain texts are nonetheless consistently classified under the name "doppelgänger." Mizuno thus rightly contends that the doppelgänger as a category is not reducible to a singular motif or image, but an assemblage of thematic resemblances, in other words, a genre.[27] Differing from Mizuno, though, I am less concerned with mapping out the generic boundaries of the discursive terrain of the doppelgänger. My understanding of genre is not as a static classificatory category based on common intrinsic aesthetic traits that can be logically identified and demarcated. Rather, I follow Ralph Cohen in apprehending genres as "open systems . . . groupings of texts by critics to fulfill certain ends."[28] Key to Cohen's understanding of genre is the recognition that they are discursive *processes* that function to govern the limits and possibilities of meaning production in texts. They are, in this sense, not natural systems but social institutions that are in history, and as such, are constantly under negotiation not only as texts identified as members in a given genre accrue, but, moreover, through the very performance of definition and classification. In other words, I treat "the doppelgänger" as a marker of historically situated discursive procedures of attribution for the purpose of negotiating the practices of organization, distribution, and reception of texts all in the interests of bringing into focus the common cultural logic of the doppelgänger, that is, how each work of doppelgänger fiction relates to another within and across geographical locations and historical moments, not to mention the social and historical forces that undergird their appearances.

Another Origin, or the Doppelgänger in Japan

This challenge of historicizing the doppelgänger's emergence as a concept within the discourse of psychoanalysis is perhaps even more salient when situated within the context of its dissemination in Japan. Given the German origins of the very word *Doppelgänger*, thus appearing to mark it off as a foreign concept, it would be all too easy to frame the analysis of the doppelgänger in terms of its cultural particularity, as a Japanese variation of an already established concept from elsewhere. Certainly, the impact of the abundant translations of European and American doppelgänger films and fictions cannot be discounted outright, and acknowledging these influences allows for the recognition of Japan's positioning within a larger global context of transnational conversations about literary concepts, movements, genres, and narrative devices, among which the doppelgänger motif is but one. Nonetheless, reading the doppelgänger in Japanese texts primarily in these terms of influence provides only a partial explanation. Even as it points out *what* sources authors of fictions of the doppelgänger in Japan drew from, it does not account for *why* the doppelgänger motif found popular appeal among these authors, and presumably their reading publics, during these historical conjunctures in the first place.

As I highlighted above, the appearances of the figure in Japanese texts tend to recur at historically specific conjunctures, namely the interwar period on the one hand, and the contemporary conjuncture on the other hand. Although the translation of doppelgänger fictions from elsewhere introduced the concept to Japanese authors, this introduction does not in itself explain the historical specificity of the motif's recurrences during the Taisho and early Showa periods. In order to account for this, it is also necessary to consider the existing social and material conditions that made the doppelgänger a meaningful signifier to a Japanese audience, so as to enable its formation as a coherent concept and literary motif at the particular historical moments in question. The effective translation and popularization of the doppelgänger motif into the Japanese context is a consequence of its parallel (yet nonetheless locally distinct) historical experience of the processes of modernization, rapid urban development, imperial consolidation, and the rise of mass cultural forms formative of the development of the German and Anglo-American Gothic traditions out of which the figure of the doppelgänger emerged. Only when a similar constellation of historical conditions had come into alignment could the doppelgänger become a viable cultural formation. It is therefore necessary to reframe the analysis, to account for these larger social transformations so as to properly articulate the stakes of the doppelgänger's recurrences in Japanese literary and cinematic culture.

For this reason, I believe that the appearances of the doppelgänger motif in Japanese texts is more productively understood as a historically specific formation, as one instantiation of what Miri Nakamura has identified as discourses of monstrous bodies that proliferated in modern Japan not as mere premodern remnants, but as figures that became visible precisely through the gaze of new scientific discourses that sought to demarcate the normal from the abnormal under conditions of modernity.[29] This is not to say that motifs akin to the double did not at all exist in other historical periods. One easily points to so-called "premodern" texts in Japan that reference motifs like magical twins as well as related phenomena such as somnambulism [*rikonbyō*]. That said, as my above discussion indicates, it is critical to account for not the existence or non-existence of texts per se, but the historicity of the formation of the doppelgänger as a coherent cultural formation. In other words, at issue here is the question of how a diverse set of texts came to be grouped together under the sign of the doppelgänger, such that preceding texts could then retroactively be read as proto-doppelgänger narratives, and subsequent texts read through the lens of an established genre. Even as images of ghosts and ghostly doubles have appeared in cultures around the world and across history, the doppelgänger's significance lies in its particularly modern inflection as a figure taken to have a psychic reality derived from the conceptualization of the unconscious.

Double Visions, Double Fictions approaches the figure of the doppelgänger not simply as the literary or cinematic representations of fixed prefigured psychoanalytic concepts, in effect subsuming the former into the terms of the latter. Rather, even as it is informed by psychoanalytic concepts, it takes as its task the examination of the doppelgänger from a historical frame of analysis in the interest of placing emphasis on the historically situated discursive processes through which the very conditions of possibility for the psychoanalytic imagination of the doppelgänger came to be constituted. Indeed, the necessity of historically situating the place of psychoanalysis in the formation of the doppelgänger as a genre takes on a particular salience when its study is refracted through the prism of its appearances in Japanese films and fictions in light of the fact that, as I noted above, the proliferation of fictional representations of the doppelgänger in the Japanese context tends to cluster around very particular historical conjunctures, namely the 1920s and the 1930s and at the end of the twentieth century. At roughly the same moment of the beginnings of psychoanalytic interest in the figure, the doppelgänger motif became the subject of a veritable explosion of literary attention in Japan. Furthermore, as if also enacting the very compulsion to repeat that the figure embodies on a historical register, a renewed wave of interest in the doppelgänger can be felt in Japanese cultural production of the recent decades.

Attentive to the historical specificity of the conceptual cohesion and recurrence of the fantasy of the doppelgänger in Japanese texts, the questions that guide the discussions of the doppelgänger in this book are as follows: What was it about these historical moments that led to the emergence of the doppelgänger as a popular and meaningful literary and cultural signifier within the Japanese social milieu? What were the social, political, and material conditions that mobilized this desire for the doppelgänger as a cultural formation precisely at these conjunctures and not others? I contend in this book that when it is situated within the historical conditions in which it recurs as a textual motif, the figure of the doppelgänger makes for a productive point of departure for illustrating the linkages and points of intersection among a constellation of cultural practices and institutions, from matters of language and visuality, to the links between colonialism and commodity culture, to the imbrications of the emergence of psychoanalysis with discourses on race and empire.

The subsequent chapters of the book will highlight two intersecting historical trajectories that I argue are formative of the emergence of the imagination of the doppelgänger in Japan during the 1920s and 1930s. The first is the condition of colonial modernity and the ways in which this produced imperial subjects based on the strategic mobilization of discourses of identity and difference. Whether in Japan or elsewhere, the economic engine of colonial expansion and the circulation of capital and mass migration of populations this enabled was not only formative of processes of rapid urbanization and the emergence of a mass consumer culture (along with their attendant social anxieties and crises); moreover, it also underpinned emergent conceptions of modern subjectivity and alterity central to the imagination of the doppelgänger. The second is the restructuring of schemas of visuality in the late nineteenth and early twentieth centuries marked especially by the increasing mechanical mediation of vision in such technologies as photography or cinema. The imagination of the doppelgänger—whether in literary or psychoanalytic terms—is closely linked to the social impacts of the emergence of cinematic technologies; in particular, the figure of the double foregrounds cinema's role in facilitating the alienation and commodification of vision, affect, and desire, which can be understood as a parallel form of colonization, which, instead of expanding outward geographically, drives inward into the psyche.

Considering how the figure of the doppelgänger is structured around the enactment of repetition, it seems only fitting that the proliferation of the motif in Japanese fictions of the 1920s sees a renewed recurrence—a repetition—in films and fictions since the 1980s, suggesting the possibility of a historical dimension to its enactment of the compulsion to repeat. While the doppelgänger's embodiment of doubling and repetition puts this issue into stark relief, the revival of interest in the figure is no isolated instance, but rather appears as a symptomatic marker of a constellation of similar patterns of repetition also visible in other areas of cultural production, manifesting most visibly in a recurrence of precisely those genres (and the historical conditions that engender them) formative of the doppelgänger's popularization. For instance, in an echo of the emerging popular interest in psychoanalysis in the early twentieth century, Saitō Tamaki has observed a resurgence of interest in psychoanalytic terms and concepts in Japan since the 1980s, manifesting in such popular phenomena as the invitation of psychologists and psychoanalysts to be commentators in mass media, in the institutionalization of counseling in education, not to mention the proliferation of trauma narratives in contemporary literature.[30] Also, parallel to this is a revival of interest since the 1990s in Japan within the genre of detective fiction in not only "new orthodox mysteries" [shin-honkaku misuteri] but also in "anti-mysteries" that restage the debates and discourses surrounding the oppositions between orthodox and unorthodox detective fictions as well as the oppositions between "pure literature" [junbungaku] and "mass literature" [taishū bungaku].[31] Finally, in the realm of visual culture, the emergence of new digital media brought about a renewed interest in early cinema, prompting a rethinking of the origins of film.[32]

The reappearance of the doppelgänger in the 1980s can thus be read as an emblematic marker of a resurgence of a neo-nostalgic historical attention to the mass culture of the Taisho period. In this regard, it presents a paralax view of history through its staging of a structure of repetition that sees a reflection in the attempts of scholars such as Karatani Kōjin to articulate a logic of historical repetition that structures capitalist modernity.[33] Taking seriously the doppelgänger's embodiment of a return of the repressed therefore means accounting for the figure's contemporary repetitions and resignifications, which entails the recognition of what has also been repressed in history, and the challenge of articulating a critique *in the present* vis-à-vis its representations of (and relations to) the past. After all, to speak of a resurgence of interest in Taisho culture is to at once indicate an earlier relative neglect of the cultural history of this period. Indeed, a popular misconception of the cultural production (and especially of the mass culture) of the Taisho period as largely derivative of European forms has often led to its critical dismissal until recent years.

Notably, the literary and historical concerns surrounding interwar Japan that an attention to the emergence of the figure of the doppelgänger effectively brings to the foreground—Japanese modernism, early cinema, mass cultural forms like detective fiction, not to mention a much-warranted historical attention to the broader backdrop of Japanese imperialism and fascism—are precisely those issues that have historically been neglected within the field of Japanese studies. Partly a consequence of the mutual desire to circumscribe cultural and historical work on the Japanese colonial empire on both sides of the Pacific in line with the interests of Cold War geopolitics, the historical period of the doppelgänger's proliferation was one that was often written off as an aberration, a wrong turn in the predetermined path to modernization. It is only in the last two decades that a much-needed corrective to this relative neglect has appeared. As such, the examination of the doppelgänger must also address the history of the present and what social and material conditions in the contemporary juncture provoke this return to Taisho.

It is here where the doppelgänger makes for an effective site of cultural critique. Because the doppelgänger foregrounds the very logic of returns and repetitions, the figure is a way to bring out the politics of the historiographic unconscious beneath not only this return to the prewar period in contemporary cultural discourse in Japan specifically, but also a range of other historical questions structured around issues of difference and repetition. Indeed, as a figure that simultaneously occupies the positions of self and other, what is most noteworthy about the doppelgänger (in its myriad manifestations) is how it brings to attention the structural limits of oppositions between such categorical terms as original and imitation, or difference and repetition. The doppelgänger is simultaneously subject and object; it is an enactment of the mirror stage of subject formation on one hand, and on the other hand it is the embodiment of the return of the repressed, the materialization of the constitutive excess of modern subjectivity. Following these premises, it will be this book's contention that the doppelgänger's embodiment of difference in repetition makes it an apt figure to serve as a conceptual lens to illuminate a host of historical issues organized around a relation between identity and difference—East and West, literature and cinema, not to mention the historical repetition in the passage from imperialism to globalization—that arise from taking up the analysis of modern Japanese culture as a site of intellectual inquiry.

Staging Problems

Double Visions, Double Fictions foregrounds the problem of relationality on a number of levels. On a micro scale, although each chapter takes up the work of a literary author or film director in whose body of work the doppelgänger motif recurs, the effort is not intended to construct an imagined unity to their works. Rather, it is to take up these literary and cinematic appearances as nodal points in the effort to historicize the doppelgänger and situate its relations within the various elements—discourses, practices, and operations—of the structures of Japanese modernity that are constitutive of the imagination of the double, even as these are interrupted and exceeded by it. While each chapter examines its own specific set of questions and concerns, they are nevertheless linked through the figure of the doppelgänger, such that taken together, they may facilitate an accounting for the different facets of the figure. Although the texts examined follow a largely chronological order, to place emphasis less on lineage and continuity and more on returns and repetition that mirror the problems of temporality embodied by the doppelgänger, the book takes on a chiastic structure, with the problems and questions raised by the first three chapters revisited in the final two chapters, thus staging the resignification of these issues in the process of historical repetition.

Chapter 1 begins with an examination of the appearances of the doppelgänger in the work of the detective fiction writer Edogawa Rampo in an effort to establish the frames of reference and terms of discussion for the rest of the book. Against approaches that would treat the doppel-gänger solely in terms of cultural influence, I consider Rampo's doubles in the context of the ideological premises of the genre of detective fiction. While the logic of detective fiction is based on a narrative drive to individuate and render the criminal other so as to disavow guilt from the broader social body, in contrast, in their confusion of positions of self and other, Rampo's doppelgängers mark the excess of the procedure. In his fictions, the positions of detective and criminal cannot be so easily demarcated. In this respect, I argue that the figure of the doppelgänger not only embodies a return of the repressed on the level of the individual subject, as psychoanalytic understandings of the figure would have it. More importantly, it brings to the surface a broader historical uncon-scious that the detective genre attempts to ideologically repress.

Chapter 2 expands upon the discussion of colonial underpinnings of the doppelgänger. Beginning from the contention that psychoanalysis is a colonial discipline, the chapter examines the figure of the doppel-gänger in the fictions of Tanizaki Jun'ichirō as a site on which ideas about race, nationality, and empire are played out. While critical apprais-als all too often frame his literary biography and body of work in terms of a trajectory that moves from immature infatuation with the West fol-lowed by a later return to Japan, Tanizaki's doppelgänger fictions suggest a more complex pattern of repetition shaped by Japan's peculiar position-ing as a racialized, non-Western colonial empire is at work. Often, these doubles' staging of what might be termed a return of a racialized repressed trouble any simple dyad between the West and Japan. Instead, Tanizaki's doppelgängers reflected the libidinal anxieties surrounding the desire to identify with the West yet failing to do so, tracking the impact of the production of racial difference while at once refracting an even deeper tension vis-à-vis the colonial subjectivity in Japan's own empire, wherein the positions of colonizer and colonized could not so easily be demar-cated in visual/racial terms.

While the preceding chapter takes up the colonial underpinnings of psychoanalysis as its point of departure, chapter 3 centers on the sig-nificance of the relations between psychoanalysis and cinema in the con-stitution of the doppelgänger as a concept. This chapter discusses the doppelgänger fictions of Akutagawa Ryūnosuke with an attention to these relations among language, visuality, and the unconscious. Along-side discussions of such fictions as "Futatsu no tegami" (Two letters, 1918) and "Hagurma" (Spinning gears, 1927), I take up Akutagawa's short story "Kage" (The shadow, 1920), which stages the event of cinematic specta-torship as a parallel experience to seeing one's own double. Through this procedure, the story effectively shows how cinematic technologies are productive of the imagination of the doppelgänger; moreover, it fore-grounds the tensions and negotiations surrounding the formation of social and spectatorial practices vis-à-vis early cinema.

If Akutagawa's fiction is illustrative of the linkages between the figure of the doppelgänger and the apparatus of cinema, what then might this mean for actual films featuring the motif? To address this question, I revisit the work of Edogawa Rampo to build upon the preceding discus-sions by considering the subject of film adaptations of his writings in chapter 4. Through a close analysis of contemporary film adaptations of Rampo's work, this chapter approaches the problem of doubling and repetition not only in terms of their staging within the texts in question or for that matter from one text to another, but also the stakes of repeat-ing a text from one historically specific moment (the 1920s) in another (the 1990s). If film adaptation is understood as a kind of doppelgänger, then at issue here is not only a textual and transmedia doubling but also a historical doppelgänger. It is therefore not sufficient to situate the dop-pelgänger's appearances only in their "original" moments of production. Beyond this, the compulsion to repeat involved in the very act of looking at the doppelgänger *in the present*—and what social material conditions provoke the desire to do so—must itself be historicized. Thus, the analy-sis in this chapter will account for the contemporary conjuncture as a second historical moment that is not only marked by the reappearance of a recurrence of the doppelgänger motif in literary and cinematic pro-duction, but also, instrumental in shaping the understanding of the pre-vious moment in its very repetition of it.

Finally, I conclude my examination of the figure of the doppelgänger by turning to the recent films of Kurosawa Kiyoshi. Through a discus-sion of his films, chapter 5 will first recapitulate some of the key issues and problems raised in the preceding chapters. From there, it attempts to draw out the broader implications of the doppelgänger's conceptual performance, especially its play on generic structures of difference and repetition. At its heart, this chapter poses the following question: if the figure of the doppelgänger is intimately intertwined with the politics of visuality and looking, then what implications might it have for the practice of cultural criticism? By addressing this question, I account for my own gaze upon the doppelgänger in my analysis, but more importantly, I also attempt to articulate the implications for critical practice enacted in the doppelgänger's disruptions of genres as categories of analysis.

1

Stalkers and Crime Scenes

The Detective Fiction of Edogawa Rampo

On the Origins of the Doppelgänger Motif

At roughly the same time that Otto Rank began writing his seminal psychoanalytic study of the doppelgänger, the first Japanese translation of Edgar Allan Poe's (1809–1849) short story "William Wilson" (1839) was published as a part of the anthology *Akaki shi no kamen* (*Masque of Red Death*, 1913).[1] The story of "William Wilson" revolves around a young student who is persistently hounded by his double in the form of another boy who not only shares a roughly similar appearance to the protagonist, but moreover has an identical name and date of birth. Soon, the other boy imitates his dress and mannerisms, and later, the protagonist discovers that the other William Wilson's face has become an exact duplicate of his own. This discovery leads the protagonist to leave school, only to have his double leave at the same time. He eventually ends up at Eton College and Oxford, where he leads a life of debauchery by swindling a young nobleman of his money in a game of cards and later beginning an adulterous affair. Yet, this does not allow him to escape the other William Wilson, who turns up wherever he happens to go. Disgusted by his double's constant pursuit, the protagonist drags him into the anteroom of a banquet hall and stabs him, only to end up taking his own life in the process when the fatal wounds appear on his body instead.

Poe's "William Wilson" makes for a useful starting point for apprehending the history of the doppelgänger motif in Japanese film and fiction for a number of reasons. Foremost among these is the fact that the story has since become one of the defining texts of a large body of work that makes use of the motif of the doppelgänger. Indeed, the German novelist Thomas Mann's comments on Fyodor Dostoevsky's own doppelgänger-themed novella "The Double: A Petersburg Poem" (1846) illustrate this point well. Mann asserts that Dostoevsky's novella "by no means improved on Edgar Allan Poe's 'William Wilson,' a tale that deals with the same old romantic motif in a way far more profound on the moral side and more success-fully resolving the critical [theme] in the poetic," implying that Poe's story had become an established standard against which other doppelgänger fictions were read and evaluated.[2] Moreover, the story became one of the key source texts—while also borrowing elements from other doppel-gänger stories, including the Faustian bargain from Oscar Wilde's *The Picture of Dorian Gray* (1890) and the contrasting personalities of each double from Fyodor Dostoyevsky's *The Double* (1846)—for Stellan Rye and Hanns Heinz Ewers's widely distributed and critically recognized film *Der Student von Prag* (*The Student of Prague*, 1913).[3] *The Student of Prague*, one of the first examples of the appearance of the doppelgänger motif in early cinema, inaugurated a series of films revolving around the motif of doubling in German Expressionist cinema, including such classic films as Robert Weine's *Das Cabinet des Dr. Caligari* (*The Cabinet of Dr. Cali-gari*, 1920), Paul Wegener and Carl Boese's *Der Golem* (*The Golem*, 1920), and Fritz Lang's *Metropolis* (1927), among others. Indeed, the film's signifi-cance in the popularization of the doppelgänger is only further reinforced by the fact that it prompted Otto Rank to begin his pioneering psycho-analytic study of the figure.[4]

By the time of the translation of "William Wilson," Poe's reputation was already established in Japan. The first translations of his fiction—namely "The Black Cat" (1843) and "The Murders in the Rue Morgue" (1841)—appeared in the *Yomiuri shinbun* as early as 1888. Motoki Tadao's biography of Poe followed in 1891. His work was also covered extensively by Lafcaido Hearn in his lectures on American Literature at the Tokyo Imperial University. Miyanaga Takashi goes so far as to surmise that of all the foreign authors whose work had been translated into Japanese, none was more widely read than Poe.[5] Consequently, given the central-ity of Poe's work in the early articulation and conceptualization of the doppelgänger motif, a claim can certainly be made that explosion of interest in the figure of the doppelgänger in fictions coming out of the Taisho and early Showa periods in Japan is but another manifestation of Poe's influence on the modern Japanese literary scene. It is certainly no accident that those Japanese authors whose writings are often purported to have drawn influence and inspiration from Poe's work themselves produced their own doppelgänger stories, wherein at times, they would even include explicit citations of Poe's work or other intertextual references to fictions of the doppelgänger. For example, Tanizaki Jun'ichirō repeatedly took up images of dolls, doublings, and automatons in such works as "Tomoda to Matsunaga no hanashi" (The story of Tomoda and Matsunaga, 1926) or "Aozuka-shi no hanashi" (The story of Mr. Aozuka, 1926). Citations of Poe's writings are also abundant in the work of Satō Haruo, ranging from the naming of a character "William Wilson" in his doppelgänger story "Shimon" ("The Fingerprint," 1918) to an extended sequence centered on the recitation of a Poe poem in "Aojiroi netsujō," (Pale passion, 1919).

As I briefly touched upon in the introduction, because of the abundance of translations of European and American fictions of the doppelgänger in this period in Japan, not to mention the German origins of the word *Doppelgänger* itself, it would be easy to fall into the trap of reducing the concept to something foreign that arrives on Japanese shores as a consequence of a process of modernization. Yet while the impact of these translations cannot be discounted outright, reading the doppelgänger in Japanese texts in these terms arguably effaces as much as it explains. While the process of translation and transplantation may indeed have been a necessary condition for the dissemination of the doppelgänger as a motif and concept into Japan, I am not convinced the historical precedence of the figure in the European context on its own serves as a sufficient explanation for the motif's popularity.

In fact, it is precisely the potential to articulate the very limits of the logic of origins that I find most compelling about the attributes ascribed to the doppelgänger. Seeing how a key characteristic of the figure of the doppelgänger is its troubling of the polarity between original and imitation, I believe that its critical force lies in its capacity to stage a critique of a discourse of origins. More to the point, by deemphasizing a rhetoric of origins and influences, my interest here is to avoid the kind of comparative approach that would premise an a priori difference between the positions of an essentialized "West" and "Japan," coupled with a notion of a temporal lag in characterizing the latter's relation to the former. This particular frame of analysis is predicated upon unsustainable assumptions and as such suffers from significant limitations in what it can illuminate. After all, there is the Eurocentric premise in the practice of reading cultural forms in Euro-America as a baseline against which their appearance elsewhere is evaluated in terms of assimilation or domestication without critiquing how the boundaries of the very categories of "Japan" and "the West" are not only porous, but more importantly historically contingent and ideologically charged ideas. Harry Harootunian has leveled a thorough critique of the fundamental assumptions upon which this logic rests. In his words, this received idea of modernization sees "development comparatively according to a baseline experience attributed to Western societies, tracking the variable locations of latecomers like Japan, and assessing the political and social costs incurred from starting later."[6] Posited by this approach is the notion that temporality is measured from a singular baseline, against which other histories are constructed on the basis of a simple question of convergence or divergence. Yet elided in such analyses are the particularities of the experience of modernization in Japan arising out of its concrete local circumstances that are not reducible to such broad historical narratives.

In this chapter I will attempt to bring attention to specific local developments and discursive contexts that created the conditions formative of the imagination and popularization of the doppelgänger in Japan. Before tackling in the ensuing chapters how the figure of the doppelgänger opens up a space for a critical cultural intervention, it is necessary to articulate the interlocking discursive sites in which its manifestations became prevalent—namely detective fiction, psychoanalysis, and literary modernism—and, more importantly, how Japanese authors employed the doppelgänger as a literary motif and critical concept within them. It should become evident that despite its ostensibly foreign origins, the particular articulation of the doppelgänger within the Japanese context is a local event, an emergent cultural response to the complex discursive space and circumstances of 1920s and 1930s Japan—from the urbanizing

effects of industrialization and its attendant consequence of mass anonymity, to the shock of the new technologies of cinema, to the commodification of everyday life—even as these circumstances are themselves
intertwined with global forces, albeit unevenly inflected by the particular historical position that Japan occupies.

Doubling the Detective Story

Perhaps more so than any other Japanese author, it is in the work of
Edogawa Rampo (b. Hirai Tarō, 1894–1965) that Poe's classic story of the
double makes its most visible manifestation.[7] One of the most famous
and popular detective fictionists of his generation, Rampo may very
well be the quintessential embodiment of the figure of the doppelgänger.
Representations of not only doubles themselves, but also other imagery
that can be linked to the motif of doubling such as disguises, dolls, mirrors, and masks feature heavily in much of his fiction. But beyond this
prevalence of doppelgänger figures and related motifs in his fiction, an
even more fundamental doubleness is immediately marked by Rampo's
choice of a nom-de-plume meant to echo the Japanese transliteration
of the name of Edgar Allan Poe as an invocation of Poe's status as the
father of detective fiction, in effect positioning himself as Poe's Japanese
doppelgänger.[8]

More than merely a point of trivia, this doubling effected by Rampo's
name has led to a tendency by critics to read his works through a logic
of bifurcation between treating them as domesticized copies of European and American detective stories, or alternatively praising them for
their divergence from foreign models and excavating a "Japanese authenticity." As Yoshikuni Igarashi observes, Rampo's name itself has functioned as a sign that sets the terms of much of the critical discourse
surrounding his fiction in a relation of binarism between Japan and the
West, the premodern and the modern, copy and original.[9] For example,
Shimizu Yoshinori has identified what he calls a "tenacious two-faced-
ness" [kyōjin na nimensei] in Rampo's body of work. In Shimizu's view,
the work itself can be broadly divided into two groups: his scientific (or
honkaku—"orthodox") detective fictions and his fantastic (or henkaku—
"unorthodox") romances, with the notion of the orthodoxy taken to mean
the rules and conventions of a putative "Western detective fiction."[10]

Shimizu's deployment of this bifurcated frame for reading Rampo is not an isolated one; a similar observation has been made by another critic, Ozaki Hotsuki, who further divides Rampo's work up on a temporal axis between early scientific and "authentic" detective fictions and later works of fantastic grotesquerie.[11] And these observations are not in themselves new; on the contrary, they carry over from the critical discourse surrounding detective fiction contemporary to the time that Rampo was actively writing. The terms *honkaku* and *henkaku* that have since become the standard classificatory scheme for not just Rampo's fiction but the broader genre of detective fiction in Japan can be traced back to the first round of the formative debates on the subject by critics like Hirabayashi Hatsunosuke and Kōga Saburo.[12] Premised on the perception that Japanese detective fiction appeared belatedly, that is, only in the wake of the emergence of the genre elsewhere, these debates set the boundaries for mapping out the discursive terrain of the genre around an anxiety of being nothing more than derivative of a putative "Western original" that is fundamentally foreign to Japan.[13]

Rampo's positioning within this schema warrants some attention. On the one hand, he is typically named as the "father" of modern detective fiction in Japan, with his work identified for pioneering the use of deductive reasoning and scientific methodologies in the detection and apprehension of criminals. This recognition began as soon as his first published story "The Two-Sen Copper Coin" appeared in the magazine *Shinseinen* (New youth), made evident by the fanfare that surrounded his debut. The story was accompanied by not only Rampo's own treatise on detective fiction, but also a piece of critical commentary by Kozakai Fuboku (1890–1921) praising Rampo's work for its successful adoption of the conventions of deductive reasoning from European and American detective narratives.[14] Rampo's subsequent literary activity after the Second World War—in particular his championing of the classic whodunit form based on principles of logic, rationality, and science as the "proper" form of detective narratives in various essays collected in *Gen'eijō* (Illusory castle, 1951)—only further cemented this status and effectively became the conventional wisdom about the detective genre in postwar Japan.

Nevertheless, Rampo's postwar advocacy of "orthodox" detective fiction stands in marked contrast to earlier stances he took in support of unorthodox detective fiction. Rampo's fiction—often taken as representative of prewar detective fictions in general—regularly faced criticism in both his time as well as more recent commentary on the genre for tending toward the bizarre and the grotesque and reflected an "unorthodox" or "inauthentic" development of the detective fiction genre. He was also seen as a spokesperson of the wildly popular literary and cultural phenomenon known as erotic-grotesque-nonsense [*ero-guro-nansensu*]. For example, Hirabayashi Hatsunosuke names Rampo specifically as one of the writers who exhibits an "unhealthy" [*fukenzen*] fascination for the morbid and the grotesque.[15] Similarly, in Kasai Kiyoshi's periodization of the history of detective fiction in Japan, he suggests that because of the extensive presence of fantasy and horror elements in detective fiction during the 1920s and 1930s, works from this period are properly characterized as unorthodox.[16]

Viewed through the lens of this *honkaku–henkaku* schema, the prominence of the doppelgänger motif within Rampo's fictions would appear to confirm Hatsunosuke's and Kasai's respective analyses. Such an understanding is certainly not without merit. After all, the employment of motifs of uncanny doublings, even if they are sometimes given explanations in terms of psychic projection or split personalities, nonetheless tends to give these stories a quality that approaches the fantastic. As such, they often fail to conform to the conventional demand for scientific rationality and deductive logic typically endorsed and privileged within the orthodoxy of the genre of detective fiction. However, I would argue that Rampo's use of the doppelgänger in his fiction is not always reducible to this schema. On the contrary, there are notable instances wherein the motif functions as an active means of interrogating the limits of the detective genre itself. Put another way, rather than simply signifying a text's exclusion from the proper boundaries of the genre, might it not be more productive to read Rampo's deployment of the doppelgänger motif in his detective fiction—not to mention his own performance of doubling—as a metacritical intervention into the ongoing critical discourse surrounding the detective genre itself, especially given Rampo's notably active participation in these debates as they were taking place?

Several examples from Rampo's body of work speak to this approach to the doppelgänger, but few are as illustrative as the motif's appearance in his *Injū* (*The Beast in the Shadows*, 1928). *The Beast in the Shadows* makes for a particularly productive case study in articulating the broader stakes that the interplay between the detective and the doppelgänger implicates because it places the relation between them at the crux of the plot and stages this relation in a self-referential and almost metafictive form. In effect, the novel does not merely make use of the doppelgänger motif. It also performs a critical commentary about the figure's recurrence in Rampo's own writings.

At the onset, *The Beast in the Shadows* sets up an opposition between two detective fictionists who are made to appear as doubles of one another. On the one hand, there is the narrator Samukawa. On the other hand, there is his enigmatic opponent who goes by the pseudonym Ōe Shundei. The novel sets up this rivalry between these two characters from its very opening passage as not only one between individuals, but also between two opposed approaches to the genre of detective fiction itself. It begins with the following words:

A thought crosses my mind at times. There are really two types of detective novelist. The first is what we might call the criminal type, an author whose sole interest is in the crime itself, and should he attempt to write a detective story in the deductive style, he would not find much satisfaction unless he is also able to describe the cruel psychology of the criminal. The second is the detective type, an author of sound mind whose sole interest is in the intellectual process of detection and who otherwise appears to be largely indifferent to the subject of criminal psychology.[17]

Immediately, with this mention of two types of detective novelists, *The Beast in the Shadows* references the debates surrounding the genre of detective fiction taking place in Japan at the time of the novel's publication. In other words, the novel sets up this rivalry between the narrator and Shundei as representative of the broader schism in the genre in Japan. Samukawa, the narrator of *The Beast in the Shadows*, asserts that while he is an example of the latter (a detective writer whose primary preoccupation is deductive reasoning), the antagonist of the story—an enigmatic and personally secretive detective novelist and erstwhile rival of the narrator's who goes by the pseudonym Ōe Shundei, is an example of the former (a so-called "criminal sort").

The story proper continues from here when Samukawa receives a request for assistance from a woman named Shizuko. He learns that Hirata Ichirō (a name that the attentive reader will immediately recognize as a playful reference to Rampo's own birth name Hirai Tarō), a former lover of Shizuko's from her youth, has been stalking and sending threatening letters to Shizuko. To further complicate things, Hirata appears to be the real identity of Ōe Shundei. As the narrator investigates and attempts to ascertain the whereabouts of Ōe, he repeatedly comes across motifs from Shundei's fiction. Taking these up as clues, he is initially led to believe that the culprit, rather than Shundei himself, is Shizuko's husband impersonating the infamous author. Upon the narrator's reaching this conclusion, though, Shizuko's husband conveniently dies in a freak accident. Thinking that the case had resolved itself, the narrator and Shizuko slip into a secret romance and sadomasochistic sexual relationship. But, after noticing odd gaps and contradictions in the time line of events, the narrator concludes that the whole thing was really a ruse by Shizuko herself—who is in fact the true identity of Shundei—to allow her to murder her husband and deflect attention from herself. Yet at the end of it all, the narrator expresses a sense of retrospective uncertainty. Lacking an outright confession from Shizuko, who subsequently commits suicide at the end of the novel following the accusations he levels against her, the narrator of *The Beast in the Shadows* wonders if he had not been in fact mistaken, if his suspicion of Shizuko was ultimately unjustified.

From the above summary, already evident is the plethora of disguises, impersonations, and false identities at play in this novel. At the center of it all is the question of the identity of Ōe Shundei, indeed whether Ōe Shundei exists at all beyond a name. Is he the pseudonym of one Hirata Ichirō, or is he being impersonated by the husband of Shizuko as a part of some twisted game he is playing? Or is his presence ultimately fictive, an orchestration of Shizuko? In itself, this attention to the true identity of Shundei is neither unusual nor surprising for detective fiction. After all, for the criminal to be apprehended he or she must be named and identified. Nonetheless, evident here is the function the doppelgänger serves within the specific context of the genre of detective fiction. Insofar as within the logic of the genre, the primary narrative drive propelling a given text forward is the challenge of identifying the perpetrator of a crime (or, "whodunit," so to speak), through its multiplication of subjectivities, the doppelgänger compounds this challenge of identification and individuation central to the task of the detective. It should come with little surprise that doubles and impersonations, given their resistance to simple demarcations of identity and difference, find a comfortable home in Rampo's detective fictions.

Rampo's fiction is significant in the notable pervasiveness of such motifs. He often calls particular attention to their deployment by way of a citation of texts that have since come to be identified as exemplars in the corpus of doppelgänger fictions. Take, for example, his short story "Soseiji" (The twins, 1924), wherein a direct reference is made to the classic doppelgänger text by Scottish author Robert Louis Stevenson, *The Strange Case of Dr. Jekyll and Mr. Hyde* (1886), and its famous split-personality protagonist. At one point in the story following one twin's murder of his brother, he ponders his future criminal activities with the words: "I would be able to enact Stevenson's fantastic tale of Dr. Jekyll and Mr. Hyde in real life."[18] Likewise, in another work, *Ryōki no hate* (Beyond the bizarre, 1930), a similar reference is made, when its protagonist—an itinerant youth named Aoki—runs into a man with the exact same appearance as a friend of his. Comparing the personalities of his straitlaced friend Shinagawa and his perverted double, he compares them to Dr. Jekyll and Mr. Hyde.[19] These intertextual citations of Stevenson have the effect of calling further attention to the figure of the double; moreover, it is indicative of the extent to which the concept has become familiar to Rampo's readers through the dissemination of its various literary representations. In none of the examples cited above does Rampo even bother to elaborate upon his citations with some form of summary or annotation; rather, the author's name and the book's title or alternatively the name of the principal characters Jekyll and Hyde are merely dropped.[20]

A more elaborate instance of a similar name-checking of Stevenson appears in *The Beast in the Shadows* as well. Close the end of the novel, following the narrator's realization that his initial belief that Shizuko's husband was impersonating Ōe Shundei is mistaken, he meets with Shizuko—who by then has become his illicit lover—in their private rented room. Combing once again Shundei's fiction for clues to his suspicion that Shizuko is herself in fact the mysterious author, he tells her:

> "Don't you think that whole thing with Shundei mingling with vagrants at Asakusa Park sounds like something straight from Stevenson's *The Strange Case of Dr Jekyll and Mr Hyde*? Once I noticed this, I scoured Shundei's fiction for other such stories, and found a couple more of them. I'm sure you know of them—there's 'Panorama Country,' a novel that was published just before he disappeared, and there's 'One Person, Two Roles,' a short story published even earlier. Upon reading these, it became clear to me just how fascinated he was by a Dr Jekyll-type technique, of one person transforming into two people, I mean."[21]

Samukawa's statement here is doubly interesting in that it offers yet another citation of Stevenson's novel, and does so in a transparently self-referential manner. The two stories of Shundei's referenced here recall Rampo's own writings that feature the figure of the doppelgänger. "Panorama Country" is an allusion to Rampo's *Panorama-tō kidan* (The strange tale of Panorama Island, 1926), and "One Person, Two Roles" shares a title with one of Rampo's own short stories. These are not isolated instances, and other similarly thinly disguised citations of Rampo's fiction—always attributed to Shundei—are scattered throughout *The Beast in the Shadows*. The most obvious of these is a reference to Rampo's "The Stalker in the Attic," which appears in the novel as "Yaneura no yūgi" (Games in the attic) when, at one point, the narrator is led to believe that Shundei is spying upon Shizuko in the manner represented in the story in question. None of these references would come as a surprise to the alert reader, though, given that the relation between Edogawa Rampo and Ōe Shundei is already foreshadowed early in the narrative through the explicit linkage made by the rendering of Shundei's supposed real name—Hirata Ichirō—as a play on Rampo's own name, Hirai Tarō.

Through these self-referential citations, Rampo implicitly points to his own fascination with stories of the doppelgänger, the so-called "Jekyll-type approach" that proliferates in his detective fiction. The character of

Ōe Shundei is linked with the actual author of the novel, implying that the criminal the narrator seeks is Rampo himself. At the same time, this fictional play of conflating the identities of Rampo with that of the character Shundei is complicated by the typical tendency to associate a text's protagonist with the identity of the novel's real-world author. When Rampo's novel began serialization in the late 1920s, a practice of reading texts specifically for their autobiographical traces, which Tomi Suzuki has termed the "I-novel discourse," had already emerged as the ascendant reading paradigm.[22] Rampo's *The Beast in the Shadows* plays upon this paradigm of reading, most fundamentally by making its narrator and protagonist an author of detective fictions. More importantly, the novel renders him almost as a cipher, with the effect of making the temptation of reading him as a surrogate for Rampo himself more compelling. His name—Samukawa—is not mentioned until the third chapter, and aside from his self-identification as a writer of detective fiction, very little else is revealed about him. This ironically makes the narrator even more of a mystery than Ōe Shundei, whom he characterizes as especially enigmatic. For the most part, he is described only through negation, only as Shundei's polar opposite. While Shundei is eccentric and eerie, the narrator claims to be virtuous; while the former's style is gloomy and grotesque, the latter's is bright and ordinary.[23] In this sense, both Samukawa and Shundei seem less like fully fleshed-out characters and more like caricatured representatives of the personalities of *henkaku* and *honkaku* detective fictions.

Since Rampo himself is known for straddling these poles of orthodoxy and unorthodoxy—for being the representative *honkaku* as well as *henkaku* detective fictionist—one effect of the novel's staging of this opposition between Samukawa and Shundei is to encourage the identification of Rampo with both the narrator and his rival Shundei. Or, to put it in the terms of the central character roles within the conventional structure of detective fiction, *The Beast in the Shadows* metafictively plays upon the idea of both the detective and the criminal—the subject and object of the narrative—as stand-ins for Rampo himself. Read against this backdrop, the citation of Stevenson's *The Strange Case of Dr. Jekyll and Mr. Hyde* takes on greater resonance. Recall the opening setup of the text, before the story itself begins. The opening chapter devotes its attention entirely to a preamble focused on the rivalry between the narrator Samukawa and his opponent Shundei. The story proper does not actually begin until the second chapter when Samukawa first meets Shizuko. One of the odd effects of this extended discussion of the characters' relationship is to generate a suspicion—especially for the genre-savvy reader—of the possibility that the Samukawa and Shundei are the same person, that the novel is itself one that takes a "Jekyll-type approach." Determining and fixing Shundei's identity therefore would demarcate self and other, that is, resolve the initial confusion between him and the narrator. In other words, the novel sets out Samukawa's task as the rendering of the criminal other, and in effect absolving himself of potential guilt.

Initially, it is made to appear that the initial setup linking the narrator with his seeming alter ego Ōe Shundei is nothing more than a red herring, with the suggestion that Shundei is Shizuko and not connected to the narrator at all. However, a closer examination of the text reveals that things are far less straightforward. Certain details hint at the possibility the narrator's act of othering—of demarcating himself from Shundei—isn't quite complete. A telling clue suggesting a challenge to the principle of narrative closure in the novel is its inversion of the conventional temporal structure of detective fiction. Typically, in detective fiction, the story of the investigation happens *after the fact of* the event of the crime; as such the detective is positioned as *external* to the story of the crime. As Tzvetan Todorov has put it, "[Detective fiction] contains not one but two stories: the story of the crime and the story of the investigation. In their purest form, these two stories have no point in common. . . . The first story, that of the crime, ends before the second begins."[24] Yet rather than following the conventional structure, in *The Beast in the Shadows*, the investigation creates the conditions for the crime to take place. By asking the narrator for assistance in investigating her supposed stalker (and secret alter ego), Ōe Shundei/Shizuko is able to set up the alibi that then subsequently allows her to murder her husband.

The significance of this reversal is only further clarified by the novel's climactic scene. Several details in the scene when Samukawa triumphantly figures out that Shundei is none other than Shizuko herself are quite telling. Here, at the moment when he confronts Shizuko with this knowledge, the two are engaged in their sadomasochistic sexual relations, with the narrator whipping Shizuko with a riding crop. Ironically, while his conclusive identification of Shundei as Shizuko effectively marks off himself as a separate entity from his rival, against the earlier gestures of the narrative, it also has the effect of hinting at his own increasing unconscious identification with the persona of Shundei as an embodiment of grotesquerie and perversion. This is further underscored through the narrative performance itself. Given that he functions as the encoded author of *The Beast in the Shadows*, one might conclude that Samukawa has now too produced his own "Jekyll-type" story, with the implication that he has in effect become Shundei, or at least the kind of author of dark, unorthodox detective fictions that he asserts Shundei to be.

Through its employment of the doppelgänger motif, what *The Beast in the Shadows* seems to suggest is that the fixing of (the criminal's) identity central to the narrative logic of detective fiction can never be a fully completed operation. The very attempt to demarcate self from other only serves to confirm their entanglement. The other reappears, albeit in the form of the self, as its double. At the same time, given that the text's two detective fiction writers, Samukawa and Shundei, function as stand-ins for orthodox and unorthodox detective fiction respectively, Rampo's novel effectively calls into question the presupposition of an a priori distinction and polarization between these two categories of detective fiction, and with that, the opposition between the authentic and inauthentic, the original and the imitation, the Western and the Japanese, embedded within this discourse. In other words, the doppelgänger's appearance marks what exceeds detective fiction on the level of both its structural logic and discursive formation. It manifests as the embodiment of the condition when the detective's compulsive task of fixing and demarcating identities—of mapping the distinctions between detective and criminal, self and other, domestic and foreign—has become untenable.

Psychoanalysis and Detective Fiction

Studies of detective fiction have called attention to how the very structural features of detective fiction implicitly function as a metafictive enactment of the procedures of textual analysis. For example, Susan Sweeney has noted how the form of detective fiction—its emphasis on suspense, on acts of reading signs, on the production of narrative closure—illustrates the workings of narrativity as such. For Sweeney, a key component is the alignment of the relationship of the detective and the criminal with an analogous relationship of the reader and author. She writes: "The genre dramatizes the interdependent relationship between writer and reader . . . the relationship between criminal and detective, mediated by the crime which one commits and the other resolves, suggests the relationship between writer and reader, mediated by the text. . . . The criminal is the author of a crime that the detective must interpret."[25] Understood in terms of this analogy, one conclusion that can be drawn is that if one of the consequences of the appearance of the doppelgänger is to implicate the detective in the crime through the confusion of the positions of detective and criminal, and with that, the refusal of the possibility of a position of exteriority for the detective, then at once implicated is the entanglement of the reader in the making of the text.

Such a gesture is evident in Rampo's *The Beast in the Shadows*, whose inconclusive ending seemingly tasks the reader with the solving of a mystery that has been left unaddressed. The novel concludes with a brief epilogue following immediately after what initially appears to be the final solution to the mystery, with Samukawa leveling an accusation at Shizuko for murdering her husband and using him and his investigation of the alleged stalking by Ōe Shundei as an alibi. Despite the seeming certainty to Samukawa's earlier accusations, he subsequently expresses doubts about his own conclusion, a problem compounded for him by the fact that Shizuko never confesses or otherwise confirms his theory, instead committing suicide after their final sexual encounter. The novel's ending brings it back full circle, to the foreshadowing of the earlier chapters when Samukawa's narrative performance hints at his apprehension at even telling the story, given all the uncertainties surrounding the event in question. Nonetheless, by retroactively casting doubt on the ostensible solution to the mystery and leaving the identity of the criminal potentially in question, Rampo refuses the imperative for narrative closure so central to the conventions of the detective fiction. As Sweeney has remarked, "Nothing is more definitive, complete, and single-minded than the ending of a detective story. It is less a resolution than an erasure: the answer to a riddle, the unmasking of a criminal, and most important, the full explanation of everything that happened in the preceding narrative."[26]

Not surprisingly, the novel's concluding chapter has caused some controversy, with critics suggesting that it is ultimately unnecessary, perhaps even making the text less effective as a work of detective fiction.[27] That said, the fact of its existence cannot simply be ignored, and so the novel's open-ended conclusion has garnered substantial discussion, with different critics reading its significance in a number of different ways. For example, Sari Kawana suggests that the novel's epilogue forms an important component of its critique of normative understandings of female criminality. Noting that Rampo's text seemingly plays on theories about the relationship between female sexuality and female criminality circulating at the time, this refusal of a categorical solution to the mystery has the effect of casting doubt on the conclusions of criminology and abnormal psychology. Since Shizuko never confirms Samukawa's suspicions, "because of her silence, the puzzle remains as hopelessly difficult as the mystery of female criminality itself."[28] Mark Silver takes a different tack, approaching the novel's ending in terms of the problem of "cultural borrowing," expressing what he sees as Rampo's profound self-consciousness and anxiety about the belatedness of Japanese detective fiction vis-à-vis the West. For Silver, the central issue with the novel's lack of a clean resolution is how the true identity of Shundei—"whether there is a Shundei who exists in his own right or whether his works are the result of Shizuko's impersonation"—is left in suspension.[29] Given the alignment of Shundei with Rampo himself, this becomes a meditation on Rampo's own status as a mere impersonator of Edgar Allan Poe.

A common thread that runs through these analyses of Rampo's metacommentary on the genre of detective fiction is the shared emphasis on the question of the categorical identification of the criminal. However, I believe that this is only one part of the picture. Overlooked in the emphasis on the matter of Shundei's true identity is the novel's hints of a doubling between Samukawa and Shundei. Viewing the novel through the lens of its employment of doubling as a motif reveals that the issue at the heart of Rampo's novel goes beyond merely the failure to fix an identity to the criminal but to stage the confusion of the very positions of detective and criminal. It is not just the concealment of Shundei's identity in the text but another, even more fundamental concealment at the level of the unconscious—in other words, a repression—that takes the form of

Samukawa's failure to recognize his own increasing identification with Shundei, indeed his functional transformation into Shundei. Through this gesture, Rampo undermines the very possibility of ascribing the position of mastery that underpins the detective's act of narrative reconstitution, in effect staging a critique of the genre's methods of producing knowledge.

In this regard, my analysis here aligns with that of Satoru Saito's, who sees in Rampo's habit of staging reversals of familiar tricks from famous detective stories as a means of not only overturning the expectations of genre-savvy readers, but also as a part of a broader "epistemological project" of addressing the limits of the detective's conventional methods and techniques. One specific element in this project was the introduction of Freudian psychoanalytic concepts. His intellectual project, "as a re-examination of the way in which an individual can be known regardless of his or her attempt to remain unknown, is a two-fold process: it begins with the rejection of a method of detection based on positivistic science and ends with the articulation of a method based on human psychology."[30] In this way, Rampo thematized and popularized for a mass readership similar concerns to those expressed by psychoanalysts of his time, which included such subjects as sadomasochism, sleepwalking, hypnosis, and others, while simultaneously making use of the language and idiom of psychoanalysis to give his detective fictions and erotic-grotesque writings a critical force beyond these genres' usual ideological dictates.[31]

Given the historical concurrence of the popularization in Japan of both psychoanalysis and detective fiction, Rampo's interest here may not be all that unusual. As early as the first decades of the twentieth century, laboratories of psychology and psychiatry had begun to appear in Japan.[32] But beginning with the publication of Ōtsuki Kaison's "Monowasure no shinri" (The psychology of forgetting, 1912), followed by a series of articles by Morooka Son, and some years later, Kubō Yoshihide's *Seishin-bunseki* (Psychoanalysis, 1919), Freud's theories of psychoanalysis made an increasingly popular cultural impact in Japan. An interesting aspect to the reception of psychoanalysis in Japan is the fact that it was especially well received among those not formally associated with the academic discipline of psychiatry. Instead, it was among literary authors and cultural critics that its impact was particularly pronounced. As a case in point, the aforementioned essays and translations by Morooka Son appeared not in a psychiatry journal but in the literary magazine *Eniguma*.[33] Furthermore, many of the leading pioneers of psychoanalysis in Japan had little, if any, psychiatric training. For instance, Ōtsuki Kenji—one of the founders of the Tokyo Psychoanalytical Association and a central figure in the project to translate Freud's complete works, culminating in a ten-volume edition that was published in 1929—was a literature graduate from Waseda University. Edogawa Rampo was very much an active participant in the early groups interested in psychoanalysis in Japan. Rampo not only had close ties with Ōtsuki Kenji (one of the central figures in the translation and dissemination of psychoanalysis to Japan), he also become a co-founder of the Japanese Psychoanalytic Association in 1931 and participated in the planning of the journal *Seishinbunseki* (Psychoanalysis), even contributing an article titled "J. A. Shimonzu no hisoka naru jōnetsu" (J. A. Symond's Secret Passions, 1933) to the journal at one point.[34]

However, the parallels between detective fiction and psychoanalysis do not end simply at their historically concurrent moments of introduction to the Japanese context. Beyond this, there is a much-noted similarity in the "formal procedures" that the detective and the analyst respectively employ, a similarity that Freud himself in fact recognized. In his "Psycho-Analysis and the Establishment of the Facts in Legal Proceedings" (1906), Freud writes that "the task of the therapist, however, is the same as that of the examining magistrate. We have to uncover the hidden psychical material; and in order to do this we have invented a number of detective devices, some of which it seems that you gentlemen of the law are now about to copy from us."[35] Developing this point further, Elisabeth Strowick notes that both detective and analyst employ procedures that are predicated upon a knowledge/power regime based on the tendency to "reconstruct the object from the clues, that is, to reconstruct the 'facts' as the very cause of those clues," in effect fabricating *after the fact* what Strowick terms the cause-effect-nexus.[36] In less abstract terms, what this means is that both detective and analyst are faced with a scene in the aftermath of an event (e.g., murder or psychic trauma) that seemingly has the appearance of an imaginary unity; the patient may not bear any outright symptoms or a crime scene may not reveal any clues that point to an obvious culprit. Upon further examination, however, cracks in this imaginary unity begin to appear. The detective may begin to notice inconsistencies in the crime scene, contradictions in the testimony of suspects, or some other telling detail; in the same vein, the analyst encounters unsaid gaps or slippages in the analysand's account. In both cases, it is through the attention to these details in the "false solution" that a different solution, a different narrative emerges. Put differently, what detective fiction and psychoanalysis have in common is their shared social function to reconstitute a narrative continuity out of the site of its breakdown. Both the detective and the analyst start off faced with a scene in the aftermath of a violent event (either a murder or a psychic trauma). They then attempt to render the incoherence of this scene coherent using similar techniques: namely the production of a narrative leading up to the event, through such means as the identification of the incongruous detail, the attention to gaps and slippages in testimony, and so on. Indeed, one might even go so far as to say that they operate in parallel; in other words, the analyst is the detective of the psyche and vice versa.

However, the important points of difference between detection and analysis cannot be overlooked. The most obvious divergence is their respective objects of investigation, with the detective's interest placed on an external world of society while the psychoanalyst's is in the internal world of the psyche. While seemingly minor, this difference brings into the picture the problem introduced by the concept of the unconscious. Whereas a criminal conceals a secret he knows from the detective, the subject of an analysis is himself or herself unaware of the secret in question. As Freud puts it, "In the case of the criminal it is a secret which he knows and hides from you, whereas in the case of the hysteric it is a secret which he himself does not know either, which is hidden even from himself."[37] Following this logic, Slavoj Žižek has argued that a crucial implication of the differences between the practices of detection and analysis is that while in the former the end point is the conclusive identification of a singular criminal with its implied guarantee of innocence in all others through the externalizing or othering of guilt, in the latter, because the object of inquiry is the unconscious, what is unearthed is the repressed otherness *within* the subject, with the implication that potential for guilt

is not something that can be so easily externalized. Instead, all are potentially guilty, all are potentially implicated in the crime. In Žižek's words,
"the detective's act consists in annihilating the libidinal possibility, the
'inner' truth that we all could have been murderers (i.e., that we are murderers in the unconscious of our desire)."[38]

Implicated here is more than the mere matter of the narrative conventions of detective fiction. More importantly, it speaks to the genre's
ideological underpinnings, the latent political charge of its techniques
of narrativization. On this point, consider Franco Moretti's analysis of
the social functions of detective fiction, in which he calls attention to
how the roles of criminal and detective map onto the positions of individual and collective, respectively. For Moretti, individuation—that is,
the fixing of a singular *individual* identity to the criminal, so as to absolve
the social body at large of guilt—forms the foundation of the genre. In
Moretti's words, "A good rule in detective fiction is to have only one
criminal. . . . [Detective fiction] exists expressly to dispel the doubt that
guilt might be impersonal, and therefore collective and social. . . . Crime
is always presented as an exception."[39] Individuating the criminal allows
for his or her differentiation from the social body, marking off the crime
as something outside the norm, as the sole cause of social disturbance,
thus preserving the presumed innocence of the social body. Any examination of social guilt, of structural violence is rendered beyond the purview of the genre's narrative system, rendered as that which lies beyond
its representation. Hence, "the perfect crime—the nightmare of detective
fiction—is the featureless, de-individualized crime that anyone could
have committed because at this point everyone is the same."[40]

Herein lies the significance of the doppelgänger's appearances in
Rampo's fiction. In hinting at a relationship of doubling between Samukawa and Shundei, it renders the othering of Shundei incomplete, with
the effect of implicating the narrator in the crime he is investigating.
Rampo's novel thus rejects of the conventional imperative in the detective genre to produce a singular scapegoat, hence bringing it into closer
formal alignment with what Žižek views as the critical potential of psychoanalysis. Furthermore, this activation of the detective's unconscious
has the attendant consequence of bringing to the surface the historical
unconscious that the very form of detective fiction seeks to repress. In

his refusal of the categorical othering of the criminal through his employment of the figure of the doppelgänger, Rampo implicitly recognizes
forms of violence that exceed representability within the narrative logic
of detective fiction. Its significance can therefore be located in its potential to gesture toward a critical practice that can account for the implication of the social body in forms of violence that cannot be reduced to
exceptions, but are instead built into its very structure, its very history.

Situating the Doppelgänger in Modern Japan

Insofar as the doppelgänger's appearances within detective fictions serve
as a figuration of a resistance to the genre's tendency toward the identification, individuation, and categorical othering of the criminal, taking
seriously the doppelgänger's features as a concept and critical prism
entails a similar resistance to treating it in terms of influence, in isolation
as something reducible to an idiosyncratic feature of a singular author's
body of work. Rather, it calls for a critical practice that is attentive to the
historicity of its appearances, that recognizes the broader social context
and structural constraints in which the figure manifests, that can account
for the material conditions that engender its recurrences at particular
historical conjunctures. This is a task that becomes particularly salient
in light of the repeated deployment of the doppelgänger motif in the
work of not just Rampo, but many of his contemporaries as well, in the
writings of such as authors as Akutagawa Ryūnosuke, Satō Haruo, and
Tanizaki Jun'ichirō, to name a few. That these writers' doppelgänger fictions also often exhibited their interest in dabbling in the techniques of
detective fiction is no mere coincidence. Indeed, it emphasizes the necessity of addressing the broader social and political function served by the
historical emergence and consolidation of detective fiction as a genre
within the specific context of interwar Japan, and with that, the significance of the doppelgänger motif's function as a marker of the ideological
limits of its techniques of narrativization.

In connection with this challenge, I would be far from the first to point
toward the interlinked processes of urbanization and the corresponding
rise of consumer culture in the first few decades of the twentieth century
as something formative of an increasingly pervading sense of a crisis in
representation in Japanese cultural life. On the one hand, the sheer pace

of growth in Japanese population centers generated new experiences of mass anonymity. This was particularly acute in the case of Tokyo. Partly as a consequence of the industrial boom experienced during the First World War, Tokyo's population growth rate reached 14.5 percent, in stark contrast to the national average of 1 percent. Much of this growth came from waves of population migration, both from the rural regions of "Japan proper" as well as the empire's colonial periphery. When the first national census was published in 1920, Tokyo's population reached a staggering 3.35 million (rising to over 5 million by 1928), making it one of the largest metropolitan centers of the world at the time. By the end of the 1920s, over half of the city's population was composed of migrants from outside of the city.[41] This process involved a double push on the one hand to undermine extant forms of identities, and on the other hand, to capture and discipline these dislocated bodies so as to facilitate their commodification and circulation as labor; or, in the words of Gilles Deleuze and Félix Guattari, "capitalism is reterritorializing with one hand what it was deterritorializing with the other."[42]

But the end of the First World War brought a sharp economic downturn in Japan, leading to significant declines in real wages and increases in the surplus population. Not coincidentally, these events led to the exacerbation of existing social problems—crime and the breakdown of communities—that consequently increased demands for greater policing. Given the anonymity of the city, procedures of individuation and the fixing of identities became a key problem in the area of crime and its detection. Of particular concern were repeat offenders. As Serizawa Kazuya has pointed out, one characteristic of the modernization of policing in Japan was a shift in focus from the crimes themselves to the criminal as a subject. Within this regime, much attention was placed on the problem of assessing the danger a given criminal posed to the social fabric, and repeat offenders (whether already realized or only potential) were assessed to be of greater risk. But the problem then was how to identify who was a repeat offender with confidence—after all, names could be changed and disguises could be adopted—thus requiring new techniques and technologies that were subsequently taken up and popularized by writers of detective fictions.[43]

Such concerns led to the development of all manner of new technologies for fixing these dislocated bodies to facilitate their commoditization and capture. For example, Tom Gunning has pointed to the operations of photography and early cinema, writing that "while the mechanical reproduction and multiplication of photographic images undermined traditional understandings of identity, within the practice of criminology and detective fiction the photograph could also be used as a guarantor of identity and as a means of establishing guilt or innocence."[44] This is especially evident in the institution of techniques like the accumulation of captured criminals' portraits that were arranged into "Rogues' Galleries" or the more advanced and complicated Bertillon system (developed by and named after French police statistician Alphonse Bertillon), which involved not only the collection and archiving of portrait photographs but also charts and measurements for classifying and systematizing the various biometric and physiognomic features. In Japan, techniques like the Bertillon system were imported through such works as Ōba Shigema's *Kojin shikibetsu hō* (Methods of individuation, 1908), which collected research on various penal and policing systems around the world. Put simply, doppelgängers, disguises, and multiple identities became more than just merely figures of fantasy, but scientific problems in the field of policing and the management of populations. As detective fiction emerged as the representation of these social problems in popular culture, it is not surprising that the figure of the doppelgänger found a home in the genre.

It was not only in the field of detection and policing that a reterritorializing response to the deterritorialized space of the city and its displaced populations became apparent. It was also against this backdrop of a lived experience of being removed from a rural collective life only to be thrust into a privatized and solitary social situation productive of new traumas and anxieties that the introduction and popularization of psychoanalytic theories took place in Japan. At the same time, writings like Kobayashi Hideo's characterization of Tokyo as a space of homelessness in his famous essay "Kokyō o ushinatta bungaku" ("Literature of the Lost Home," 1933) gave expression to these anxieties. For Kobayashi, the rapid and repeated transformations witnessed by Tokyo—punctuated particularly by the devastation wrought by the Great Kanto Earthquake of 1923 that leveled much of the city—meant that it could no longer serve as stable ground for the accumulation of memory; it had become dream-like, a shifting, phantasmal place.[45] His characterization of modern life as permeated by the feeling of homelessness readily brings to mind Freud's concept of the uncanny or un-home-like (*unheimlich*), which the figure of the doppelganger embodies in its simultaneous evocation of the familiar and the alien. Further compounding this sense was the mass production of new consumer products, more specifically, their display and advertisement, which had the effect of saturating urban spaces with commodity spectacles. This brought about the production of new affects and desires and the increasing commodification and alienation of all aspects of culture and human subjectivity. In Kobayashi's observation, "Both the capacity and the patience to dream for oneself are lost. Yet the craving to dream remains. How convenient, then, for people to just go and stand dumbfounded in the city streets, where the high-speed, man-ufactured motion seems already dreamlike."[46] Put another way, the effect Kobayashi describes here is akin to the externalization of dreaming and the unconscious, its materialization outside one's body. It is perhaps only apt that the doppelgänger became a favored literary metaphor for the experience of dislocation and disorientation symptomatic of a pervading sense of crisis in representation and subjectivity in 1920s Japan.[47]

It is this historical backdrop that served as the formative context for the emergence and popularization of not only the genre of detective fiction and the practice of psychoanalysis, but also a range of other inter-linked reterritorializing cultural practices. This common social function places both psychoanalysis and detective fiction within the broader discursive context of modernist writing oriented around a desire for narrative of a larger scale, an attempt to apprehend the totality of history and everyday life against the context of alienation that had become the normative structure of feeling in modern Japan during the period between the two world wars.[48] In her study of 1920s and 1930s Japan, Miriam Silverberg emphasizes the underlying logic of montage that shaped the conditions of the period. The collision of different codes of everyday life differentiated along the axes of multiple social classes, subcultures, ethnicities, and lifestyles coexisting within the rapidly changing space of the city formed a complex and hybrid culture of modern life that necessitated the development of new techniques for apprehending and negotiating one's immediate social and material environment.[49] Against this backdrop came the appearance of such discursive practices as modernist experiments with new literary forms, the desire for representational immediacy expressed through the rise of the so-called "I-novel" or *shishō-shetsu*, or the meticulous ethnographic documenting of the transformations of everyday markers of modernity (language, fashion, the body, etc.) of such activities as Kon Wajirō's practice of "modernology." Indeed, an argument can be made that both detective fiction and psychoanalysis functioned as testing grounds for techniques subsequently adopted by other cultural practices.

One particularly visible manifestation of this can be found in the rise of what Silverberg calls a "documentary impulse"—a desire to segment and rationalize the new collective mass of dislocated human bodies—in various mass cultural practices of the time. These practices often drew upon techniques of detailed observation and classification alongside the supposition that hidden secrets (whether consciously concealed or only unconsciously present) can be uncovered through attention to these surface details, both of which were central tenets of both psychoanalysis and detective fiction.[50] Similarly, in the literary field, a consequence of the rapidity of urbanization and the consolidation of mass culture was a breakdown in the institution of literature as an autonomous and depoliticized space, provoking the reevaluation of literary form to incorporate ethnographic and documentary techniques such as tailing, spying, detailed observation adopted from detective fiction on the one hand, and the rise of confessional modes of writing as a reactionary formation on the other hand.[51]

The underlying logic uniting these discursive practices was the articulation of a desire for what Ernst Bloch has called "a remoter something"—an essential clue or symptom that might reveal a hitherto unknown coherence to the "nightmare of history"—so as to uncover its hidden origins and make it possible to give it narrative form.[52] Through their respective narrative techniques, these modernist discourses, in the words of Harootunian, "attacked the problems raised by capitalism at the level of representation, each, in its own way, trying to find a stable ground and referent capable of guaranteeing the possibility of representation."[53]

Principally, this entailed the adoption of a position of visual mastery over the other, that is, a position to observe without oneself becoming the subject of a parallel opposite observation. But if Rampo's doppelgänger fictions are indicative of anything, it is that this procedure is never quite so simple. The doppelgänger threatens to reverse and return the gaze, thus subverting any attempt to produce coherence out of incoherence. If modern narration is undergirded by the drawing of stark boundaries between interiority and exteriority, as Karatani Kōjin has famously put forward, the doppelgänger can be understood as enacting a reversal of this process; its staging of a collapse of the distinctions between self and other—between interiority and exteriority—breaches the boundaries of subjective sovereignty.[54] In this sense, the doppelgänger's proliferation as a cultural formation becomes significant in that it functions as a figure that marks the point of intersection of these various discursive practices by way of a subversion of their logics and a foregrounding of the historical unconscious that underwrites their emergence.

Many of Rampo's doppelgänger fictions capture the interplay of these dynamics. Take, for example, the case of his 1930 novel *Beyond the Bizarre*. The story revolves around the activities of a wealthy yet bored married man by the name of Aoki. It begins with Aoki wandering in a street festival in Tokyo, where he runs into someone who by coincidence has the exact appearance of his close friend Shinagawa, but turns out to be someone else altogether. A turn toward the bizarre takes place when Aoki tails the "other" Shinagawa to a flophouse that houses a secret attic where participants in a thrill-seeking group organize sexual encounters and other spectacles. After bringing Shinagawa with him to observe his double performing sadomasochistic sexual activities from behind a peephole, the story begins to fragment, with Shinagawa receiving a letter from one of his double's lovers and Aoki suspecting that his wife (or her double) is also involved in the activities within the secret flophouse. Ultimately, the novel culminates in the rather contrived conclusion wherein all the various doubles turn out to have been engineered through extensive plastic surgery as a part of an insane scheme concocted by a mad scientist from Shanghai to encourage all manner of vices and delinquencies among the members of the secret club.

Aside from the central place of the doppelgänger motif in its story, what makes *Beyond the Bizarre* noteworthy is the extent to which it prominently features several cultural practices that speak to the discursive context of interwar Japan. Foremost among these is Aoki's so-called "curiosity-hunting," which sets the stage for the events of the novel to unfold. His initial encounter with Shinagawa's double takes place as a direct consequence of his habit of wandering the streets of Tokyo in search of spectacles and cheap thrills. Moreover, this encounter develops into his secretive tailing and close study of Shinagawa's double to first ascertain his identity and then to draw vicarious pleasure from the act of observation itself. Both actions incorporate important cultural practices taking place in Japan at the time. On the one hand, Aoki's curiosity-hunting [*ryōki*]—that is, his obsessive desire for the stimulation of the senses by seeking out all manner of bizarre and titillating sights and sounds—had real-life counterparts in the proliferation of journals of the bizarre and the erotic-grotesque that documented all manner of "odd" phenomena such as paranormal sightings, exotic colonial artifacts, or accounts of perverse sexual encounters.[55] On the other hand, his tailing and close observation of others finds a parallel in the documentary impulse of the meticulous recording of minutiae—gestures, fashion, vectors of movement—at the heart of Kon Wajirō's urban anthropological project of "modernology."

Aoki's incessant desire for thrills echoes Georg Simmel's famous observation that the overstimulation of the senses among metropolitan consumer-subjects elicits a blasé outlook in them, so that increasingly escalating sensations become necessary to activate any affective response.[56] Not only does the novel suggest that its protagonist Aoki has a tendency to confuse fact and fiction [*jijitsu to shōsetsu o kondō shite*], but also the novel ends by hinting that the fantastic events depicted in the story take place only in the protagonist's imagination.[57] This particular plot device has doubtless become a cliché. However, considered in the context of the rapid expansion of consumer capitalism, Aoki's dreamlike confusion of fact and fiction—of object and its image—is not just a rhetorical sleight of hand, but is emblematic of the lived experience of its consumer-subjects. As Mark Driscoll describes in his analysis of the links between erotic-grotesque culture and the history of Japanese imperialism, this "declining rate of pleasure" is a phenomenon that takes place parallel to the tendency toward a decline in the rate of profit within the structural logic of capitalist production. Just as the fall in the rate in profit engenders a crisis that demands the opening up of hitherto unavailable markets through colonial expansion on the one hand, and the commodification of even human desire and subjectivity on the other, the production of new affects and surplus pleasures became necessary within the image-commodity saturated environment of urban metropoles.[58]

Aoki's so-called curiosity-hunting—his flânerie—responds to these conditions. At the same time, what enables his activities in *Beyond the Bizarre* is precisely the cover of anonymity provided by the mass circulation of bodies in urban spaces. Aoki's actions here recall Walter Benjamin's famous observation that "the original social content of the detective story was the obliteration of the individual's traces in the big-city crowd."[59] The observational techniques of the detective give rise to the mobilized observer embodied in the figure of the flâneur that Benjamin associates with the development of the industrialized urban form from the nineteenth century onward. The flâneur adopts the detective's gaze only to turn it into a different purpose. Nonetheless, they share the same position of acting as observer without themselves being the object of observation. This relationship is one that *Beyond the Bizarre* foregrounds fairly early in its narrative. Its preface opens by relating the ennui that drives the curiosity-hunter's desire to seek out greater and greater thrills to the detective fictionist's need to stage even more lurid crimes from one story to the next, and it ascribes this shared sense to their subjects' respective positioning as consummate third-person observers [*akumademo daisansha de ari, bōkansha da kara de aru*].[60] Later in the novel, Aoki's desire for third-person observation is made explicit when, after participating in an orgy at the secret club, he decides that he has a voyeuristic preference for observing others' sexual acts rather than participating in them. So, he transforms himself into the classic spectator, seated anonymously in the darkness as a consumer of image-commodities. In effect, he has come to desire the spectacle of sexuality over sexuality itself.

But if the detective's gaze is based on a principle of visual mastery, conversely, the doppelgänger enacts a reversal of this gaze in *Beyond the Bizarre.* When Aoki first informs Shinagawa of his encounter with his friend's doppelgänger, Shinagawa expresses concern. While Aoki expresses a sense of enjoyment in the whole situation, for Shinagawa, it is a cause for alarm. He says: "You say he's a criminal. Picking someone's pocket may be a petty offense, but what if he commits something more serious, like murder for instance? I look just like him, so there's a chance I might get entangled in some mix-up. I can neither stop nor predict his crimes. What if I don't have an alibi? It's really quite frightening to think about."[61] In other words, the presence of his double effectively precludes Shinagawa from the kinds of thrills Aoki enjoys. He can no longer take a position apart from the crowd, but has instead become literally *another face* in the crowd. Shinagawa's distress is only further amplified when he accompanies Aoki to witness the other Shinagawa engage in rather intense sadomasochistic sex inside the secret club. Shinagawa finds himself unable to watch the whole thing as he is tormented at the sight of his own double. The visual pleasure of spectatorship is only possible when one can occupy a position detached from the images before one's eyes. Rather than consuming the images before him, Shinagawa has become the image-commodity itself, foreshadowing the novel's conclusion, which depicts the mass-production through plastic surgery of people's faces and likenesses, that is, the commodification of the very markers of identity.

Colonial Doppelgängers

In sum, what Rampo's fictions of the doppelgänger appear to highlight is the linkage between the figure's proliferation in Japanese literary texts during the 1920s and 1930s and the experience of living through the process of modernization, with its attendant introduction of all manner of interlinked social and material technologies including new systems of industrialized mass production and new forms of image and media cultures, not to mention new modes of interiority and subjectivity. Scholars such as Marilyn Ivy have noted that one by-product of these processes is the experience of the uncanny, of encountering what was once familiar reappearing in an alien and threatening form, manifesting in such discourses as persistent expressions of a sense of loss, a sense of homelessness.[62] Or, to put it another way, if indeed the doppelgänger embodies this sense of the uncanny, as Freud suggests in his seminal work on the subject, this understanding must be understood within the broader context of the uncanniness of the experience of modernity itself. In Japan, this experience tended to be conflated with the foreign, hence translated into a language of cultural colonization by foreign commodities and cultural products.[63]

However, this is only one part of the picture. Overlooked in such an emphasis is how Japan's metropolitan capital was at once an imperial capital. The rapid urbanization and rise of a mass consumer capitalism in Japan since the First World War is inseparable from its colonial expansion and economic encroachment into other parts of East Asia. As Driscoll points out, even as the expansion of consumer capitalism in Japan's metropolitan centers functions as a form of subsumption of human desire and sensation into the capitalist economy, it is crucial to also recognize that this process was predicated on a more conventional colonial economic engine underpinned by wide-scale overexploitation of its colonial peripheries in Korea and northern China. Put another way, had it not been for Japan's practices of colonial expansion and exploitation, the sheer pace of urbanization and development of a consumer-capitalist economy in the metropolitan centers of Tokyo and Osaka may very well not have occurred. Through such means as coolie labor, the trafficking of opium and women, land appropriations, and other tactics, Japan's colonial periphery accumulated and directed wealth and human bodies to the metropolitan centers in an illustration of what Driscoll calls the peripheral a priori: "the spatiotemporal prioritizing of peripheral marginalia as the primary agents of culturo-economic change."[64] The periphery of Japan's colonial empire functioned as a laboratory wherein not only forms of economic exploitation, but also sociocultural practices and techniques of social control and policing were practiced and perfected prior to their adoption in the metropolitan centers.

With this context in mind, the question of what is at stake in the various reterritorializing processes and practices that make themselves visible in 1920s and 1930s Japan can be better articulated. Indeed, highlighting this peripheral a priori leads to a number of implications, not the least of which is the recognition that the aforementioned sense of crisis and anxiety of dislocation in Japan's urban centers is traceable to the lived experience of colonial modernity. At one level, because a significant constitutive component of the workings of the economy is located elsewhere, the totality of the lived experience of everyday life in the metropolitan centers is rendered ungraspable or unrepresentable.[65] At another level, metropolitan capitals increasingly became sites for the interpenetration of the colonial periphery into the center, rendering them into what Mary Louise Pratt has termed a "contact zone," a "space of colonial encounters, the space in which peoples geographically and historically separated come into contact with one another, usually involving conditions of coercion, radical inequality, and intractable conflict."[66] One symptom of such a condition of coercion is precisely the reactionary desire (and the power to enact this desire) to re-mark boundaries, to exclude and designate the colonial subject as other.

That the disciplinary desire of detective fiction emerges out of this context is no accident. It is not uncommon for crimes that take place in the urban centers to be represented as originating from the colonial periphery in detective fictions, thus marking the latter as a site that is just as central in importance as the city for the genre.[67] In the case of Arthur Conan Doyle's Sherlock Holmes fictions, for instance, the titular character and his partner (and focalizer of the narrative) Watson's first meeting is enabled by the latter's injury during a military campaign in Afghanistan that compels him to return to England. Moreover, the criminals in these fictions were often, if not "foreigners" literally, nevertheless characterized as bearing some kind of foreign taint, reflecting in literary form the racist component of the discipline of criminology at the time and its inseparability from Britain's colonial expansion. As Ronald Thomas's reading of the detective as "a designated figure of authority" who "gains the power to tell 'the truth' by acquiring the right to tell someone else's story against his or her will" emphasizes, the relations of power between detective and criminal mirror the asymmetrical relationship between colonizer and colonized.[68] The profound linkage between not only the historical but also the narratological relationship between the devices of detective genre and techniques of colonial governance is difficult to overlook.

Not coincidentally given its aforementioned parallels with the narrative techniques of detective fiction, a similar argument can be raised vis-à-vis the discourse of psychoanalysis in that it emerges as a discipline at the height of colonial expansion all over the world. In her book *Dark Continents: Psychoanalysis and Colonialism* (2003), Ranjanna Khanna argues that psychoanalysis is itself a colonial discourse, a "colonial intellectual formation [that] disciplines a way of being as much as it establishes a form of analysis based in the age of colonialism and constitutive of concepts of the primitive against which the civilizing mission could establish itself."[69] What this means is that the condition of possibility for the psychoanalytic construction of the modern, masculine, and "civilized" self is the demarcation of its others—the feminine, the primitive, the savage—that is enabled primarily through the contact zone of the colonial encounter. In other words, the coming into being of psychoanalysis is predicated upon colonial structures of exclusion, with colonized subjects incorporated into its logic as its excess, its own constitutive repression. Analogous to the pattern we see in the case of detective fiction, individual subjective violence is conditioned by a background of objective violence; the psychoanalytic theories that posit the birth of the sovereign subject as something that comes out of trauma themselves only became thinkable in the context of historical traumas and violences of a larger scale.

Psychoanalytic treatments of the doppelgänger provide an illustrative example of the colonial underpinnings of the discipline. This is especially evident in the work of Otto Rank, whose *Der Doppelgänger* is generally considered to be the pioneering psychoanalytic study of the figure. While Rank's primary interest is to examine the doppelgänger in terms of psychoanalytic concepts, he also delves into myth and performs armchair anthropology in an effort to show "the common psychological basis of the superstitious and artistic representations of these impulses."[70] In his analysis, Rank suggests that the modern conception of the double (and its association with foretelling imminent death) is an inversion of an earlier understanding of the double in so-called "primitive cultures" as representing the immortal soul, that is, as a ward against death. Through this move, Rank extends his analysis of the doppelgänger as a manifestation of a return of the repressed to give it a historical dimension as well; just as the doppelgänger's uncanny effect is the product of the familiar returning in alien form, its modern form is the primitive double turned threatening. To arrive at his argument wherein the origin of the doppelgänger figure is traced to the moment of childhood narcissism prior to the demarcation of subject from object, Rank goes back in time by way of folklore read through the colonial anthropological practice of the early twentieth century in an attempt to identify a "primitive" and "pure" doppelgänger, prior to modern civilization. In other words, he had to rely on a hierarchical schema of "civilizations"—a kind of "civilizational childhood" upon which narcissism could be ascribed in racial and cultural terms.[71]

Yet if, as Karatani Kōjin has argued, the category of "children" had to be "discovered"—that is, invented—in modernity,[72] then the uncanny appearance of the doppelgänger cannot be reduced to a return of an original childhood narcissism, to "a regression to a time when the ego had not yet marked itself off sharply from the external world and from other people," as Freud put it.[73] Rather, it is more productively understood as a sign marking the breakdown in the foundational demarcation of child from adult (or premodern from modern) on which the teleology of modern subjectivity (and modernity) rests. In addition, Karatani's point here can be broadly aligned with other arguments surrounding the constitution and structuring of historical narratives of colonial modernity that note how their underlying logic rests on a foundational schism located on a temporal axis. Dipesh Chakrabarty, for example, has asserted that a "historical construction of temporality (medieval/modern, separated by historical time) is precisely the axis along which the colonial subject splits itself. Or to put it differently, this split *is* what is history; writing history is performing this split over and over again."[74] The condition of possibility for historical time itself (as it has come to be conceived in colonial—and by implication—capitalist modernity) is a structure of exclusion; the "premodern" (or the "precapitalist") had to be overcome and repressed and rendered docile by locating it as chronologically prior to "the modern" or "the capitalist." What is called modern history is the compulsion to repeat this foundational repression, this constitutive violence of capitalism and colonialism.

Indeed, in the particular case of Japan, the compulsion to repeat this splitting takes on a doubled dimension in that it performs the roles of both colonizer and quasi-colonized mimic at the same time, with the consequence of calling attention to the discursive spaces and structures of colonial modernity that an analysis of the doppelgänger in a different context may very well overlook. As the subsequent chapters will discuss further, it is precisely this potential to disclose a practice that is attentive to these historical violences that I see as the broader critical significance of the doppelgänger's manifestations in Japanese cultural production. Just as the figure of the doppelgänger manifests in the work of Rampo as the excess to the detective's act of narration, its recurrent appearances at specific junctures seemingly mark a desire to unearth the historical unconscious that underwrites various narratives of modernization. What is therefore intriguing about the figure of the doppelgänger, especially in its appearances in the Japanese context, is how the very features and characteristics most often ascribed to it already engender a critical practice that is attentive to the very historical conditions of possibility of its emergence as a literary motif and psychoanalytic concept.

2

Repressing the Colonial Unconscious

Racialized Doppelgängers

Tanizaki's Double Fictions

It cannot be said that the work of Tanizaki Jun'ichirō (1886–1965) has suffered from any critical neglect. Not only were his fictions some of earliest and more extensively translated into English among twentieth-century Japanese authors; more importantly, they have been consistent objects of attention, with various debates and discussions about his work persisting through the decades in both Japanese and English-language scholarly writings.[1] Beyond the standard literary-historical overviews and biographical accounts of the trajectory of his career, all manner of approaches to Tanizaki's fiction have appeared in recent years, from considerations of his employment of the femme fatale figure, to studies of his writings on cinema and aesthetics, to examinations of his accounts of his travels to China, among others. No doubt, his long and storied literary career, not to mention the various turns he took through his life, contributed to making his body of work eminently readable through a disparate range of approaches, themes, and theoretical frameworks.

Tanizaki received initial recognition with his early decadent fictions such as his debut story "Shisei" ("The Tattooer," 1910) or "Himitsu" (The secret, 1911), which featured the themes of sexual fantasy, sadomasochism, fetishism, and perversion that would continue throughout his career. His dabbling in film production led to the writing of not only several screenplays, but also novels that took up cinematic themes such as *Nikukai* (A lump of flesh, 1923) or *Chijin no ai* (*Naomi*, 1924). His move to the Kansai region in the aftermath of the Great Kanto Earthquake of 1923 prompted an exploration of the classical arts and literatures of Japan, culminating in writings like *Tade kuu mushi* (*Some Prefer Nettles*, 1929) and *Yoshino kuzu* (*Arrowroot*, 1931) and an effort to produce a translation of the *Genji monogatari* (*The Tale of Genji*, 1939–1941) into modern Japanese. Moreover, Tanizaki's persistent meditation on his shifting (and often ambivalent) positions vis-à-vis the relationship between Japan and the West presented an accessible entry point for all manner of cultural hermeneutics within the field of Japanese studies.

However, one facet of Tanizaki's writing that has thus far seen relatively less attention is his employment of the doppelgänger motif. At various points during his long literary career, Tanizaki wrote several works of fiction that featured the figure of the doppelgänger. For example, in the aptly titled "A to B no hanashi" (The story of A and B, 1921), two individuals, one good and another evil, who are both writers and ostensibly cousins, agree to a pact wherein A surrenders all the recognition he has earned as a writer to B as proof of his desire to redeem B from his criminal ways. Another example is "Aozuka-shi no hanashi" (Mr. Aozuka's story, 1926), which centers on an actress who reads about the manufacture of lifelike dolls with her face in her husband's diary after he passes away. Evident in both these examples are traces of the prototypical features commonly associated with fictions of the doppelgänger. In the former appears an almost schematic example of the splitting of the characters who are otherwise symmetrical—indeed in this case, punctuated further by the reduction of their identities and names to anonymous initials—on an axis of a moral binary, and their subsequent interchangeability. With the latter, more fleshed-out text, there are clear echoes of E. T. A. Hoffmann's "The Sandman" and its female dolls, posited by Freud in his discussion of the doppelgänger as an emblematic icon of uncanniness.[2]

It is worth examining Tanizaki's doppelgänger fictions in more detail for several reasons. First, his employment of the doppelgänger motif—with its staging of notions of narcissism, the uncanny, and the compulsion to repeat—calls attention to the thematic overlaps between his writings and psychoanalytic theories. As Margherita Long has observed, despite the fact that there is little evidence to suggest that Tanizaki was all that familiar with the work of Sigmund Freud, one of the more curious characteristics of Tanizaki's body of literary work is the way many of his fictional narratives seemingly speak to several concepts at the heart of psychoanalysis.[3] Consider, for example, Tanizaki's relentless examination of fetishes, covering everything from expressions of his infamous foot fetish, which recur throughout his writings, to fetishes for visual pleasure manifesting in repeated scenes of photographing women's bodies, to obsessions with matters of (perceived) racial difference, appearing most famously in his novel *Naomi*. In addition, one cannot neglect to mention Tanizaki's repeated exploration of the theme of masochism, which is visible as early as his debut short story "The Tattooer" and recurs throughout the many fictions he authored across the span of his literary career. It is therefore difficult to overlook how Tanizaki's work recalls the long-debated question of the suitability of employing psychoanalytic concepts for cultural analyses within the specific sociocultural milieu of Japan.

Objections to psychoanalysis on the grounds that it is ill suited to the Japanese cultural context have been voiced since its introduction to Japan in the early twentieth century. To the extent that such questions compel the recognition of the contingent historical circumstances in which psychoanalysis emerges as a discursive formation, there is some merit to these objections. However, often, the premise underlying such concerns is a culturalist fantasy of a fixed, homogenous "Japan" *different from* a unitary (and universalized) "West."[4] As such, the perception of a poor fit between psychoanalysis and Japan is underpinned by Orientalist forms of knowledge. In fact, I would suggest that such claims serve as gestures that disavow the discursivity of psychoanalysis *in general.* Implied in the argument that psychoanalysis is unsuited to a specifically Japanese context are two interlinked presuppositions: that there were not in fact multiple expressions of psychoanalytic concepts that emerged *within* the Japanese context, and that psychoanalytic theories would fit in other sociocultural milieus without raising similar concerns. In other words, the issue at hand is not that the Japanese context is somehow uniquely unsuited to psychoanalytic theories. On the contrary, what the history of the introduction and reception of psychoanalysis to Japan has the potential to illuminate is the fact that the deployments of psychoanalysis—and for my purposes here, its concepts like the doppelgänger, the uncanny, or narcissism—are historically situated within a broader economy of discourses shaped by the structures of modernity, *regardless of location*.[5]

If Tanizaki's writings appear to echo psychoanalytic concepts, it is because he too occupied a set of historical circumstances that mirror those that engendered the emergence of psychoanalysis in the first place. This brings me to a second point of interest for Tanizaki's doppelgänger fictions, namely, their portrayal of cross-racial and cross-ethnic doublings, with the consequence of foregrounding the relations between the psychoanalytic themes typically ascribed to the doppelgänger and questions of race, empire, and history. More than merely affirming and recapitulating received conceptions of the figure of the doppelgänger or, alternatively, producing a localized "Japanese" version, what is significant about Tanizaki is his explicit linking of the motif of doubling to questions of race and empire not only within the particular historical circumstances of interwar Japan, but also as a more general problem.

Psychoanalysis and Colonial Mimicry

It should no longer be controversial at this juncture to assert that the development of psychoanalytic theories of the unconscious is historically wedded to the techniques of interpreting the other introduced by the burgeoning discipline of ethnography.[6] This linkage is made especially explicit in the early theorizations of the doppelgänger around the concept of narcissism. In "On Narcissism" (1914), Freud suggests that what takes place in the passage from the stage of childhood narcissism to adult sexuality is the repression of primary narcissism through the displacement of desire from oneself to a substitute "ego-ideal," who is typically the father figure. Freud's analysis does not stop there, though. Rather, he takes up this mechanism of the formation of an "ego-ideal" and expands it from the family system to larger social formations, noting that: "The ego-ideal opens up an important avenue for the understanding of group psychology. In addition to its individual side, this ideal has a social side; it is also the common ideal of a family, a class, or a nation."[7]

It is this aspect of the Freudian conception of narcissism that Otto Rank subsequently develops in his initial theorization of the doppelgänger.

Following Freud, Rank posits narcissistic autoeroticism as a fundamental feature of a phase of childhood, which the subject normally overcomes in the passage to adult sexuality. However, the encounter with one's doppelgänger is symptomatic of a regression to a state of childlike narcissism. It is, in Rank's words, "a functional expression of the psychological fact that an individual . . . cannot free himself from a certain phase of his narcissistically loved ego-development."[8] But in this process of regression also comes an externalization and inversion of the subject's excessive self-love, leading to its appearance in a defensive, disavowed form as an expression of a "suicidal" desire to murder one's own double, hence the conventional understanding of the doppelgänger as a harbinger of death. Rank then takes this narrative of childhood development and expands it to a civilizational scale, suggesting that because "primitive cultures" lack the multiple artificial groupings of "civilization" and with these, the overlapping ego-ideals formed in such social structures, they can be understood as fundamentally narcissistic. Or, as Rank puts it, if the structures to enable the displacement of narcissism do not exist, one can understand "primitive man, just as of the child, as being exquisitely narcissistic."[9] In this sense, so-called "primitive cultures" serve as the "fossilized" remnants of an earlier phase in the evolution of "civilization" for Rank. This enables him to argue that parallel to the process of inversion and externalization of self-love involved in the encounter with one's doppelgänger on an individual level, the common association of the doppelgänger with impending death in modern literature is a consequence of a similar reversal of the function of the shadow in "primitive cultures" as a ward against death, as a guarantor of immortality.

Immediately evident here is how Rank's psychoanalytic approach to examining the doppelgänger reflects what Johannes Fabian has characterized as the "denial of coevalness," that "persistent and systematic tendency to place the referent(s) of anthropology in a Time other than the present of the producer of anthropological discourse" so typical of the colonial gaze of the discipline of anthropology.[10] It reflects psychoanalysis's complicity in the reproduction of narratives of "civilization" through the production of and bifurcation from the imagined category of the "primitive" other, thus revealing the colonial underpinnings of its practice. In the words of Ranjanna Khanna, psychoanalysis is a "colonial intellectual formation [that] disciplines a way of being as much as it establishes a form of analysis based in the age of colonialism and constitutive of concepts of the primitive against which the civilizing mission could establish itself."[11] Indeed, insofar as an analogy with an imagined primitive subjectivity serves as a foundational basis for the conceptualization of the figure of the neurotic, the theories of psychoanalysis must be understood as inseparable from the global system of colonial conquest and subjugation.[12] In this regard, what is noteworthy about Rank's interest in the doppelgänger is how it calls attention to the very structures of exclusion that condition the emergence of the concept of the modern ego within colonial modernity.

Almost at the very moment of its consolidation as a modern capitalist nation-state, Japan engaged in colonial expansion—first with the annexation of the Ryukyu kingdom and Ezo as the prefectures of Okinawa and Hokkaido, respectively, and then moving into Taiwan in 1895 following the Sino-Japanese War and Korea in 1905 in the aftermath of the Russo-Japanese War. There is certainly a case that can be made that the same colonial logic through which the imagination of the doppelgänger was constituted was very much in operation in the Japanese context as well. However, such an analysis only goes so far. Complicating the picture are particularities in Japanese colonial policy and practice that warrant consideration. A key element is how the prevailing dominant discourses of Social Darwinism and scientific racism—which claimed an absolute demarcation between West and non-West as white and nonwhite, or for that matter, civilized and primitive—that served in part as an ex post facto ideological cover for colonial expansion could not be fully deployed in the case of the Japanese colonial empire. Despite emerging as a colonial power, Japan was nevertheless still also the object of the same orientalizing and racializing discourses deployed against its own colonial periphery. As such, its own positionality vis-à-vis its colonial subjects could not adopt the same transcendent normative invisibility conferred by constructions of the notion of "whiteness." In contrast to the Euro-American experience of imperialism wherein racial difference could be posited as a stark division, in the Japanese empire, because the colonial periphery was not geographically or culturally so far removed from its metropolitan centers, this demarcation and differentiation of colonial subjectivity appears masked and further abstracted by the absence of visible and easily reifiable racial differences.[13]

Put simply, in Japan, the legitimation of colonial power operated on the basis of the simultaneous production of both similarity and difference. One way to apprehend the workings of these techniques of power is by comparing them to Homi Bhabha's concept of colonial mimicry and ambivalence. To briefly summarize, Bhabha asserts that mimicry—the generation of an image of a "reformed, recognizable other, *as a subject of difference that is almost the same, but not quite"*—is an important mechanism of colonial rule in that it serves as a technology of identity imposed upon the colonized subject so as to discipline and regulate otherness. Yet at the same time, Bhabha also sees it as a potential site of its disruption, containing within it a structural ambivalence to the operations of colonial power.[14] The Japanese colonial empire arguably makes for an even more effective illustration of Bhabha's analysis than the historical circumstances of South Asia under British rule that serves as his primary object of examination.

On the one hand, Japan's status as what Oguma Eiji has called a "colored colonial empire" [*yūshoku no shokumin teikoku*] made it necessary to produce and deploy colonial discourses based not on the *absolute* exclusion of a racialized other.[15] Instead, these discourses had to be negotiated in conjunction with an ideology of assimilation while nonetheless maintaining a level of structural exclusion so as to reproduce the necessarily uneven relations of power in the colonial situation. If racialized categories of identity proved to be the mechanism for regulating otherness elsewhere, such a technology could not be fully operational in the Japanese context. On the other hand, the Japanese case introduces another dimension to this mimicry, operating not only with respect to the position occupied by the colonial subjects of the Japanese empire, but also at the level of the Japanese empire's own relation to the global system of imperialism itself. In the words of Leo Ching, "caught in between the contradictory positionality of not-white, not-quite and yet-alike, Japan's domineering gaze towards its colonial subjects in the East must always invariably redirect itself, somewhat ambivalently, to the imperialist glare of the West."[16] Put differently, this two-faced operation of assimilation and exclusion in Japanese colonial discourse is itself mirrored on a larger scale in Japan's own position among the various colonial empires at the time, rendering Japan itself as arguably the colonial mimic par excellence by itself becoming a colonial empire.[17]

If the notion of "civilization" can be understood as broadly functioning as a form of the "ego-ideal" through which primary narcissism is repressed, as Freud argues, then what the case of the Japanese empire and the specific character of its relations with its colonial periphery shows is the consequence of the incomplete assimilation and identification with this "ego-ideal" stemming from the particular position of the Japanese empire within a system of racial hierarchy wherein it cannot assume the unmarked and invisible position that whiteness confers. Thus, with respect to the problem of thinking about the doppelgänger, the case of Japan renders particularly visible the processes of racialization at work during this historical juncture, turning the doppelgänger's staging of a return of the repressed into what might be termed a return of the racialized repressed.

Return of the Racialized Repressed

It is precisely this incompleteness of assimilation brought about by this process of racialization that lies at the heart of the appearances of the doppelgänger in Tanizaki's fiction. Consider, for instance, the case of Tanizaki's novella "Tomoda to Matsunaga no hanashi" (The story of Tomoda and Matsunaga, 1926). At a glance, the setup of its story immediately brings to mind the opposition between the West and Japan in that it features a man living out a double life as a purportedly "Westernized" Tomoda and a "traditional Japanese" Matsunaga. Despite this setup, "The Story of Tomoda and Matsunaga" nonetheless offers a narrative that goes beyond merely reproducing a stark opposition between Japan and the West (despite what may appear at first glance) by instead attempting to complicate and interrogate the very logic of this opposition.

"The Story of Tomoda and Matsunaga" opens when the narrator, a professional writer identified only as F.K., receives a long, elegantly crafted letter from a woman residing in Yamato (Nara) who requests his assistance in locating her missing husband. In this letter, she reveals to the writer that her husband, one Matsunaga Ginsuke, has once again—in a cycle that apparently repeats every three or so years—left home without

providing her with any information as to his whereabouts. Upon searching his belongings for clues, she finds (along with an amethyst ring
and several photographs featuring women in indecent garb) a postcard
from F.K. addressed to a man named Tomoda Ginzō. With this as her
only clue, she contacts the narrator in the hope that he might be able to
clear up the situation. She wonders if through this Tomoda, he might be
able to assist her in locating her husband.

Indeed, the narrator is familiar with Tomoda, whose own periodic
disappearances curiously line up with Matsunaga's, leading him to suspect that they are in fact the same individual. However, the photograph
of Matsunaga he receives from the woman challenges his immediate suspicions. It shows a man who looks nothing at all like his friend Tomoda.
Whereas Tomoda is a young rotund man who almost does not even
appear Japanese, Matsunaga, in contrast, is an old and emaciated man.
Whereas the narrator knows Tomoda to be a lustful glutton, the photograph of Matsunaga he receives makes him appear to be dull and de-
pressed, as if they were not only different individuals, but total opposites.
In the narrator's description, the two men appear as follows:

> Tomoda was a corpulent, one might even say a morbidly obese, man. But
> the Matsunaga in this photograph was a tottering slender man. Tomoda's
> rotund face swelled as if his cheeks would burst right out from it. Matsu-
> naga had haggard, sunken cheeks that gave his face the shape of an inverted
> triangle. The two were as polar as polar opposites could be, with one bright
> and hearty and the other dark and melancholy.[18]

Despite their seemingly stark differences, the possible connection between
the two men marked by the alignment of their respective times of departures and disappearances intrigues the narrator. This leads him to seek
out his friend Tomoda in Yokohama. But when they meet, Tomoda
denies any knowledge of Matsunaga and claims to have no idea how the
postcard the narrator sent him ended up among Matsunaga's posses-
sions. His only explanation is a recollection that his bag had been stolen
some time ago. Not completely satisfied, the narrator continues to investigate. Through various plot twists and turns, with a telling one involving
a ring that Tomoda wears (which is oddly concealed in the photographs

Tomoda hands to the narrator to forward to Mrs. Matsunaga) that bears a striking similarity to the amethyst ring left in Yamato, F.K. is eventually able to surmise the solution, which is (mostly) confirmed by Tomoda's eventual confession at the end of the story. Finding himself suffocated by the marriage foisted upon him by his mother, Matsunaga first fled to Paris and reinvented himself as a Frenchman named Jacques Morin, transforming not only his behavior but his very body through persistent acts of gluttony until he became a man no longer recognizable as Matsunaga, or even as someone Japanese, for that matter. But then, Tomoda falls ill after three years of his raucous lifestyle. This forces him to return to his hometown. The illness causes him to lose his appetite and so he once again becomes the emaciated Matsunaga. Three years later and fully recovered, he takes off again, this time for Shanghai, once again becoming a large rotund man and taking on the new name of Tomoda Ginzō. And thus begins a repeating three-year cycle of departures (subsequently to Yokohama, Tokyo, and finally Kobe) and returns, each time involving drastic bodily transformations and reversions.

On its face, "The Story of Tomoda and Matsunaga" does not take the form of the classic doppelgänger story in the vein of Poe's "William Wilson"; instead, one might say that it appears closer to the version of the figure in Stevenson's *The Strange Case of Dr. Jekyll and Mr. Hyde*, which appears like the mirror image in that rather than two individuals of the same bodily appearance, it features a single person who seemingly occupies two seemingly distinct bodies, two separate identities under two separate names. That said, with its narrative framed as a mystery based upon the confusion of the identities of Tomoda and Matsunaga, its underlying logic is nonetheless not all that different from the typical doppelgänger narrative. In both cases, conflict arises from the unfixing of individuated identities from singular bodies; Tomoda emerges as the excess that the subjectivity of Matsunaga is unable to contain (and vice versa), forging a separate persona that is, if the constant oscillation between the two identities is any indication, never quite completely and neatly divisible. In this sense, Tanizaki's story enacts a similar narrative of the return of the repressed, albeit couched not in the terms of individual psyches and the unconscious, but in the language of corporeal bodies, and in particular, in terms of racialized bodies and the lived experience of colonial modernity.

Picking up the phrase "the specter of comparisons" [*el demonio de las comparaciones*] from Filipino author and revolutionary nationalist icon Jose Rizal, Benedict Anderson has described the lived experience of modernity in non-Western locales as akin to living a double life, as characterized by "a new, restless double-consciousness which made it impossible ever after to experience Berlin without at once thinking of Manila, or Manila without thinking of Berlin."[19] Something similar to this double life is certainly visible in the doubling of identities in "The Story of Tomoda and Matsunaga." However, in Tanizaki's novella, this tension in the experience of modernity is made corporeal, inscribed upon the very bodies of Tomoda and Matsunaga. Given expression in the story is not only a case of a doubling of personalities and psychical identities, but the doubling of bodies. Tomoda/Matsunaga's corporeal body itself becomes the site of the tensions ascribed to the double consciousness of non-Western modernity. He does not only identify with the West as Tomoda at a psychical level, but also transforms his body to the point of effacing any racialized features that mark him as "Japanese." To achieve the transformation from the gaunt Matsunaga to the obese and "Westernized" Tomoda, the character makes himself a glutton. He literally "assimilates" the West into his own body. But his body can take in only so much, such that every three years, he falls ill, and is forced to return to his hometown of Nara to once again become Japanese, become Matsunaga and recuperate. Matsunaga thus returns as a kind of remainder of Tomoda's racial shadow, whose weakness of body in the end cannot sustain the lifestyle Tomoda leads. He thus repeatedly enacts the process of racialized subject formation, which Frantz Fanon has characterized as a process predicated upon a traumatic identification with one's inferior position, so as to render one unable to fully assimilate into a given (white, Western) ego-ideal. It is to be ineluctably other, even to oneself. In the context of Japan, as well as other locations marked as "non-Western," this logic comes to be coded, literally inscribed upon the body in the process of racialization, or what Fanon has called a process of "epidermalization."[20]

In its incessant attention to these concerns, "The Story of Tomoda and Matsunaga" prefigures Tanizaki's later and more famous treatise on Japanese aesthetics *In'ei raisan* (*In Praise of Shadows*, 1933). Often read as the culmination of Tanizaki's so-called "return to Japan," *In Praise of Shadows* deals with a range of subjects, from architecture, to food, to women. An overarching logic that encompasses these various topics is the contrast between light and shadow that is coded consistently as "Western" and "Japanese," respectively. Whereas Tanizaki characterizes Western aesthetics (and "white" bodies) as constantly seeking illumination and clarity, the prevalence of shadow in Japanese aesthetics (and likewise, the bodies racialized as "Oriental") serves to capture a subtlety that is lost under the bright lights of the modern, even as it serves as a means of concealing the taint of color inscribed upon the surface of the Japanese body as yellow skin. As Tanizaki puts it: "For the Japanese complexion, no matter how white, is tinged by a slight cloudiness. . . . But the skin of the Westerners, even those of darker complexion, had a limpid glow. Nowhere were they tainted by this gray shadow. . . . It is natural that we should have chosen cloudy colors for our food and clothing and houses, and sunk ourselves back into the shadows."[21]

Similar language appears in "The Story of Tomoda and Matsunaga" as well. Tomoda's confession at the end of the story offers a clear example. In this confession, Tomoda explains the motivation for his desire to become a Westerner as stemming from his disgust with Japan, and more importantly, with the racial identification of being Japanese. He tells the narrator:

> I find the sight of the yellow faces of us Orientals discomfiting. You could say that my one regret in life was that I too possess such a face. Each time I saw myself in the mirror, all I could see was the sorrow at having been born in a yellow nation. As long as I stayed in this yellow nation, I felt that my face will just turn more and more yellow. My one wish was to flee from this dim, this dispiriting country of shadowy illumination and escape to the West. There I will find not some warped taste for spirit or elegance, but a music that celebrates earthly pleasures.[22]

One particular detail Tomoda brings up in this explanation—the characterization of Japan as a country cloaked in shadowy illumination [*usugurai kuni*]—clearly portends the sentiments expressed in Tanizaki's later writings on the subject. However, the two texts differ in the values ascribed to the respective positions of "Western" and "Japanese." Whereas in "The Story of Tomoda and Matsunaga" the culture of shadow that Tanizaki associates with Japan is rejected as ugly and distasteful, seven years later in *In Praise of Shadows*, the same observations are noted, but this time seemingly valorized. No doubt, these points of similarity along with the seeming reversal of their evaluation makes it easy to read "The Story of Tomoda and Matsunaga" in terms of the literary-biographical narrative of early infatuation with the West followed by a "return to Japan" that is usually ascribed to Tanizaki's career.[23]

But can *In Praise of Shadows* simply be considered a closing off of what has been held in tension—that is, an expression of the triumph of the traditional (or the Japanese) over the modern (or the Western)—in the final analysis? Interestingly, a number of odd shifts and ironic reversals permeate this text upon closer inspection, in effect hinting that something more than a straightforward valorization of Japanese aesthetics is at work in it. Particularly in passages dealing with issues of racialization, a sentiment of abjection seems to erupt from the text in several places, revealing descriptions that do not quite contradict those found in his earlier writings, such as in "The Story of Tomoda and Matsunaga." For instance, when Tanizaki describes the Japanese complexion as "tainted by gray" or "tinged by a slight cloudiness," the sentiment appears less celebratory and more resigned.[24] A racial shadow, perhaps otherwise repressed but returning when juxtaposed against the Westerner, nevertheless remains. With this in mind, I believe that there is merit to Long's perceptive suggestion that Tanizaki's purported valorization of Japanese aesthetics is more productively understood as a kind of fetish response. Following the psychoanalytic understanding of the fetish as a compensatory object that redirects the subject's attention so as to displace or disavow an underlying trauma, Long argues that the "Japan" to which Tanizaki returns in his writings cannot be characterized as something "original," that is, as something from prior to the formation of a national subjectivity as a response to its encounter (and desire to identify with) the West. Instead, Tanizaki's "Japan" is one that becomes imaginable not by overcoming the racializing gaze upon it, but instead only upon passing through and internalizing this process of racialization. In effect, it is a shadow object that is generated as a result of the founding trauma of Japan's emergence as a modern nation-state under the paternal racializing gaze of the West. It functions as a palliative, that is, as a means of displacing or disavowing this trauma.[25]

Long's arguments about Tanizaki's ambivalent sentiment toward Japan expressed in *In Praise of Shadows* find resonance when they are considered in conjunction with Tanizaki's "The Story of Tomoda and Matsunaga." At no point does Matsunaga (or any other character) speak of "Japan" in positive terms. Neither does he make much of an appearance in the text outside of his mediation through Tomoda, suggesting that the conception of "Japan" has coherence only when defined negatively, through the voice and perspective of the ostensibly Westernized Tomoda. In what appears like an almost literalized enactment of the fetish character of the identification with "Japan," Matsunaga takes on a role as a palliative function for Tomoda. By returning home and becoming Matsunaga again for a period of three years, the character is gradually able to recover his health. This is not a permanent return, however, for once he recuperates, he again departs to engage in the gluttony and debauchery that once more transforms his body into Tomoda.

In this regard, Tanizaki's "The Story of Tomoda and Matsunaga" can be read as a staging of what Paul Gilroy and Anne Anlin Cheng have respectively called "postcolonial melancholia" or "racial melancholia."[26] In "Mourning and Melancholia" (1917), Freud describes melancholia as one type of response to a traumatic loss. In contrast to what Freud terms mourning, which he characterizes as a finite response that eventually overcomes the loss, melancholia is a persistent and pathological response, refusing to let go of the lost object. Instead, the melancholic obsessively fixates on the lost object, culminating in its consumption, in its devouring.[27] This process entails the incorporation of the lost other into the self, resulting in the turning back of the libido toward the ego in what is, in essence, a compulsion to repeat primary narcissism, which is the psychological mechanism behind the appearance of the doppelgänger. Racial melancholia, then, is what takes place when this psychical process overlaps racial or colonial relations, when the lost other in question on which the melancholic fixates is racial difference.[28] Parallel to Freud's contention that the relation of the ego-ideal "to the ego is not exhausted by the precept 'you ought to be like this (like your father).' It also comprises the prohibition: 'you may not be like this (like your father)—that is, you may not do all that he does; some things are his prerogative"[29]—*national* subject formation in Japan (and the non-West more generally) is structured around a similar contradictory injunction to "become like the West/you may not be like the West." It is this contradictory injunction that generates the trauma of racialization, when the subject becomes aware of the historical traces inscribed upon the body that render the demand to identify with whiteness and the West impossible.

In alignment with Freud's theories, in "The Story of Tomoda and Matsunaga," the protagonist acts out by compulsively repeating the literalized devouring of whiteness through bouts of excessive gluttony in an attempt to incorporate and assimilate it into his own body so as to erase the traces of his racialization. The result is the appearance of a doppelgänger that functions as a restaging of primary narcissism along a racialized self/other axis. More importantly, in line with Freud's linkage of trauma and melancholia with the compulsion to repeat, Tanizaki's story presents the temporality of the "return to Japan" as something that does not take on the teleological trajectory taken by most narratives of return that posit Japan as a natural end point following a brief youthful dalliance with the West. Rather, it takes the form of a compulsive repetition without necessarily providing a conclusive resolution or overcoming, hence opening the door to future repetitions. This enactment of the compulsion to repeat that Tomoda/Matsunaga performs can also further be extended to an intertextual level. The tension between the West and Japan in "The Story of Tomoda and Matsunaga" is not finally closed and concluded with the "return to Japan" of *In Praise of Shadows* following a seemingly linear path. Rather, it is less a conclusion, less a return, and more aptly characterized as another repetition that does not necessarily resolve into a neat identification with one pole or the other of the West/Japan binary.

Of course, one might argue that even "The Story of Tomoda and Matsunaga" suggests an eventual resolution to these tensions. Indeed, at the end of Tanizaki's story, Tomoda suggests in his confession to the narrator that for reasons of health his next transformation will likely be his last, that when he next becomes Matsunaga again, it will this time be permanent. Yet is it not telling that the final confession is delivered not by Matsunaga upon the completion of his repeated departures and returns, but by Tomoda, who clearly laments how his age and failing health might prevent him from becoming Tomoda again in three years' time? The "sad look" [*kanashige na metsuki*] Tomoda is described as casting upon the narrator suggests that the home Matsunaga represents is not at all a familiar, reassuring space, but rather, an uncanny one that was never really a home in the first place.[30] Allowing the final word and primacy of voice to Tomoda belies any supposed "victory" of Matsunaga. Given that the rhetoric of confession is based on performatively producing the appearance of transparency and truth, implied in having the confession uttered in Tomoda's voice is that the "Westernized" Tomoda is more than merely the disguise—the performed alter-ego—of an original and authentic "Japanese" Matsunaga. Instead, it is the apparent authenticity and originality of Matsunaga that is the performance. In effect, rather than offering a resolution, Tomoda's confession only further deepens the confusion between authentic and inauthentic, original and imitation.

But the larger point here is that to even pose the problem of whether it is the Westernized Tomoda or the Japanese Matsunaga who triumphs is unproductive, in that this question is premised on the idea that such identities as "Western" and "Japanese" remain stable and mutually exclusive through the course of the story. However, it is arguably just such a supposition that the narrative movement in "The Story of Tomoda and Matsunaga" calls into question. When Tomoda first travels, his destination is Paris. But subsequent trips take him only as far as Shanghai, then Tokyo and Yokohama, and in his last incarnation before the story ends, Kobe. That Tomoda closes his confession with a remark about the nearness of Kobe to Matsunaga's hometown in Nara only punctuates this spatial movement.[31] This logic of oscillation problematizes any understanding of the relation between East and West in Tanizaki as a simple linear movement away from the West to the East. On the contrary, if in the end Kobe can stand in for the position of the West, then the assertion of East and West as bounded and clearly demarcated positions cannot be sustained. Rather, they imbricate one another and consequently, can be inhabited in the same places, indeed even in the same body, as coexisting contradictions.

Cosmopolitan Contact Zones

There is another dimension to the staging of a geographic collapse between the poles of East and West in Tanizaki's "The Story of Tomoda and Matsunaga." Examining the various destinations at which Tomoda arrives in his travels (namely Paris, Shanghai, Tokyo, Yokohama, and finally Kobe) reveals a slippage in the West/East polarity. In addition to the aforementioned gradual decrease in the distance from Matsunaga's hometown of Nara in each iteration, it is striking that Tomoda's travels include the city of Shanghai as one of the sites mapped onto the position of "the West." Since even Japanese cities like Kobe can occupy a "Western" positionality in Tanizaki's story, that Shanghai can do so as well is perhaps not in itself significant. However, there is more to the space of Shanghai than just another step in the geographical compression of the distances involved in Tomoda's travels. In light of the significant position that Shanghai occupies within the history of not only Japanese imperialism specifically but also imperialism in East Asia in general, I would contend that the inclusion of Shanghai in Tomoda's itinerary is not an arbitrary detail. It is instead an element that signals a critical complication to the West/Japan binary by introducing a third term to the schema in the form of Japan's relation to the colonial subjects generated as a result of its own territorial expansion and incursions into the rest of East Asia.

An important feature of many of the literary treatments of Shanghai during the early twentieth century is its perceived cosmopolitanism. As Meng Yue has observed, the city is often apprehended by way of a comparison with the imperial metropoles of Europe and America, as for example, the "Paris of the East" or "New York of the West."[32] Such statements speak to the profound ambivalence about how Shanghai is situated in the world. In Meng's analysis, Shanghai is a "doubly dislocated" city; what distinguishes it from many other places is that it occupies a position reducible to neither core nor periphery. It was neither a mere non-Western version of a European metropolitan capital in that it did not serve as the core of any imperial power, nor an example of a simple colonized city on the periphery in that its political status as a treaty port resulting from China's defeat in the First Opium War (1839–42) gave the city a more complex "semicolonial" sovereignty that was not under the exclusive formal control of any one colonial power but was instead subject to a shared occupation—with rights of extraterritoriality and considerable economic control—by several imperial powers.[33] It was a city at the intersection of multiple empires, the meeting point of the "overlapping histories" of the various imperialisms and emergent cultural practices and negotiations in the wake of the declining Qing Empire. As Meng succinctly puts it, "Shanghai, in short, was not merely a site that housed different worlds; rather, it was the result of their meetings and interactions."[34] In other words, the city's semicolonial status rendered it arguably the most cosmopolitan city in East Asia, while at once revealing the colonial violence that is the necessary condition of possibility for cosmopolitanism in the first place. In this regard, more so than any other location at the time, Shanghai may very well be the paradigmatic example of those "social spaces where cultures meet, clash, and grapple with each other, often in contexts of highly asymmetrical relations of power, such as colonialism, slavery, or their aftermaths as they are lived out in many parts of the world today" that Mary Louise Pratt calls "the contact zone."[35]

Japan's imperial expansion played an important role in the construction of Shanghai as a contact zone of semicolonial cosmopolitanism. Although Shanghai was not formally a part of Japan's colonial empire, the city was nonetheless a key site in which Japanese interests ranging from textile factories to the sex trade operated. Indeed, by the time of the publication of "The Story of Tomoda and Matsunaga" in 1926, the Japanese presence in Shanghai had already grown to rival even British economic interests. The city's place within the economy of Japan's empire as a whole was becoming even more significant than that of its formal colonies of Korea and Taiwan.[36] Events in the preceding year only serve to accentuate Japan's growing influence in the city. Following a strike against Japanese cotton mills in February 1925 and the subsequent killing of a Chinese worker in mid-May, wide-scale protests were called, culminating in a demonstration in the middle of Shanghai's International Settlement. When Chinese and Sikh constables opened fire on the crowd, killing more than a dozen demonstrators, tensions escalated into a general strike and protests directed against the Japanese and British imperial presence in the city.[37]

Although Tomoda's stay in Shànghai supposedly takes place some years prior—according to the story, a brief period between the summer of 1912 to the fall of 1915—it is difficult not to consider Japan's own colonial presence in Shanghai as a context here, especially given Tanizaki's own trip to the city in 1926 before the publication of "The Story of Tomoda and Matsunaga."[38] In fact, this was Tanizaki's second trip to China. A previous trip in 1918 produced a range of Sinophilic travelogues, essays, and fictions that take up China as an aesthetic image. Notably, these trips coincide with what Atsuko Sakaki has identified as a significant ambivalence and historical shifts in the treatment of China in Japanese literary and cultural discourse from the centripetal movement toward the center of civilization to a material fetishization of Chinese objects, in alignment with the changes in the political relationship between Japan and China. While Japan was historically located in the periphery of Chinese cultural hegemony, the appearance of Europe as a new cultural hegemon in the region disrupted this relationship, effectively creating an "ambiguous cultural hierarchy" between China and Japan.[39] With this in mind, although Tanizaki's second trip in 1926 resulted in comparatively little Sinophilic literary production other than this brief reference to the city of Shanghai in "The Story of Tomoda and Matsunaga," it is nonetheless worth reading the use of Shanghai in the text as a part of Tanizaki's broader engagement with China in his writings, all of which take place against this historical backdrop.

Of particular significance here is how China introduces a mediating third term that complicates the purported simple trajectory from Western fetishism to nativism in Tanizaki's work. One important way that China—or more precisely, the specific space of Shanghai at this historical conjuncture—complicates the West/Japan dyad is through its ability to bring into open view the fundamental contradictions that underpin the formation of national (and, by implication, imperial) subjectivities within the milieu of Japanese colonial modernity. Because it was a treaty port at which multiple imperial territorialities overlapped, in Shanghai, Japan's doubled status as a colonial presence identified with the European powers and as a racialized, non-Western nation becomes starkly visible. On the one hand, Japanese subjects in the city were accorded extraterritorial privileges like freedom of movement within the International

Settlement or criminal immunity from the Chinese legal system. On the other hand, because of the lack of visible distinguishing traces inscribed on the skin itself as racial difference, Japanese nationals were nonetheless still subject to the same experience of racism directed toward semicolonized Chinese nationals. In this sense, Shanghai is a location wherein the experience of racial melancholia becomes particularly acute; more than any other, it is perhaps the site that most profoundly provokes the return of a racialized repressed in that it is a place in which the mechanisms of identification with the ego-ideal of Western imperialism easily comes undone.

In "The Story of Tomoda and Matsunaga," this manifests in a concrete form in the very hybrid subjectivity of the purportedly Westernized Tomoda himself. Notably, in his first trip to Paris, the identity he assumes is not that of "Tomoda" but of a Frenchman named "Jacques Morin." It is only in his second round of travels, this time bound for Shanghai, that "Tomoda" makes his first appearance.[40] Why does he adopt the hybridized identity of Tomoda in his latter transformations? What accounts for the possibility of erasing racial signifiers that mark him as "Japanese" in his earlier but not later corporeal transformations? Here, the location of his travels is significant, in that it is precisely in contact zones like Shanghai that the vigorous policing of racial identities manifests; through the institutions and operations of colonial relations of power and knowledge, the racialized repressed returns, thus rendering the complete transformation from Matsunaga to Morin impossible. In this sense, despite the fact that Shanghai plays only a peripheral role in it, Tanizaki's story effectively illustrates how spaces like Shanghai are marked by the production of hybrid subjectivities stemming from the peculiar position Japan occupies within the larger global system of imperialism. It speaks to how Japan's relationship with its colonial others is marked less by racialized differences and more by what may very well be characterized as something akin to racial doubling with all its attendant tensions between identification and differentiation.

Another of Tanizaki's fictions—his earlier unfinished novel *Kōjin* (Sirens, 1920)—echoes this treatment of the tensions woven into Japanese imperial subject formation through its employment of the doppelgänger motif in conjunction with a play on themes of ethnic and gender passing as a means of performing secret identities. While the motif itself makes only a brief appearance in the text, it serves as an illustrative punctuation to an ongoing commentary that manifests at various points throughout the novel about the historical shifts in Sino-Japanese relations taking place at the time, thus opening up a space for complicating the conventional approach to apprehending Japanese modernity in relation to an imagined Western frame of reference. Set in the Asakusa district of Tokyo in the year 1918, the narrative of *Sirens* largely revolves around a pair of Japanese itinerant intellectuals (named Hattori and Minami) and their encounters and interactions with a troupe of actresses involved in the Asakusa theater scene. In the novel's opening section, these two intellectuals—who fancy themselves artists—take on the roles of highly opinionated tour guides for the benefit of the reader as they provide extended commentary on all manner of subjects, from Western and Chinese art, to theater and the opera, to the bodies of the women performing on stage. But at the forefront of all these conversations about mass culture and modern life are Hattori's and Minami's observations about the Asakusa district itself, which the novel characterizes as a space of excess and earthly pleasures, marked by the dizzying circulation of commodities, spectacles, and human bodies.

Just as its visitors come from all walks of life, a pandemonium of all manner of pleasures await here. Even if I were to list just a few, there's the traditional plays, musicals, modern plays, comedies, motion pictures (be they Western or Japanese, Douglas Fairbanks or Onoe Matsunosuke), acrobats, equestrian feats, *naniwa bushi, gidayū,* merry-go-rounds, flower gardens, the Asakusa twelve-stories, shooting ranges, prostitutes, and restaurants of all kinds (whether Japanese, Chinese, or Western—the Rai-Rai ken, wonton noodles, oysters, horsemeat, snapping turtles, eels, and the Café Paulista). . . . In other words, what makes Asakusa Park distinct from all the other entertainment districts is not just the size of the place, but how the hundreds upon hundreds of different elements inside it violently crash into each other.[41]

This vision of Asakusa as the exemplary site for the chaotic experience of mass culture and modern life is by no means unique to Tanizaki. On the contrary, his depiction is a part of the broader public imagination of the place, anticipating multiple similar characterizations from other literary authors and cultural commentators such as Hori Tatsuo (1904–1953), Kawabata Yasunari (1899–1972), and Soeda Azenbō (1872–1944), all of whom portrayed Asakusa as a play space—a site of popular amusement and corporeal pleasure. Or, as Miriam Silverberg has put it, popular depictions of Asakusa made it out to be an erotic space: "It celebrated the sensuality of both men and women, a sensuality encompassing an overwhelming number of sensations (a montage of senses, as it were), including taste, the thrill of motion, and a gaze defined not necessarily by domination but by exploration and imagination."[42] However, for the two itinerant intellectuals of Tanizaki's *Sirens*, the pleasures of Asakusa also come with an attendant vulgarity and ugliness. It is a place where the trappings of modern life in Tokyo manifest in a raw and intensified form, where the incessant parade of new spectacles and curiosities presents an almost perverse sham—a bad mimicry—of modernization.

As a counterpoint to Asakusa, the novel offers China as a kind of point of origin or lost homeland for Japan.

And now [Minami] has returned from China. Parting from the venerable continent from which Japan's old civilization sprang forth, he would forever be back here living as a Japanese man. In place of the reclusive and contemplative Beijing, before his eyes looms this shallow and vulgar Tokyo. . . . But in this Japan of the present where he had been born, in this Japan of the present where a Western fetishism (and a half-hearted Western fetishism at that), the purity of nature whose beauty he sought was now being destroyed.[43]

In Tanizaki's *Sirens*, China is presented as an object of nostalgia and a space outside of history. While this reproduces an all-too-typical gesture in colonial discourses at one level, at another level, there is also a crucial point of difference in the expression of identification with the imagined space of China. The passage above suggests that whatever fetish for assimilation into Western culture Tokyo might present, China nevertheless still embodies a far deeper connection for modern Japan. Indeed, especially noteworthy here is Tanizaki's effort to present China as a point of origin for Japanese civilization. In a move that participates in the discursive construction of Japan's orient [*tōyō*], which functioned as an attempt to locate Japan's place in history in response to both Western orientalism alongside its attempt to negotiate its shifting historical relationship to China, evident here is a nostalgic desire not for a traditional Japan per se, but instead for China as a further, second-order space to which one might seek to return.[44] The lament about the inability to return to it, though, has the effect of constructing China as a kind of "homeland" that cannot be characterized in the simple terms of familiarity or domesticity, but rather one fraught with ambivalence, one that is literally uncanny.[45] Tanizaki's vision of the space of China perfectly captures the sense of something simultaneously familiar and alien, a home that is not a home, of something that activates the sensation of, in other words, the un-home-like (*das unheimlich*). Because it evokes feelings of both intimacy and fear, Tanizaki's China is characterized by a certain vagueness and intangibility that provokes a compulsive return to it even as it is disavowed. From this perspective, the imagination of China in Tanizaki's writing can be understood as operating allegorically as a kind of doppelgänger.

The subsequent appearance in the later sections of the novel of the character of Hayashi Shinju, a Japanese actress in the Asakusa Opera who specializes in musical renditions of the plays of Shakespeare, only further emphasizes this doubling. At one point in the story, one of the itinerant intellectuals recalls that Hayashi Shinju once traveled to Shanghai. While there, she performed a scene from a Chinese classic, appearing therein as the Chinese male character Yan Qing. Midway through her performance, however, an elderly Chinese man named Wang appears on stage. On stage, the man makes the astounding claim that Hayashi is in fact his lost son Lin Zhenzhu (whose name is written using the same characters as "Hayashi Shinju"). When the actress Hayashi Shinju is first confronted onstage with the suggestion that she is the lost son of a Chinese man, it is curious that her response is not amusement or dismissal of what on its face appears to be a patently absurd claim (in that not only is it a cross-ethnic double but a cross-gender double), but shock, as if there is more to the story—a secret, perhaps even to Hayashi Shinju herself—that is left unrevealed. As Tanizaki terminated his writing of the novel to work on film productions when it was only partly completed and never returned to it in later years, the mystery of Hayashi Shinju's identity remains unresolved, thus keeping the gender and ethnic identities undecidable, indeed perhaps suggesting that it is ultimately irresolvable. Yet regardless of this lack of resolution, what can nevertheless be inferred from this sequence of events is the hint that Hayashi Shinju's past is nevertheless haunted by another identity, by an uncanny Chinese doppelgänger of nearly the same name.

Pointing to this and other episodes in Tanizaki's unfinished novel, Atsuko Sakaki observes how the cross-ethnic performance in the text associates a feminizing movement with China and a masculinizing movement with Japan.[46] This is a pattern that not only aligns it with narrative tropes in other Sinophilic fictions that Tanizaki produced early in his career but also parallels similar tendencies in other orientalizing discourses that gender the East as a feminized and eroticized other. At the same time, however, Tanizaki's employment of a cross-ethnic doppelgänger in this brief episode in *Sirens* discloses the linkage between its colonial gaze toward China and the desire to identify with it as a marker of Japan's past and the origins of its civilization. In doing so, it brings to the foreground his consciousness of the different positionality vis-à-vis an imagined "Orient" he inhabited as a Japanese subject. It speaks to a sense of imperial ambivalence that at once articulates an imperial nationalism *and* its subversion. This ambiguity often manifests in the form of occasional slippages of identification across his various writings. As Thomas Lamarre has noted, there are moments in Tanizaki's various writings when he takes up the subject position of "Japanese" while at other times when he identifies as "Oriental" in his performative utterances, with the effect of affirming an identification with China and other parts of East Asia.[47] Thus, rather than confirming Japan's supposed "Westernization" through a disavowal of the trauma at the core of its constitution as a nation-state and ethnocultural identity, Tanizaki's production of an imagined "China," through what at first glance appears like an enactment of an orientalizing gaze, paradoxically complicates and brings to the foreground the immanent contradictions of Japanese colonial discourse.

For this reason, Oguma Eiji's caution against an uncritical adoption of Edward Said's critique of "Orientalism" into the context of Japan has much merit.[48] In Oguma's argument, ascribing a simple reproduction of Euro-American practices of Orientalism has the paradoxical effect of reinforcing a rhetoric of modernization that separates Japan from the rest of East Asia. In his words, "the more researchers emphasize the fact that an Orientalism existed in modern Japan just as it did in the West, the more they 'prove' that Japan had accomplished a modernization that could be compared to that experienced by Western nations."[49] For Oguma, then, the critique of Japanese colonial discourse solely in terms of its own deployment of an orientalizing practice (without accounting for the specific conditions and contradictions in which such takes place, Japan's own positioning as a racialized other in Euro-American discourses) ironically reproduces what may very well be a key discursive move through which the contradictions of the Japanese colonial order were managed at the time.

Indeed, critics such as Kang Sang-jung have argued that one of the consequences of Japan's imperial expansion was its effective assimilation of the same colonial discourses and practices employed by European and American colonial empires, not the least of which is the employment of a colonial gaze that produces the image of the colonial other as monolithic and ahistorical.[50] However, it cannot be forgotten that this is only one dimension of the overall structure of colonial discourse in the Japanese context. It is further complicated by the knowledge—though often repressed—of Japan's own functional self-colonization. The work of Komori Yōichi is instructive on this point. Employing a Freudian rhetoric, he suggests that Japan's peculiar position as the only non-Western colonial empire in history engendered a dynamic marked by the interplay between a "colonial consciousness" [shokuminchishugiteki ishiki] associated with the manifest ideologies of imperial expansion, and a "colonial unconscious" [shokuminchishugiteki muishiki] connected to the external colonial pressures exerted upon Japan, that is, the threat of Japan's own colonization by Western imperial powers. For Komori, it is this threat of colonization—of being rendered into just another Asian colonized territory of a European empire—that served as the foundational trauma that prompted the modernization process, leading the Japanese nation-state to remake itself—to self-colonize—in the image of Western "civilization." Expanding the empire outward and internalizing the European colonial gaze in this process became a technique of introjection, a method of repressing this foundational trauma through the discovery of its own "savages" beyond its border, that is, the creation of its own colonial other, thus disavowing any racial identification with the other parts of Asia.[51]

It is precisely the breakdown of the orientalizing apparatus that Tanizaki's doppelgänger fictions stage, with the consequence of prompting the return of the repressed colonial unconscious. Tanizaki's obsessive meditations on "race," which manifest in his doppelgänger fictions as a cross-racial or cross-ethnic doubling, stage the failure to demarcate a racial other to buttress a conception of Japanese national subjectivity as "civilized." Rather than disavowing the "colonial unconscious" in line with Komori's argument, there is instead a persistent foregrounding of it. Tanizaki's doppelgängers consistently bring the colonial unconscious back to life in the form of a racialized uncanny, that is, the melancholic return of a racialized repressed, or the haunting of a racial shadow. Staged in Tanizaki's writings is an attempt to displace the foundational trauma of the formation of a Japanese national subjectivity through the enactment of its own colonial expansion, its own casting of an orientalizing upon its others. Yet ironically, by provoking an uncanny encounter and the traumatic repetition of seeing oneself as other, this very act becomes its own subversion. Thus, if these texts are any indication, Tanizaki's cross-ethnic doppelgänger calls attention to the fundamentally colonial and racialized constitution of the figure of the doppelgänger, with the effect of rendering contingent and undecidable the racial and cultural categories presumed to be fixed and natural.

Colonialism and Visuality

To close my discussion of Tanizaki's racialized doppelgängers, let me turn to a final significant dimension of his employment of the figure, namely the question of the circulation of bodies in colonial space within a specifically visual register. That the subject of visuality should manifest in Tanizaki's doppelgänger fictions is not out of the ordinary. It is by no means an unprecedented move to highlight the unmistakably visual character of the figure of the doppelgänger. Indeed, it has been the object of attention of several existing critical writings on the figure. Andrew J.

Webber, for example, identifies the "characteristic visuality of *Doppel-gänger* texts" as the very first premise of his analysis.[52] Likewise, Fried-rich Kittler asserts that film, not to mention all manner of other optical technologies from panoramas to the railways, served as "the point of departure for [Otto] Rank's study of the Double" and psychoanalytic approaches to the doppelgänger more generally.[53] However, what Tani-zaki's employment of the figure of the doppelgänger in explicitly racial-ized terms allows for is the reframing of this visual character of the figure to foreground the linkage between the twinned historical processes of visual modernization and colonial expansion.

The historical underpinnings of Tanizaki's doppelgänger fictions can be located in the circulation of colonial images as commodity spectacles that Anne McClintock has identified as an important material basis for the mass dissemination of the ideologies of a global project of empire and the reproduction of the subjectivities of both colonizer and colo-nized. In McClintock's argument, although the fantasies and ideologies of empire had already begun to take shape by the eighteenth century, these ideologies mutated during the passage into the nineteenth century. Of particular interest here is what McClintock identifies as a shift from an older model of "scientific racism" to a newer "commodity racism." Whereas discourses of scientific racism circulated primarily through "anthropological, scientific and medical journals, travel writing and eth-nographies," with commodity racism, these circuits are superseded by "advertising and photography, the imperial Expositions and the museum movement" with the effect of transforming imperial ideologies of prog-ress and racial hierarchies from a (pseudo) social-scientific discourse into image-commodities for mass consumption.[54] By effectively turning colonial discourse into a commodity spectacle, this shift had the con-sequence of spreading all manner of colonial images—ranging from hygiene and domesticity to racialized and gendered differences—beyond the sole purview of a literate elite to provide it a mass audience.

To McClintock's various examples of commodity spectacles—travel-ogues, postcards, photographs, and so forth—can also be added theater. It is no mere accident that the doubling and concurrent gender and border crossing of Hayashi Shinju in Tanizaki's *Sirens* is enacted on stage. This detail is of no small significance, because the story is set in a historical

period following the aftermath of major shifts in the conceptual understanding of theater, and in particular, acting, which is itself intimately
interwoven with discourses of Orientalism as imperialism through the
gendering and racialization of performance. Per Ayako Kano, by the end
of the Meiji period, important changes in the practices surrounding theater and acting—and especially women's acting—played a significant
part in a shift to "a definition of womanhood grounded in the physical
body, rather than constituted in performance."[55] In sum, women on stage
became defined less by the learned gestures and performances, and more
by her (often bared) visible body in itself. In this respect, the actress in
modern theater contributed to the formation of a conception of gender
that was biologically fixed, or to put it a differently, a conception of gender as emanating from the physical body outward and given expression
in performance, as opposed to gendered identities as the product, the
very effect of these performances.

Telltale traces of this shift certainly manifest in Tanizaki's *Sirens*. In
Hayashi Shinju's cross-gender and cross-ethnic performance of the role
of a Chinese man on stage (which the text makes out to be largely con-
vincing), what is suggested is the privileging of performativity over the
physical body. Yet in the aftermath of the old man's publicly claiming
that Hayashi Shinju is his lost son Lin Zhenzhu, when there is an attempt
to resolve the confusion, the means to do this is the baring of the physical body to "prove" that Hayashi Shinju is indeed a Japanese woman and
not a Chinese man. Nevertheless, the mystery is ultimately left unresolved,
and indeed complicated further, in that the attempt to prove Hayashi
Shinju's identity as a Japanese woman results in the revelation of another
doubling, this time in the form of Lin Zhenzhu's sister, who is described
as appearing like a twin to the stage actress.

Implicated in this shift in the modes of gendered and racialized iden-
tifications that Kano identifies are not merely matters specific to the modernization of theater. More importantly, these transformations signal
toward a broader historical shift marked by the emergence of a modern
regime of visuality that would transform the body into an object of vision,
encompassing not only theater, but a larger constellation of disciplines
that includes biology, medicine, policing, and statistics, among others.
The work of Michel Foucault is instructive here. Consider, for example,

his analysis of how modern penal systems revolve around the metaphor of the panopticon and how its ever-present surveillance created the conditions for the self-discipline and the production of docile bodies.[56] Similarly, in his examination of modern medical techniques, Foucault takes up the emergence of what he calls the "medical gaze"—which he characterizes as a mode of looking at and observing the patient's body as a material and biological fact that purports to be transparent and unmediated by discourse—as constitutive to its formation as a discipline.[57] The crucial point to recognize here is that these were historical developments that cannot simply be understood as movements toward greater realism and to the discovery of the empirical "truth" of the body, but were *political* processes of knowledge production about the body by way of its visual observation.

Less often noted though is the fact that these disciplinary procedures and techniques of vision were constituted precisely in the colonies, which often functioned as laboratories of modernity, generating what Pratt has called "massive experiments in social engineering and discipline, serial production, the systematization of human life, the standardizing of persons."[58] In the case of the visuality of theater specifically, of relevance here is the historical role that the stage played as an institution and instrument of cultural diplomacy in Japan's relations with the outside world alongside other spectacles and visual practices for international consumption like panorama halls and world's fairs. A telling detail that Kano references is the commentary surrounding a number of theatrical performances that the actress Kawakami Sadayakko and her troupe staged on tour in Europe and the United States in 1899, performances that, as Kano notes, were gazed upon and read in terms laden with Orientalist tropes.[59] As such, in this context, the inscription of gender upon the material body as its natural expression is inseparable from the parallel biologism of the racializing discourses concurrently in operation. Sadayakko's body was not only gazed upon (and constituted through this gaze) as a woman, but specifically, as a Japanese woman. An important implication that can be drawn here then is that to properly account for how the visible body came to be produced as an object of knowledge, it is necessary to recognize that this process does not take place on an even visual field. Rather, the emergence of modern techniques and technologies of vision are intimately wedded to colonial discourses of the body in the rendering of some bodies as marking an excessive visibility, turning them into objects of ethnographic knowledge.

From this perspective, the transformations in acting and the conception of the body in modern theater can be understood as preparing the ground for the appearance of the visual practices and their structuring of the traffic of gazes in later technologies and commodity spectacles. It is therefore unsurprising that Tanizaki's writings that deal with cinema exhibit certain similarities with the doppelgänger fictions discussed above in their engagement with the racial politics of visibility and corporeality. Take, for example, his "Jinmenso" ("The Tumor with a Human Face," 1918). This short story is loosely structured in two parts. Its first half opens with a summary of a film within the fiction (also titled *The Tumor with a Human Face*). This is subsequently followed by an investigation of the origins of the mysterious film by the actress Utagawa Yurie, who has no recollection of ever having made the film at all despite of the fact that she had supposedly been cast as its lead actress.[60] The story of the film centers on a Japanese courtesan who elopes with an American sailor. While the two are successful in escaping Japan and smuggling her to the United States, the courtesan finds that she develops a tumor on her knee that bears the hideous face of a beggar she had previously spurned (and who had killed himself afterward). Persistently tortured and goaded by this tumor, she ends up murdering her husband, and then subsequently transforming into a femme fatale who seduces, robs, and kills a series of other American men, only to end up killing herself when the tumor on her knee reveals itself in public. The story does not end here, though, and in the remainder of the text, the focus shifts to the investigation into the origins of the film by the actress who plays the courtesan. Having no memory of ever making such a film, she questions a film technician friend of hers who works at her studio. But neither he nor anyone else seems to be able to trace when or how the film was made. Furthermore, the film itself is apparently haunted by the tumor as well; those who have viewed the film alone in the dark have all inexplicably died or lost their minds later.

The motif of doubling manifests in several different forms in "The Tumor with a Human Face." There is the doubling between the actress and the role of the courtesan she plays on-screen. On top of this, there is the doubling of the man the actress spurned and the tumor that grows on her knee. But a final set of doubles is also implied in the possible encounter with one's doppelgänger that can take place in the very act of viewing a film alone. In their discussion of the mysterious film, Yurie's technician friend points out to her the strange sense of the uncanny that film spectatorship provokes, especially when the film in question happens to include images of oneself: "Should some actor project and watch a film wherein his image makes an appearance," he says, "no doubt it would feel like it was his self appearing in the film who was truly alive, while his self sitting still and watching in the dark was nothing more than a shadow."[61] The image on the screen collapses the distance between spectator and image, with the consequence of inverting the relationship between them. A sense of terror erupts at the threat of one's becoming image, of being replaced by the image on the screen. Or, to put it in the terms of Rank's understanding of the doppelgänger, the very act of identifying with one's own image on the screen in narcissistic self-love also produces a suicidal desire for self-destruction.

Tanizaki's depiction of the terror at the encounter with the magnified close-up of the face on the screen here anticipates Gilles Deleuze's famous discussion of the process of facialization as central to the constitution of the spectator's subjectivity. In Deleuze's theorization, facialization is a central component in the process of subject formation, functioning as a "locus of resonance" through which the operations of signification and subjectivization must pass. In cinema, it is through the close-up that the face is given shape. Rather than existing a priori to being shot in close-up, the very notion of the face as a signifying surface is produced through the shot. In Deleuze's words, "There is no close up of the face. The close up is the face." However, while instrumental in the process, this is not where the operation of the close-up ends for Deleuze in that immanent to this very procedure is its disruption. An effect of the magnification of the face is to render it excessive; it inspires attention to what would otherwise be invisible minute oscillations, intense vibrations, and micromovements on the surface of the face, which hold the potential to threaten to break free of the limits of the face: "The close up has merely pushed the face to those regions where the principle of individuation ceases to hold sway . . . the facial close up is both the face and its effacement."[62]

This sense of effacement—this breakdown in the process of individuation—is what lies at the heart of the sense of dread in seeing oneself in close-up in Tanizaki's story. That said, it should be noted that Yurie and her friend's discussion of the terror in an actor's encounter with his own face on the screen is only hypothetical in nature. None of those who are said to have viewed the film and subsequently suffered ill effects are in fact actors. Instead, they are film technicians and the company president. But if this encounter with the double on the screen is what provokes the experience of terror, then to what do the spectators of the film within the story "The Tumor with a Human Face" identify, if it is not necessarily their own individual faces? Given how descriptions of the fictional actress Utagawa Yurie are marked by their obsessive corporeality and visibility in both racialized and gendered terms, I wonder if it is not in terms of these categories that the process of identification takes place. At the onset of the narrative, she is described as having a "smooth, full figure that was the equal of any Western actress" and as possessing a charm that "tempered Occidental coquetterie with Oriental modesty."[63] Tellingly, when the famous roles she has played are listed in the story, they point to familiar archetypal figures with clear gendered and racialized overtones such as the geisha or the dragon lady. In addition, there is the face of the tumor itself, which is described as having "a corpulent face and dark glaring eyes that made it hard to say whether he's a Japanese man or a South Seas native."[64] More than anything else, this description identifies the man as possessing a racially marked face, and it is with these racial markings that the film's spectators overidentify and encounter as an uncanny double that provokes a traumatic experience of racial melancholia.

In Tanizaki's story, the screen of cinema is taken up as a practice and product of a contact zone that is productive of the appearances of the figure of the doppelgänger. In this respect, it is not unlike the stage in *Sirens* or Shanghai in "The Story of Tomoda and Matsunaga." Where cinema differs from the theater or an urban space, however, is in its mechanical reproducibility. Whereas the site of a city or the spectacle on the stage is accessible only to those physically present before it, photography and cinema disseminate their images across the capitalist networks of production and distribution. The rather ominous conclusion of

"The Tumor with the Human Face" calls attention to this point with the words "So what fate awaits this film once it comes into the Globe Corporation's possession, I wonder? Since it's the shrewd Globe we're talking about here, I'm certain that they'll print multiple copies and give it a wide distribution. Yes, there is no doubt at all that this is what they'll do."[65] Indeed, if McClintock is correct in her suggestion that commodity spectacles—from advertising, to photography, to films—were important channels through which embodied alterities in both racialized and gendered terms came to be encountered, classified, fixed, and domesticated, then the circulation of these images would have the effect of collapsing geographical distances.[66] In other words, the dissemination these mechanically reproduced images of photographs and cinema multiply the contact zones in which colonial encounters may take place. In this sense, if in Tanizaki's *Sirens* and "The Story of Tomoda and Matsunaga," the stage and the city serve as one set of sites wherein the contradictions embedded in the logic of Japan's colonial empire come to the foreground in the form of the doppelgänger, "The Tumor with a Human Face" hints at the mechanization of image production in the cinema, with the consequence that such sites wherein gendered and racialized identities come to be formed and fixed—as well as the possibility of their breakdown marked by the doppelgänger's appearance—increasingly multiply, making it possible to encounter them everywhere.

3

Projections of Shadow

Visual Modernization and Psychoanalysis

Shadows of *The Student of Prague*

Technologies of visuality played a crucial mediating role in the conceptual articulation of the figure of the doppelgänger. From the very beginnings of its theorization, with Otto Rank's pioneering work on the figure in his *Der Doppelgänger* (*The Double*, 1925), cinema featured as the impetus behind the examination of the doppelgänger as a psychoanalytic concept. Rank opens his study of the doppelgänger with a discussion of the "banal subject" of film, recounting from memory his experience of viewing Hanns Heinz Ewers and Stellan Rye's *Der Student von Prag* (*The Student of Prague*, 1913), which he describes as "shadowy, fleeting, but impressive."[1] Even as Rank appreciates the film's ability to evoke the quality of dream-work with vivid clarity, and in his words, finds "the uniqueness of cinematography in visibly portraying psychological events" intriguing and effective in bringing attention to psychoanalytic concerns, he nonetheless suggests that the film itself does not provide a sufficient explanation for its spectators to fully comprehend the imaginative representation before them. To do this, the modern interpreter must trace the doppelgänger motif's appearances in literature, folklore, and mythology in order to highlight how its meaning can be located in the essential problem of the ego.[2]

Although Rank does not return to the subject of film in the rest of the book, his opening nonetheless hints at how the technology of cinema played an important role in making visible the psychoanalytic conception of the doppelgänger.[3] In part, what made *The Student of Prague* particularly effective in facilitating the figure's popularization is its deployment of many of the motifs and plot formulae that have since become familiar elements of the films and fictions classified together under the sign of the doppelgänger. The film portrays what should now be a familiar story of a young man (named Balduin) who becomes romantically obsessed with a wealthy countess and sells his reflection in the mirror in exchange for great wealth to enable him to pursue her. Of course, things do not end there. Despite winning the Countess Margit's affection, his mirror image—who has become his haunting doppelgänger—begins appearing everywhere to torment him, leading eventually to the ruin of his affair. In retaliation, Balduin confronts his double and attempts to force him back into the mirror. After a struggle, he then draws a gun and shoots his reflection in the mirror. However, it is Balduin who falls to the ground dead.[4]

Immediately apparent from the above summary of the film is the extent to which many elements that appear in it are likely to sound vaguely familiar to many, regardless of whether they have in fact seen this specific film, or its several remakes through the intervening years.[5] This is not all that surprising when one considers that Edgar Allan Poe is credited as one of the writers of the film. His seminal work of doppelgänger fiction "William Wilson" (1839) was one of the film's primary inspirations, indeed, to such an extent that *The Student of Prague* may very well be considered a loose adaptation of Poe's story. In addition, the film recapitulates what would become the standard tropes and formulae identified with doppelgänger fictions—the mysterious double that haunts one's every move, the Faustian bargain, the unleashing of hedonistic sexuality and violence, not to mention the conclusion wherein the man who murders his own mirror-image ends up killing himself—drawn from such preceding sources as not only the aforementioned "William Wilson," but also E. T. A. Hoffmann's *Der Sandmann* (1816) and Oscar Wilde's *The Picture of Dorian Gray* (1890), among others. What is therefore significant about *The Student of Prague* is how its appearance marks the consolidation of the doppelgänger as a coherent concept and genre, thus rendering the motif legible for subsequent authors to adopt, with the further consequence of facilitating its transmission to other contexts and cultural milieus.

Such was certainly the case in Japan, where the film played a significant role in the introduction and popularization of the doppelgänger motif at roughly the same moment when it served as the impetus for Rank's psychoanalytic investigations.[6] As Watanabe Masahiko contends in his discussion of the doppelgänger motif in Japanese literature, its proliferation during the 1920s can be traced less directly to the arrival of psychoanalysis and more to the widespread impact of the mass popularization of cinema in the early twentieth century.[7] Indeed, several examples of doppelgänger fictions published in Japan during this time—from authors such as Edogawa Rampo (1894–1965), Satō Haruo (1892–1964), Tanizaki Jun'ichirō (1886–1965), Akutagawa Ryūnosuke (1892–1927), and others— comment on the impact of the emerging film and visual culture of the time, in some cases even explicitly referencing Ewers and Rye's film.[8] For example, Satō Haruo's "Shimon" (The fingerprint, 1918) evokes both film culture and Poe's classic double fiction "William Wilson" with its story that revolves around the paranoia of a man who believes he was witness to a murder perpetrated by an actor named William Wilson after seeing the man's face in a film, whom he recognizes from an earlier encounter in a Shanghai opium den. Likewise, Tanizaki Jun'ichirō's "Jinmenso" (The Tumor with a Human Face," 1918), discussed in the previous chapter, takes these allusions further with direct citations of star Paul Wegener's performances in *The Student of Prague* and *Der Golem* (*The Golem*, 1915).

Several factors conspired to make the medium of film particularly effective in circulating images of the doppelgänger, not the least of which is the fact that the dissemination of film, in contrast to that of literary or critical texts on the doppelgänger, was less subject to the temporal lag inevitable in the production of any literary translation. This was the case not only in the specific example of Ewers and Rye's *The Student of Prague*. In many instances, film adaptations of fictions of the doppelgänger appeared nearly simultaneously to the translations of their source texts in Japan, if not prior to them.[9] But the significance of these preceding films featuring the figure of the doppelgänger goes beyond merely the popularization and facilitation of the dissemination of the concept in their capacity as a mass-produced cultural form. More importantly, what also warrants attention here is the formative role cinema played in the development of a discourse on the doppelgänger at the level of the technology of cinema itself. Specifically, Watanabe calls attention to the twinned effects of film's capacity to produce doubles out of its actors and the voyeuristic intimacy of its spectatorship, which, working in tandem, have the potential to create the impression in audiences that the actors they see on the screen lead double lives because they see the same faces play different roles in different films.[10]

My discussion here builds upon the previous work of critics like Watanabe to articulate the visual underpinnings of doppelgänger's appearances in Japan by historicizing the mechanisms through which it came to be constituted within the broader regime of visual modernization taking place in the early twentieth century. Of particular interest for me are the linkages between visual technologies, mass culture, and imperial expansion and consolidation. The preceding chapter touched upon the role visual culture played in transforming imperial ideologies into commodity spectacles, with the effect of extending the reach of these ideologies to a mass cultural audience. If colonial encounters in the contact zones were productive of racial discourses and notions of civilizational hierarchy instrumental to the psychoanalytic conception of the doppelgänger, then one consequence of these commodity spectacles is the multiplication of potential contact zones, and with it, the proliferation of potential sites that could engender colonial doublings and mimicries. This chapter continues this discussion by examining how cinema itself also functions as a form of involuted imperialism, how cinema operates through the dispossession and colonization of visuality, in effect alienating vision from its spectator and thus preparing the ground for imagining the doppelgänger. My contention is that the popularity of literary representations of doubles in early twentieth-century Japan can be read as a phenomenon that emerged in response to these historical developments.

In this effort, I focus my attention on the various writings of Akutagawa Ryūnosuke that feature the figure of the doppelgänger. The work of Akutagawa makes for an illustrative test case for examining these issues for several reasons. Not only did Akutagawa actively engage with the sociocultural impact of the techniques and technologies of cinema in stories like "Katakoi" (Unrequited love, 1917) and "Kage" ("The Shadow,"

1921) as well as the pseudo-screenplays "Yūwaku" (San Sebastian, 1927) and "Asakusa kōen" (Asakusa Park, 1927), moreover, he was also closely associated with the image of the doppelgänger. The earliest appearance of the figure in Akutagawa's fiction is in "Futatsu no tegami" (Two letters, 1917). But the more well known example is its appearance in a brief, yet nonetheless crucial scene near the end of his semiautobiographical work "Haguruma" ("Spinning Gears," 1927), published posthumously after his suicide in July 1927 in a move that seemingly signals his approaching death. Taken all together, these fictions of Akutagawa present a picture of the shifting relations among language, visuality, and subjectivity in early twentieth-century Japan focalized through the repeated deployments of the figure of the doppelgänger.

The Doppelgänger as Media Allegory

Watanabe Masahiko is by no means alone in emphasizing the visual character of the figure of doppelgänger. Andrew Webber, for example, identifies visuality as one of the key features of the double in all its myriad manifestations, writing that it is foremost a "figure of visual compulsion."[11] Likewise, Bahareh Rashidi has criticized the focus on story in much of the existing analyses of the figure, often eliding the fact that "its appearance—whether as a visual shock or sublime feat of technology—always also foregrounds the uncanny magic of the cinematic apparatus."[12] This should perhaps not come as a surprise given the close association between the doppelgänger and visual culture that is not peculiar to its appearances in Japan. On the contrary, the very features most often ascribed to the doppelgänger—for instance, its embodiment of the uncanny or its collapse of the distinctions between original and copy—mirror the more general conceptual concerns thrust into the foreground by cinema in its capacity as a technology of the copy, of the industrial reproduction of the image. One might even go so far as to suggest that it is the most emblematic figure for illustrating Walter Benjamin's famous statement that "the camera introduces us to unconscious optics as does psychoanalysis to unconscious impulses."[13]

It is no accident that Jean Baudrillard uses *The Student of Prague* as an example of what he sees as a sense of uncanniness engendered by the doubling effect of the combination of an indexical quality and mass reproducibility of photography and the cinema. In Baudrillard's words: "There is unease in front of the photograph . . . an unease, more generally, in front of any technical equipment. . . . There is already a little sorcery at work in the mirror, but how much more there would be were the image to be detached from the mirror, transported, stockpiled, and reproduced at whim."[14] Moreover, this reproducibility of the image ties together with the doppelgänger's role as a portent of forthcoming doom. After all, photography (and especially portrait photography) and cinema produce what are perceived to be indexical images that threaten to replace the subjects they capture; they bring forth copies that will survive their subjects. As Jacques Derrida has observed, such images "will be reproducible in our absence, because we know this *already*, we are already haunted by this future. . . . We are spectralized by the shot, captured by spectrality in advance."[15] In this sense, the photographic or cinematic image foreshadows the coming of one's death, in effect mirroring the superstition that associates the encounter with one's doppelgänger as an omen of one's imminent death. Is it any surprise that photography has long been associated with death, with superstitions that the capture of one's image also entailed the theft of one's soul?

Considering these conceptual affinities, the media theorist Friedrich Kittler's proposition that the doppelgänger is more productively apprehended less as a signifier of psychoanalytic concepts and more as a form of media allegory warrants attention here. Succinctly, Kittler argues that "the doppelgänger motif films the act of filming itself."[16] Films such as *The Student of Prague* bring attention to the parallels between the discourses surrounding reproductive technologies of vision (e.g., cinema, photography) and the conceptual features of the doppelgänger. In other words, Ewers and Rye's film—and perhaps doppelgänger films in general—are not simply films *about* the doppelgänger. More importantly, they make use of the image of the doppelgänger to metacinematic effect, meditating on the mechanisms of cinematic representation and reproduction as itself a form of doubling. The geographical collapse effected by cinema and its ability to circulate images as a consequence of their mechanical reproducibility discussed in the previous chapter cannot be separated from the more fundamental perceptual collapse that the encounter with the cinematic image generates. Not only was cinema instrumental for its role in literally making visible the doppelgänger and as a consequence consolidating the concept, but also for showcasing the ability of cinematic technologies at this historical moment to *literally* produce doppelgängers through optical as well as editing tricks, that is, to take the figure from the realm of dream and fantasy to a scientifically (re)producible possibility. In other words, film had the power to transform the doppelgänger from an abstract literary concept to a concrete image, to something literally visible on the screen.

It is for this reason that Kittler critiques the central position that psychoanalysis occupies in the discourse surrounding the figure of the doppelgänger. Against this tendency, Kittler contends that while it was the mobilization of the imaginary through the apparatus of cinema and other visual technologies that "prepared the way for psychoanalysis," this fact has been repressed.[17] He points to several things in support of this claim. There is of course Rank's viewing of *The Student of Prague* as the initial impetus behind his analysis of the doppelgänger. In addition, Kittler also highlights how the technology of the camera and its capability to record "24 pictures per second by chopping up the body before the viewfinder" was deployed to produce photographic traces of patients' bodies as proof of hysteria in early psychiatric research.[18] Put simply, for Kittler, cinema is the repressed unconscious—perhaps the doppelgänger— of psychoanalytic (and also arguably literary) discourse. Cinema does not merely offer the possibility of visually representing the doppelgänger. Rather, it is the technologies of the cinematic apparatus that enables psychoanalysis to apprehend the figure of the doppelgänger as one of its concerns in the first place. When Rank treats the cinematic double as little more than a repository of psychoanalytic concepts, the effect is to elide the change in technical media, creating the appearance of a simple continuity from literature to film, from German Romanticism to German Expressionist cinema. Against this, Kittler argues that the "chain of the fantastic . . . has nothing to do with Hoffmann or Chamisso and everything to do with film."[19]

Following Kittler, the modern doppelgänger is therefore more productively understood not in terms of a line of continuity from literary predecessors in myth or Romanticism but as an image that arises out of the impact of visual technologies. Cinema and the visual techniques it engenders, in other words, made the doppelgänger thinkable by consolidating the motif into a coherent set of recognizable features on the one hand, and, on the other hand, by literally making the figure visible, by giving its appearance a concrete manifestation through the technical means of the reproduction of the actor's body in the form of an image on the screen. Rather than merely mobilizing an unconscious that a priori exists, the cinematic apparatus is what instantiates its coming into being in the first place. As a case in point, consider the psychoanalytic model of the structure of the gaze, which, for Jacques Lacan, is always already in the field of the other, with the subject only emerging as an effect of the gaze, constituted in the desire of the other. In Lacan's words, "In the scopic, the gaze is outside, I am looked at, that is to say, I am a picture."[20] But if, as Lacan suggests, subjectivity emerges in the field of the visible under the gaze of the other, then it can further be argued that what enables this procedure is a historically specific condition wherein vision has become autonomized and alienated from the spectator through the cinematic apparatus. Consequently, a proper analysis of the doppelgänger's popularization must account for the doppelgänger's underpinnings within an emerging media ecology or discourse network marked by the rise of new technologies of vision like film and photography, not to mention the broader historical process of visual modernization, or more specifically, the industrialization of the image under a capitalist mode of production.

Language and Visuality in Modern Japan

I have gone into these historical links between cinema and psychoanalysis in relation to the image of the doppelgänger because they provide an important critical context for the figure's appearances in the modern Japanese literary milieu. Indeed, Kittler's contention that the very conception of the doppelgänger appears in response to the development of cinematic technologies can be extended to its literary appearances in Japan as well. The historical concurrence of interest in the doppelgänger among Japanese authors with the beginnings of psychoanalytic interest in the figure takes place in the wake of its cinematic manifestations. As such, it would appear that the figure's travel to Japan cannot be reduced to a simple line of influence from its literary precedents elsewhere. Rather, it involves a more complex relationship mediated through the development of the technology of cinema and the broader historical event of visual modernization.

In fact, there is an argument to be made that the perceptual reconfigurations that underpinned the coming into being of the institution of "literature" in Japan are wedded to historical process of visual modernization in the first place. Recall the work of Karatani Kōjin on the relation between literary language and the constitution of modern subjectivity in late nineteenth-century Japan. To briefly recapitulate, the critical thrust of Karatani's analysis is that the conjoined conceptions of an interiorized subject (*naimen*) and its differentiation from an exterior object or "landscape" [*fūkei*] came into being in the 1890s as a consequence of a transformation in perceptual configuration. Put simply, it is the projection of a space that exceeds the interior, that is, the exterior landscape, which allows for a process of introjection that draws the boundaries of the modern interiorized subject. Crucially, Karatani traces this process to the emergence of a movement to promote a standardized literary language known as *genbun-itchi*—literally, the unification of speech and writing—based on a phonocentric model tied to an ideology of transparent representation and expression. Although *genbun-itchi* was ideologically posited as the result of the need by the new "modern subject" for a language to communicate its inner being transparently, Karatani's analysis inverts this understanding. He suggests instead that the literary conception of this interiorized subject is an effect (and not the cause) of *genbun-itchi* in the sense that it is precisely this configuration of writing premised on the possibility of representing from a fixed transcendent position that enables the emergence of an inner voice of the modern subject, with writing reduced to its expression.[21]

Although the *genbun-itchi* revolution is often understood largely as a literary problem, parallel transformations were taking place in other dimensions of cultural practice such as, for instance, reforms in theater, performance, and visual arts. Karatani's account of the development of a modern literary language in Japan in the late nineteenth century cannot be read in isolation. On the contrary, it must be considered as just one manifestation of a broader historical process of visual modernization, a process that entailed a transformation of the scopic regime, which was itself inseparable from the radical reconfiguration of knowledge and social practice taking place during this time.[22] Indeed, Karatani's understanding of the mechanism of the landscape–interiority demarcation constituted in the logic of *genbun-itchi* takes on a notably visual character. This incessant visuality manifests in a number of ways, not the least of which is Karatani's repeated references to modern revolutions in painting and especially to the development of Cartesian perspective. For Karatani, the Cartesian placement of the subject of vision in a transcendent position with visual mastery over the object of its gaze engendered the modern conception of "landscape" alienated from the subject. In sum, visual modernization was a process whose impact could be felt not only in ostensibly visual objects (e.g., painting, photography, cinema), but also all manner of social and cultural institutions, among which is "literature," which effectively became another site in which the techniques and practices of modern visuality operate.[23]

If Karatani is correct in his contention that the demarcation of interiority and landscape built into the structure of Cartesian perspective is formative of modern literary practice, then one implication that can be drawn here is that "literature" comes into being as a means of recuperating classical visual practice in response to the social and cultural effects of visual modernization. This brings Karatani's analysis in alignment with Rey Chow's rereading of Chinese writer Lu Xun's famous account of watching a newsreel of the execution of a Chinese man observed by a crowd of onlookers. Against the standard literary-biographical account of this event, Chow places the problem of visuality at the very center of the sense of shock Lu Xun experiences at witnessing this spectacle. In other words, it is not simply what is represented in the images that is traumatic, but the encounter with the cinematic image as such; as Chow puts it, "If we say that he sees the horror of an execution, we must also say that he sees the horror of the activity of watching."[24] Chow presents Lu Xun's traumatic encounter with the cinematic image as a kind of autoethnographic mirror stage. It provokes an act of identification with the projected image of one's own (national) self, in so doing at once enacting an identification with the very gaze through which one is produced as subject.[25] In effect, a logic of seeing the (national) self as other—a logic of the doppelgänger—structures this traumatic encounter. Analogous to Chow's contention that the origins of literary modernism in China must be located in the trauma of a technologized visuality, the reforms to standardize literary language that Karatani critiques in his work might then be understood in a similar fashion, that is, as a reterritorializing reaction to the shock of the image through the reconstitution of the Cartesian logic of classical visuality. "Literature," Chow writes, "is a way to evade the shock of the visual"; it is a response whose function is to contain and repress the shock of modern visuality and the material and social consequences it entailed.[26] In effect, it functions as an attempt to reterritorialize, to render legible and come to terms with the deterritorializing visual trauma operating in parallel to Kittler's characterization of the obsessive schematization of the unconscious seen in psychoanalytic discourse.

While Karatani focuses on the formation of a conception of modern subjectivity in the late nineteenth century, by the 1920s, fractures had begun to appear in this schematic configuration. Several transformations in the Japanese cultural milieu contributed to this historical development. The late 1910s and early 1920s saw not only the unmooring of extant forms of living through processes of urbanization and the increasing mechanization and commodification of all aspects of everyday life, but also the rapid expansion and widespread dissemination of new forms of popular entertainment and mass media spectacles, foremost among which was cinema, whose popularization arguably played an instrumental role in rendering this foundational schema of literature and subjectivity untenable by the 1920s in Japan. If in the nineteenth century, cinema was still a nascent technological curiosity, by the early twentieth century, it had established itself as a dominant medium of mass entertainment to the extent that a cinematic rhetoric permeated much of the cultural discourse of the time. Elaine Gerbert has already written on the role of the display of new commodity spectacles and cinematic technologies in transforming Japanese literary production, suggesting that this period "marked the moment when new vision technologies began to transform the relationship between the eye and the world and open new possibilities of consciousness and literary art."[27] Likewise, Miriam Silverberg has called attention to the influence of cinematic techniques like montage and tracking shots in not only the narrative styles employed by modernist writers of the period, but also the overall constellation of discourses that included ethnographies, cultural commentaries, and mass culture.[28]

One consequence of this development was to undermine the position of dominance occupied by the novel within the cultural milieu, such that cultural commentary began lamenting the impending demise of the novel as literary texts are reduced to just another form of commodity within a world of mass-produced commercial cultural activity.[29] More fundamentally, though, it is not just the institution of literature and its centrality within the regime of cultural production that becomes subject to challenge; the epistemological basis undergirding the very conception of "modern literature" itself is called into question. Famously, Walter Benjamin has observed how cinematic spectatorship is tied to a loss of aura and distance. In "The Work of Art of in the Age of Mechanical Reproduction," he contrasts the film camera to the painter. Whereas the painter works by maintaining a certain perceptual distance, the camera's reproductive capability collapses this. Moreover, because of the speed and all too often magnified scale of the images on the screen, for Benjamin, the cinematic experience breaches the boundaries of the body. Thus, while distance in painting invites contemplation, the images of film in contrast generate a shock to the spectator.[30]

This brings me back to the question of the doppelgänger's appearances in early twentieth-century Japan. The response to such experiences of speed and shock and the attendant questions about the adequacy of existing literary forms to communicate the accelerated pace of modern life they engendered—"the crisis of modernity over the stability and reliability of forms of representation," as Harry Harootunian once put it—came in the form of all manner of literary experiments to produce discursive forms capable of capturing these sensations that marked the lived experience of the time.[31] These took shape through such approaches as Yokomitsu Riichi's (1898–1947) experiments with perspective and sensation, styles of narration based on practices of flânerie and urban ethnography in the work of authors like Kawabata Yasunari (1899–1972) or Hori Tatsuo (1904–1953), or for that matter, the rise of the confessional mode in the so-called I-novel [shishōsetsu] as a reactionary formation, and others. To this, I would add the popularization of the doppelgänger motif as yet another manifestation, whose appearances function as an allegory of the breakdown of the subject–object or interior–exterior relations that underpin modern literary language and form through the staging of a return of the repressed, albeit one that spotlights not the unveiling of some psychical truth, but the revelation of the historical unconscious of visual modernization.

Akutagawa's Doppelgängers

It is precisely this historical unconscious of visual modernization that finds clear expression in the doppelgänger fictions of Akutagawa Ryūnosuke, whose writings often place their attention on linking the figure of the double with the aforementioned breakdown of literary language and modern subjectivity. For example, in his "Two Letters" the doppelgänger's disruption features not only as a figure represented in the narrative, but also in the very form the performance of the narration takes. The short story takes on an epistolary form, introduced and framed by a narrator (*yo*) as a pair of letters that he happened to get a hold of and is forwarding to the chief of police, to whom they were originally addressed. What appears to be another individual named Sasaki (*watakushi*) is the author of the letters themselves. The first letter begins with its encoded author's odd insistence on his own sanity through an extended treatise on various philosophical and psychological works attesting to the scientific validity of the phenomenon of encountering one's doppelgänger.[32] It is only following this that he explains his predicament: Apparently, three times already, he has witnessed his own doppelgänger—each time with his wife (or her own double). Shortly after, rumors that his wife was having an affair begin to surface, and he and his wife become the object of various acts of harassment. Believing these two events to be connected, he suggests all this is a manifestation of his wife's desire to travel outside their home, and his neighbors have mistaken her psychical projection of his image for another man. He requests police assistance in quelling the harassment. His explanation falls apart, however, with the second letter, which reveals that his wife has disappeared. Moreover, this second letter is cut short following his declaration that he now intends to do research on supernatural phenomena. The framing narrator (*yo*) explains that he cut the rest of it since the letter turns into nothing more than incoherent philosophical ramblings from that point on.[33]

The above summary makes clear that the most salient feature of "Two Letters" is its depiction of the breakdown in its own act of narration, which functions as a performative signifier of Sasaki's descent into madness. This element is further given particular emphasis by the letter writer's almost obsessive emphasis on proving his sanity (despite the apparently supernatural encounter with his own doppelgänger) early in the story through the various citations of doppelgänger-related psychological research, and in so doing, paradoxically calling his sanity to attention and into question. Given the way that the story unfolds, it seems only logical to read Sasaki's (*watakushi's*) two letters as narratives produced in response to his increasing psychic fragmentation, as attempts at forming a coherent narrative for the purpose of assuaging his emergent personal crisis punctuated by his repeated encounters with his doppelgänger.[34] In this regard, Akutagawa's story has some formal affinities with the detective fictions of Edogawa Rampo discussed in Chapter 1. Analogous to the role that Rampo's detectives play in resolving the disruption provoked by a crime through the production of a narrative, the letters in Akutagawa's story are an attempt to construct a coherent narrative that can explain the spread of rumors of the supposed infidelity of the narrator's wife, which he believes to be a false accusation. Indeed, Ichiyanagi Hirotaka goes so far as to argue that "Two Letters" is formally organized around the conventions of detective fiction: "The charge of a crime is brought, and the protection of the victims is sought. The criminal is 'society' [*seken*]. The crime is the harassment of the narrator and his wife. The motive, the wife's infidelity."[35] However, Sasaki's attempt is ultimately unsuccessful. His narration is revealed to be unreliable, reduced to incoherent rambling in his second letter, and ultimately the mystery is left unresolved. Consequently, as Ichiyanagi argues, "Even as 'Two Letters' abides by the conventional forms of detective fiction, these are shifted and inverted into a parody of detective fiction."[36]

The most overt manifestation of this is, of course, the second letter's so-called incoherent rambling, which Watanabe Masahiko reads as indicative of a schizophrenic author behind the narrative performance of the letters.[37] Indeed, this particular aspect of the narrative of "Two Letters" arguably prefigures the notion of "schizophrenia" as it is deployed by Fredric Jameson in reference to what he deems to be the concept underlying the loss of historicity in postmodernist fictions. Borrowing from Lacan's ideas on the role of language in subject formation, for Jameson, schizophrenia is characterized primarily by a failure of language, by "an experience of isolated, disconnected, discontinuous material signifiers which fail to link up into a coherent sequence."[38] In "Two Letters," the repeated encounters with the doppelgänger in Akutagawa's story foreshadow the return of the repressed, from a moment prior to the demarcation between subject and object constituted through language. With the second letter, all that remains is the breakdown of the capacity for coherent language and narrative production, such that by the end of the story, it appears that the original narrator has completely disappeared, thoroughly dominated and replaced by his double (*yo*), to whom is left the task of framing the narrative and forwarding the letters to their addressee.

This linkage between the breakdown of language and the appearance of the doppelgänger finds an echo in Akutagawa's more well known final work of, namely the posthumously published "Spinning Gears." Although it does not utilize the same kind of formal play exhibited by "Two Letters" in terms of the narrative strategies it deploys, like the previous story, "Spinning Gears" is also a first-person account of a narrator who is increasingly exhibiting signs of mental breakdown and fragmentation. In the story, the narrator proceeds through several seemingly uneventful days loosely strung together into a plot beginning with his attendance at a wedding reception, visits to the famous Maruzen bookstore, and periods of time spent writing in a hotel room, among others. In the course of these events, though, he begins to exhibit the symptoms that suggest the deterioration of his mental stability such as regular bouts of insomnia, and most obviously, periodic hallucinations of images of silver wings as well as the titular "spinning gears" [*haguruma*]. But the most persistent of these symptoms is a sense of linguistic disorientation. For example, early in the narrative, after overhearing a hotel bellboy utter the English phrase "all right," the narrator finds himself unable to clear his mind of the words, such that when he decides to write, he cannot help it when his pen fails him; instead, "just when it finally began to move, it wrote nothing but the same words again and again: 'All right . . . All right . . . All right . . . sir . . . All right . . .'"[39] Later, in a conversation with a friend, he finds that he is unable to pronounce the name "Shu Shunsui" or the last syllable of the Japanese word for "insomnia" [*fuminshō*].[40] Finally, there are the repeated instances of the narrator's overhearing of the English word "mole," which in the narrator's mind is transfigured into the French *la mort* [death]. Indeed it is following one such instance, after receiving an odd telephone call wherein the voice on the other end of the line said nothing but this word, that he considers the idea of the doppelgänger:

> For the first time in a while, I stood in front of the mirror and faced off against my own image. Of course, my image smiled back at me. As I stared at it, my thoughts recollected my second self. My second self—what the Germans call a Doppelgänger—I am fortunate that I have never had to face it myself. But the wife of my friend K, who had become a film actor in America, had come upon him in the lobby of the Imperial Theatre. (I remember my confusion when she said to me without warning, "Sorry I didn't have a chance to speak with you the other night"). After that, there was another time when a certain now dead one-legged translator came upon my second self in a Ginza tobacco shop. Perhaps death was coming for my second self and not me.[41]

The juxtaposition of the French phrase "*la mort*" with the narrator's sudden recollection of the alleged presence of his doppelgänger serves to highlight not only the conventional association of the figure with a forewarning of death, but also the overlap between the collapse of the subject through the breaking apart of language and the destabilization of self–other relations foregrounded through the figure of the doppelgänger. Recall that Karatani locates the formation of modern Japanese literature in the process of demarcating of interiority from exteriority (that is, of subject from object) facilitated by the development of a modern, vernacular literary language. Building on this analysis, Seiji Lippit suggests that what manifests in Akutagawa's "Spinning Gears" is a staging of a reversal of this process, the unraveling of "literature" itself. Or, as Lippit puts it, it is "like a translation in reverse, as though modern Japanese were being separated into its various foreign components."[42] It is therefore only fitting that this breakdown of language is accompanied by the fragmentation of modern subjectivity, materializing as the literal embodiment of the collapse of the demarcation between self and other in the form of the doppelgänger.

With the fragmentation of language and subjectivity comes the loss of a capacity to produce a coherent narrative. This has the effect of turning the two stories' respective protagonists into little more than technical media, capturing every mundane and ephemeral detail before it. In "Two Letters," this is suggested in the excised sections of Sasaki's second letter. While they are not themselves made visible to the reader, the first letter certainly hints at its content given that it too presents his wild philosophical ramblings (on the subject of the doppelgänger), whose chief characteristic is its excess of arbitrary detail, formally mimicking the camera's indexical property that allows it to capture and record all that is in front of it. In contrast, "Spinning Gears" turns this experience into an optical hallucination, with the narrator repeatedly seeing the image of spinning gears floating before his eyes. It is as if he were seeing a materialization of the optical unconscious, a glimpse of something that would normally be invisible to the naked eye but visible to the camera's machinic gaze. But while this visual dimension to the encounter with one's doppelgänger is only hinted at by the above stories, Akutagawa's "The Shadow" makes the point explicit, vividly staging the encounter with the double against the specific backdrop of not just cinematic spectatorship itself, but a broader set of social and cultural practices structured around the traffic of gazes in a modern visual regime.

Initially, the story of "The Shadow" takes on a seemingly conventional appearance. Narrated in the third person, it opens in Yokohama with the protagonist Chen Cai, a Chinese businessman, receiving an anonymous letter—apparently another in a series of them he has been periodically receiving—informing him of his wife Fusako's infidelity. After informing his wife on the phone that he will be working late and so will miss the final train back to their home in Kamakura, he secretly returns home in an attempt to catch his wife. It is when, under the cover of darkness, he returns home to spy on his wife through the bedroom window that he encounters his doppelgänger. Rather than finding another man with Fusako, Chen Cai finds another Chen Cai in the bedroom of his home. As Chen Cai watches from a corner of the room, the other Chen Cai strangles the sleeping Fusako. It is not until the final scene of the story, however, when a frame narrative replaces the first, that it is revealed that the preceding section is in fact a film being watched by two spectators.

From this point, the story shifts into a first-person narration with a man (the narrator) wondering if he has dreamed the film—also titled *The Shadow*—that forms the body of the first part of the story. When he confers with his female companion, she points out to him that no film by that title appears in the program, yet curiously acknowledges a vague recollection of it when the narrator describes its plot to her.

Evident from this summary of Akutagawa's "The Shadow" are many of the familiar established tropes of doppelgänger fictions, particularly the conventional characterization of the shadowy doppelgänger as an externalized projection of an individual's unconscious, especially his or her repressed violent urges that can only end in a murderous finale. When juxtaposed to Rank's discussion of *The Student of Prague*, however, it is difficult to miss the similarity between Rank's aforementioned attempt to put into writing his recollection of the film's scenes and the characterization of the narrator's experience of cinematic spectatorship as almost hallucinatory, and the ensuing doubt and uncertainty it engenders in the final scene of Akutagawa's "The Shadow." To put it another way, Akutagawa's story goes beyond the mere reproduction of the established tropes and plot patterns of doppelgänger fictions that have appeared thus far. More importantly, it gestures toward a parallel between film work and dream work, especially in its ending, wherein the narrator wonders whether he has dreamed the film he has just seen. It thus foregrounds the role played by the cinema as both a technical and social apparatus—in its production of images, its modes of display and distribution, its mobilization of desires—in the constitution of modern subjectivities through which the conceptual articulation of the figure of the doppelgänger is made possible.

Indeed, unlike other fictions of the doppelgänger—for example, Poe's "William Wilson" wherein the two William Wilsons interact on a physical level (one William Wilson kills the other and ends up killing himself in the process)—it is striking that the primary interaction of the two Chen Cais in Akutagawa's "The Shadow" is primarily that of looking. Indeed, from its very beginning, at earlier points in the narrative before even the protagonist's encounter with the doppelgänger takes place, various moments of spying and voyeurism (and an attendant paranoia at being spied upon) appear. For example, in a flashback sequence embedded into the first scene, labeled "Yokohama," the protagonist Chen Cai's recollection of his first meeting with his wife Fusako centers on an exchange of gazes:

> . . . Cigarette smoke, the fragrance of flowers, the clatter of knives and forks upon plates . . . Melody from *Carmen* drifting dissonantly from one corner. Amid the chaos, glass of beer before him, Chen sat entranced with his elbows on the table. Before his eyes, not one thing was not in dizzying motion—waitresses, customers, even the ceiling fans. Only Chen was still, gaze cast upon the woman by the cash register all throughout.[43]

This sequence is noteworthy for its telling excess of arbitrary detail, which gestures toward the property of the cinematic apparatus to make visible all manner of ephemera by virtue of its capacity to repeat and reproduce the scene it captures. It is no coincidence that the story sets up the scene as an act of spectatorship. Here, Chen sitting immobile as the rest of scene is in constant motion serves further to call to mind the experience of cinematic spectatorship (and hence foreshadows the ending of the story), a point that is only punctuated when the flashback sequence ends with Chen in the darkness, once again *gazing* at the night sky. Later, other scenes hammer the point home further. Several scenes show Chen (as well as his assistant Imanishi) gazing upon his wife's photograph. At one point, Fusako has a strange sense that someone stands behind her, gazing at her, almost hinting at an awareness of her existence as a character in a film. In another, as if a voyeur, Chen peers through a keyhole into his wife's bedroom. But perhaps the most telling instance is a moment when Chen stands in the darkness of the garden, gazing up toward the window of his wife's bedroom in an attempt to catch her in an act of infidelity in which he mistakenly believes she will engage.

> "Fusako." As if a groan, Chen longingly uttered his wife's name.
> It was right at that moment. Far above on the second floor, a blinding light filled a room.
> "That's, that window—"
> Swallowing his breath, Chen grasped the trunk of a pine and stands on his tiptoes in order to get a better view. The window—the glass panes of the window of the second floor bedroom were wide open and the bright

interior showed itself. The light from inside the room casts shadows upon the tree branches, which seem to float against the night sky.

But that was not where the mystery ended. A single shadow, a dim silhouette approached the window. The light comes from deep within the room and his face remains in shadow. One thing was certain though. It was not a woman's silhouette.[44]

It is at this moment in Akutagawa's story when the doppelgänger makes its appearance. So convinced is Chen Cai that his wife is having an affair after having repeatedly received typewritten letters that his rage overcomes him and it materializes in the form of the silhouette that appears before the window, despite the evidence to the contrary that she is alone in their home (a private investigator whom Chen meets on the way home informs him as much). Even when this other man is later revealed to be nothing more than his double—a projection of his own violent urges—when he subsequently enters the bedroom and discovers another Chen Cai inside, his jealousy is undeterred and the embodiment of this jealousy proceeds to murder his own wife.

On its face, the appearance of Chen Cai's doppelgänger in "The Shadow" seemingly aligns with the conventional psychoanalytic understanding of the doppelgänger as a projection of an unconscious content—in this case, jealousy and a murderous urge—onto an external image or figure.[45] However, what Akutagawa's story also spotlights is an intimate linkage between the psychical "projection" that produces the figure of doppelgänger and the mechanism of "projection" at the heart of the signifying mechanisms of the cinematic apparatus, in terms of both the literal projection of light through which the images appear on the screen as well as an act of projection by the spectator through which these images are given meaning. The moment when Chen Cai sits in the darkness peering through a window into his wife's bedroom enacts an event analogous to the concluding scene of the story with the two spectators seemingly projecting into existence a film that does not exist. Just as a film spectator would, Chen Cai sits immobile in darkness, viewing a scene through a screen (the window to his wife's bedroom), and in so doing manufactures an image (his double) through the act of projection.[46] Moreover, in both instances, the event of film spectatorship (literally or allegorically) brings about the appearance of the doppelgänger. In the case of Chen Cai and his peering through the window into the bedroom where his wife sleeps, this takes on a more overt form. With the final scene of the story with the two spectators musing about the mysterious film they had just viewed, this is more obliquely suggested through the unnamed first-person narrator's observation that his female companion's "melancholy" [yūutsu na] eyes remind him of the eyes of Fusako in the film *The Shadow*, in effect indirectly implying his own identification with, and as such, doubling of the Chen Cai of the film.[47]

In her analysis of Akutagawa's story, Carole Cavanaugh argues that this linkage between the event of film spectatorship and the projection of a doppelgänger enacted by Akutagawa's "The Shadow" is demonstrative of the emergence of a transcendental subjectivity. By this, what Cavanaugh refers to is the process or mechanism wherein a specular subjectivity is formed when the spectator identifies with the positionality of the camera/projector and with this, the act of seeing itself. Cavanaugh's frame of reference here is Christian Metz's psychoanalytic theorization of the psychic mechanisms involved in the act of cinematic spectatorship in *The Imaginary Signifier* (1982). Citing, for instance, the seeming total fabrication of the film by the narrator of "The Shadow" in the closing scene, made apparent when his female companion points out that no such film titled *The Shadow* appears in the program (hence suggesting that he had "dreamed" the film), Cavanaugh suggests that this shows the "identification of the subject with his own ability to make coherent what happens on the screen."[48] This is in agreement with Metz's characterization of the spectator's position as a kind of voyeur, placed before the screen as "all-perceiving . . . as a pure act of perception: as the condition of possibility of the perceived and hence as a kind of transcendental subject."[49] Thus, for Cavanaugh, the staging of cinematic spectatorship in Akutagawa's "The Shadow" inaugurates an idea of transcendental subjectivity that takes hold in such naturalist literary forms as the I-novel (*watakushi-shōsetsu*).

Contrary to Cavanaugh's reading, in Akutagawa's "The Shadow," I would argue that the predominant sense one receives from the story is not visual mastery but ambiguity and unease. Consider, for instance, the final scene of the story with the pair of perplexed spectators. In this scene, neither the narrator nor his companion can account for the film they had just seen, which does not appear in the program, yet even the woman who points this out expresses her own vague familiarity with the film's story line, making it difficult to characterize the pair of spectators in "The Shadow" as particularly transcendent or all-perceiving. Further to this, the allegorical representation of cinematic spectatorship in the film within the story takes on a similar character. When Chen Cai first encounters the doppelgänger as a distinct physical and material body, his first response is shock, and the stability of the metaphorical camera-as-subject's field of view is destabilized in the scene of the encounter. Although the doppelgänger is already foreshadowed by an earlier scene wherein Chen Cai spies the silhouette of a man through the window to the bedroom, until the moment Chen Cai opens the bedroom door, the narrative is still focalized through him. However, the scene cuts at the moment he enters the bedroom into another scene back in Yokohama where it is revealed that Imanishi (Chen Cai's personal assistant) is the one typing the letters "informing" Chen Cai of his wife's infidelity. But when the story cuts back to Chen Cai's home in Kamakura, it has already become impossible to determine which of the two Chen Cais is the "original" one followed from the story's beginning.

> Immobile in the corner, Chen Cai stares at the two bodies lying atop one another on the bed. One was Fusako—or perhaps *something* that was once Fusako until moments before. The entire face is swollen and purple, the tongue protrudes halfway from the mouth and the partly closed eyes gaze toward the ceiling. The other one is Chen Cai, not one bit different from the Chen Cai in the corner.[50]

Although the Chen Cai in the corner functions as the subject of the gaze at this particular moment in the narration, as a result of the previous scene cut and the jump in time, continuity with the previous scene wherein Chen Cai is forcing open the bedroom door is broken. As a result, it has become impossible to tell if the "original" Chen Cai of the previous scene is the one lurking in the corner or the one atop Fusako on the bed. This confusion is further compounded when the Chen Cai atop Fusako's body rises and realizes that there is another Chen Cai in the room. The following words are exchanged: "'Who are you?' Standing before the chair, he almost chokes on his words. 'So you were the one who went through the pine groves . . . who sneaked in through the back gate . . . who stood by this window looking out . . . who . . . my wife . . . Fusako.'"[51] As both of them are at this moment standing before the chair, which of the two Chens is actually doing the speaking has become indeterminate. Only the uncertain "he" [*kare*] marks the speech of the speakers, potentially referring to either of the pair. Indeed, it is even impossible to tell if these two lines constitute an exchange of dialogue or the second is merely a follow-up spoken by the same person, further making the task of distinguishing the two difficult. All that is certain is that one or the other has murdered Fusako. With this in mind, I would contend that what is at the heart of the doppelgänger's appearance in Akutagawa's story is not the confirmation or illustration of the visual mastery of the spectator, but is instead a staging of the voyeuristic gaze of the subject in crisis.

The more fundamental problem with apprehending the doppelgänger's appearance in terms of the model of spectator identification that Metz articulates, as Cavanaugh does, is the anachronistic character of such an approach in that it presupposes a model of film spectatorship that had arguably yet to become dominant by the time of the publication of Akutagawa's story. Scholarship on the practices of early cinema has shown that the practice of spectatorship engendered by narrative cinema (and especially narrative cinema in the mold of the classic Hollywood film) is but one mode among many coexisting possibilities that existed at the time. Indeed, it was not always the dominant mode, in Japan or elsewhere. Notably, in contrast to the film theories that appeared from the 1970s onward, the commentary surrounding photography and early cinema at the time—by the likes of Béla Bálàzs, Jean Epstein, or Walter Benjamin—placed their emphasis not primarily on the content or narrative of the films, but instead on the transformative, even revolutionary character of cinematic technologies, that is, the capacity of the very apparatus of cinema itself to produce an experience of shock that entrances its spectator.[52] While film theorists of Metz's generation saw in the cinematic apparatus an ideological institution that operates on the principle of a systematic structuring of identification so as to mobilize the spectator's affects, desires, and fantasies, an earlier generation of writers saw in cinematic technologies the shocking potency of the spectacle.

Politics of Looking

In his work on early cinema, Tom Gunning has rightly emphasized the need to avoid the trap of reinscribing the hegemonic position that narrative cinema has taken since its introduction and popularization.[53] This entails not merely treating early cinema as proto-narrative-film, in effect implying that the shift from one to the other was simply a natural linear progression. Instead, early cinema operated with its own logic, its own set of distinct social and spectatorial practices. Gunning calls these institutions and practices surrounding early film "the cinema of attractions," which he characterizes as a mode of film viewing based less on an emphasis on film as a storytelling medium and more on film as an exhibition of an unabashed visual spectacle. Only later in the history of the technology does the narrativization of cinema take place, and only through a concerted industrial and ideological effort rather than any kind of natural, continuous evolution. Even then, Gunning points out that "the cinema of attractions does not disappear with the dominance of narrative, but rather goes underground, both into certain avant-garde practices and as a component of narrative films, more evident in some genres (e.g., the musical) than in others."[54]

A similar process of disciplinization of cinema, wherein the unruly multiplicity of early cinematic practices increasingly gives way to narrative cinema in the classical Hollywood mold, takes place in 1910s and 1920s Japan. In his analysis of the discursive history of cinema in Japan—that is, the history of how cinema was talked about, defined, and redefined in its first few decades in Japan—Aaron Gerow provides an important corrective to many existing histories of cinema in Japan by pointing to the fact that cinema did not appear in Japan as a fixed and fully formed technology and set of institutional practices at the turn of the twentieth century. Rather, cinema was a site of interconnected and contested discursive articulations. In Gerow's words, "cinema was written in early Japanese film history before it was filmed."[55] Put differently, even before there was film-making, there were statements and narrations about the proper conceptions and directions of style, narrative, and spectatorial practice, and for that matter the very conception of cinema as such. Consequently, in Gerow's analysis, these debates and discourses set the terms for the historical developments of how cinema came to be understood in complex ways that can neither be taken as a simple product of the cinematic ontology of the apparatus itself, nor reduced to a teleology that inevitably leads toward the form of classical narrative cinema.

When the technology of motion pictures (*katsudō shashin*) first made its way to Japan through Edison's Kinetoscope or the Lumières' Cinematographe (in 1896 and 1897, respectively), it arrived not as a fully formed and discrete thing but was instead subsumed into the existing discourse on *misemono* side-show spectacles.[56] Film, in other words, initially became another instantiation of these *misemono*. Only later did it emerge as a distinct medium and distinct problem, as "film" [*eiga*].[57] Subsequently, another constellation of discourses—the Pure Film movement—brought further attempts at defining film by promoting a particular set of formal and narrative devices deemed to be properly cinematic, transforming not only the practices of filmmaking, but also the very conception of film itself. Only through such concerted efforts did Japanese cinema introduce innovations in style and production that would align with not only the aesthetics, but also the Fordist industrial practices of Hollywood film, thus transforming cinema into a mass-produced cultural commodity and foreclosing any alternative visions of what cinema could become.[58]

This history is especially relevant for the analysis of doppelgänger fictions in Japan, given that such texts appeared precisely during the period of intense discursive negotiation and contestation over the conception of cinema. In light of how the figure of the double melds the theme of the uncanny with the technology of film—often directly linking the fragmentation of the subject with the cinematic apparatus—its repeated appearances in fictions of this period arguably act as popular interventions into the space of debates and discursive articulations of cinema and its spectatorial effects that would transform conceptions of cinema during this time. In the case of Akutagawa's "The Shadow," while the depiction of the film within the story (itself titled *The Shadow*) makes it out to be a work along the lines of what the Pure Film reformers envisioned (seeing as how it presents a self-contained, coherent narrative system structured around multiple scenes that emerge out of the text itself, without any hint of the use of a live *benshi* narrator), at the same time it makes clear that this vision of cinema had yet to be consolidated, its spectator yet to be habituated. The portrayal of cinema in the story reveals its status as a technology of representation that remains unfamiliar, making use of the metaphor of doubling to express an anxiety over the machine's repro-duction and doubling of reality. In effect it treats the cinematic image as something all-too-real, such that it poses a potential threat of replacing the original profilmic reality it ostensibly represents.

These rhetorical gestures in Akutagawa's "The Shadow" effectively link the doppelgänger's appearance with the process of cinematic moderniza-tion and its turn toward the mass production of images as commodity spectacles. The doppelgänger serves as an allegory for the alienation of vision within a regime of the industrialization of image making. It speaks to the production of, in the words of Jean Baudrillard, "potentially iden-tical objects produced in an indefinite series" relationship that "is no longer one of an original and its counterfeit, analogy or reflection, but is instead one of equivalence and indifference. . . . The extinction of the original reference alone facilitates the general law of equivalences, that is to say, the very possibility of production"[59] What is significant about the doppelgänger is its potential to pose the question of what is at stake in the shifting conceptions of cinema at the time. The media-allegorical function of the doppelgänger implicates not only matters of the develop-ment of a style or form of cinema in a narrowly aesthetic sense, but more importantly, it offers an entry point for apprehending the larger social force of cinema within historical processes of industrialization and mod-ernization, with all its attendant transformations in conceptions of social class, culture, and the nation. It is a figure, in other words, that emerges out of the development of what Guy Debord has called "the society of the spectacle," that development of capitalism and commodity fetishism into a state wherein social life is increasingly mediated through the image.[60]

Jonathan Beller's articulation of what he calls "the cinematic mode of production" is instructive here. Against Christian Metz's argument that the primary function of cinema's mobilization of spectatorial desire is the production of its own consumers, Beller argues that cinema's constitu-tion of its own consumer-spectators is only a symptom. Beyond this, the mechanical production of affects and subjectivities serves as an enabling condition for the larger project of expropriating and capitalizing an emerging order of productive labor from its spectators—attention—and through images as surplus-value bearing commodities. In Beller's words:

> Cinema and its succeeding (if still simultaneous) formations, particularly television, video, computers, and the internet, are deterritorialized factories in which spectators work, that is, in which we perform value-productive labor. It is in and through the cinematic image and its legacy, the gossamer imaginary arising out of a matrix of socio-psycho-material relations, that we make our lives.... What is immediately suggested by the cinematic mode of production (CMP), properly understood, is that a social relation that emerged as "the cinema" is today characteristic of sociality in general.[61]

In calling cinema a mode of production, Beller suggests that what takes place on the site of cinematic spectatorship and in the process of the mechanization of vision is not restricted to just the cinematic experience within the film theater, but is increasingly becoming a decisive component of social organization as a whole. In other words, "cinema" is not merely an issue of the spectator before the screen, but a part of a broader expansion and reorganization of the capitalist mode of production. Developing the point further, he posits two forms of labor performed by the spectator. The first kind of labor is the valorization of the images (or more accurately, image-commodities) through the attention given to them in acts of viewing. One need to only think of celebrities or image-commodity franchises to realize the value produced by increased visibility. Cinema becomes, in other words, an extension of the working day into visual terrain. The second form of labor implicated in Beller's work is performed by spectators upon themselves. The act of spectatorship produces desires, affects, and subjectivities that function as the condition of possibility for the production of value. Spectators are, in effect, not only productive of value in the image-commodities they consume, but are also consumed by and become images themselves. As Beller explains it:

> Early cinematic montage extended the logic of the assembly-line (the sequencing of discrete, programmatic machine-orchestrated human operations) to the sensorium and brought the industrial revolution to the eye.

> Cinema welds human sensual activity, what Marx called "sensual labor," in the context of commodity production, to celluloid. Instead of striking a blow to sheet metal wrapped around a mold or tightening a bolt, we sutured one image to the next (and, like workers who disappeared in the commodities they produced, we sutured ourselves into the image).[62]

Understood in this sense, the shifts in the practices of spectatorship surrounding early cinema might then be grasped as a parallel historical process to the passage from primitive accumulation to the development of a capitalist economy and subsequently repeated in imperial conquest and expansion, albeit taking place on the order of the visual. Put another way, if imperialism can be grasped as the geographic expansion and intensification of capital—its "spatial fix," in the language of David Harvey—in response to its periodic crises of overaccumulation, then in analogous terms, the emergence of the cinematic mode of production functions as a significant component of the drive to commodify other latent yet previously uncommodified aspects of human life: affective labor, desiring production, indeed the unconscious itself.[63] It therefore stages a colonization inward parallel to the outward colonial expansion of capital.

In Japan, these historical developments manifested not only in the specific site of cinematic discourse, but also as a literal image-commodification of the very space of the city. Tokyo, for example, increasingly became a screening space on a number of levels. On the one hand, as Mitsuyo Wada-Marciano has discussed, Japanese cinema of the interwar period—and especially in the aftermath of the 1923 Kanto earthquake—often functioned as a document of the process of rebuilding the city, as films shot on location "shaped the image of Tokyo in the popular imaginary."[64] In effect, these films played an integral role in generating and disseminating the cultural codes that would mediate the production of urban space as images. On the other hand, the city streets themselves were at once increasingly transformed into a site of signification through the proliferation of technological media and visual spectacles, especially in locations like Asakusa or Ginza. Not just movie theaters but also advertisements and mannequins displayed on shop windows, peep shows and pornography, revue halls, and other consumer amusements all turned the streets of the city into spaces for the commodification of attention and desire. The circulation of these image-commodities and the general expansion of consumer culture in Japan's metropolitan centers represented by cinema and other forms of mass culture were underpinned by colonial expansion through the extraction of surplus from the colonial peripheries. Moreover, it was itself a form of involuted imperialism, a preparation of the ground for what Antonio Negri has called a "real subsumption" by capital of all aspects of human life.[65] Just as the force of capital breaks apart existing structures of social relations only to capture the displaced bodies produced by this process and discipline them into workers, on the order of vision, the existing structure of social relations within one scopic regime is undermined, such that the sensorium and the unconscious could be alienated, commodified, and surplus value extracted from it.

Akutagawa's "The Shadow" gestures toward these historical developments in two ways. First, there is the character of Chen Cai himself, a Chinese businessman whose otherwise unexplained presence in the story hints at the interpenetration of the colonial periphery back into the metropolitan center of Tokyo, with the consequence of making him a target for harassment. This suggests that the traditional demarcation of colonial interiority from exteriority has become increasingly difficult to maintain. Lurking in the background of Akutagawa's story is the ushering in of a new phase in Japan's colonial expansion, when, as Mark Driscoll has discussed, wealth and human bodies "centripetally flowed back into and impacted Japan's inner circle metropoles, where they became normal means of capital accumulation after they emerged in the outer."[66] This brings us to the second manifestation of this new phase of colonial expansion. Accompanying this historical development is the colonization of the human sensorium in new forms of image-commodities and cultural productions, with cinema's capture of attention as a source of surplus value foremost among them. In his role as both the peripheral body that returns to the metropole and the subject of its visual alienation and colonization, Akutagawa's Chen Cai, in this sense, embodies the passage from formal to real subsumption, or, to use Driscoll's terminology, the shift from a biopolitical to a neuropolitical mode of exploitation.[67]

Signs of this emerging regime of alienated vision manifest in Akutagawa's "The Shadow" primarily as a sense of temporal alienation. Not

only is the narrative cut up into discrete scenes marked by their locations, but also, these scenes themselves are broken apart by several flashback sequences that enter suddenly and without any preparation for the
reader. All that identifies the shift from one temporal frame to another
are ellipses that mark the transition from one scene to the next. Indeed,
in one instance, the shift takes place in the middle of a yet-to-be completed statement by Chen, as he recalls a moment from the early days
of his marriage to Fusako, only to be interrupted by the ringing of a telephone.[68] With "the cut," filmic practice begins its shift from the unabashed
exhibitionism of the cinema of attractions to the grammar of narrative
cinema and the alienation of vision that organizes the logic of the scopic
regime to which it belongs. Akutagawa's story can thus be understood as
articulating the ambiguities and tensions surrounding the temporal
effects of the then emergent form of narrative cinema.

That Akutagawa's "The Shadow" appeared at the moment when the
cinema of attractions was arguably beginning to be displaced by narrative cinema is perhaps no mere coincidence. At this moment in the history of visuality in Japan, the shift from one set of practices to the other
had yet to be fully routinized or familiarized, opening the possibility for
the doppelgänger to make an appearance. In the first place, it is the development of film editing techniques that makes possible the cinematic
representation of the doppelgänger by splicing together multiple images
of the same actor. More to the point, in the same logic of the cut that
organizes the grammar of narrative cinema can also be located its point
of potential breakdown should it fail to produce a suturing effect crucial
to the constitution of the spectatorial subject. Slavoj Žižek describes the
standard suturing process in cinema by way of the mechanics of the
shot/reverse-shot sequence.[69] While the disembodied first shot produces
a sense of anxiety in the spectator, this is contained in the subsequent
reverse-shot through its anchoring in a specific character within the
screen. A figure such as the doppelgänger, however, disrupts this procedure by confusing the positions of the subject and object of the gaze. Consequently, it produces not a suturing effect but what Žižek calls "interface,"
which is a more radical operation marked by the "condensation of shot
and reverse-shot within the same shot" so as to give the filmic enunciation
an uncanny "spectral dimension."[70] Through this enactment of interface,

the figure of the doppelgänger opens up a space for that which is ideologically excluded or constitutively repressed in the shot to return.

What these temporal shifts in Akutagawa's story suggest is that within the cinematic text, time has become externalized. The experience of time is no longer necessarily organized around the subject. Instead, temporal movements move at the standardized speed of the mechanized running of film, at the rate that its discretely divided still images are projected onto the screen. I do not believe it is overreaching to suggest that what is evident here is the emergence of an assembly-line logic of the spectator's temporality, a mechanization of the eye parallel to the mechanization of the body. Cinema took on a role analogous to the techniques of "scientific management" articulated by Frederick Taylor, wherein the bodily gestures of workers on the assembly line were isolated and routinized so that it became possible for the speed of their movements and intensity of their work to be organized around the bare minimum time needed to run the production lines, as opposed to their own subjective rhythms. "The Shadow" attempts to represent in literary language this mechanization of vision, which brought about an experience of narrative temporality in which the passage of time is organized around not a narrator but an abstracted and rationalized logic.

Subjective time thus becomes, in other words, "cinematic time," to use the terms of Mary Ann Doane. As Doane explains, "the representation of time in cinema (its 'recording') is also and simultaneously the production of temporalities for the spectator, a structuring of the spectator's time."[71] Indeed, for Doane, in its role of enabling the representability of time itself, cinema was a key participant—along with other discourses and institutions such as psychoanalysis, statistics, and other emerging "scientific" discourses—in this effort to reify, rationalize, and standardize time in the nineteenth and early twentieth centuries. This was part of a process in the organization of a capitalist mode of production and its regimented and divisible conception of time necessary for the functioning of the working day.[72] To this, it now appears also possible to add that cinematic time became, at once, itself an extension of this same working day, transforming spaces of mass consumption into sites of industrial image production and thus proliferating the potential sites for an encounter with one's doppelgänger.

Violence and Visual Modernization

In sum, the appearance of the doppelgänger in Akutagawa's "The Shadow" depicts an encounter not only with the embodiment of one's own psychical fragmentation, but also the larger historical forces of visual modernization that engender this fragmentation in the first place. Functioning as a self-reflexive allegory of the media ecology in which it appears, the repressed that returns in Akutagawa's "The Shadow" is its own historical unconscious, its own conditions of possibility in the development of cinematic technologies and modern visuality. It thus opens up the space of analysis to consider the figure's significance not just in terms of its function as a psychoanalytic concept, but more importantly, as a means of providing a metacommentary on the place of psychoanalysis within a historically specific constellation of discourses and cultural technologies.

When viewed in this context, the latent content of the obsessive schematization of the unconscious seen in psychoanalytic discourse can thus be understood as an attempt to reterritorialize, to render legible and come to terms with deterritorializing visual-economic trauma marked by the expropriation and alienation of vision operating in parallel with the literary modernizations that Rey Chow and Karatani Kōjin have discussed. Or, as Beller articulates the point, "The eruption of the unconscious through the structure of the gap emerges as a crisis of signification, and psychoanalysis appears as linguistic endeavor to remedy a breakdown in language."[73] Both literary and psychoanalytic discourses operate in tandem as acts of narrativization for the purpose of recuperating the subjective anxieties provoked by an excess of the image, an excess of visuality. In doing so, they also prefigure cinema's own historical move from the spectacle of actuality films to narrative filmmaking. Doppelgänger fictions in the vein of Akutagawa's "The Shadow," then, serve to denaturalize this historical passage. Through the portrayal of the uncanny experience of doubling as a self-conscious allegorization of the experience of cinematic spectatorship, it brings to the foreground the construction of the unconscious as a problem of industrial image production, and with it, the violence of visual expropriation and alienation. One might very well take Sigmund Freud's statement that "the feeling of something uncanny is directly attached . . . to the idea of being robbed of one's eyes" as a literal observation of the alienation of visuality that the doppelgänger's appearance brings to attention.[74]

Yet despite this defamiliarizing potential, the figure of the doppel- gänger is not without its more disturbing qualities as well. Insofar as the capitalist economy is structured around uneven development, then it is also necessary to recognize the unevenness of the effects of the develop- ment of scopic regimes. If the figure of the doppelgänger foregrounds the power of the cinematic apparatus to make image-commodities out of its spectators—to make objects out of the subjects of observation—then it should also be noted that some bodies are more readily transformed into images than others, some acts of looking are more readily alienable than others. One crucial way this manifests is on the axis of gender. Indeed, it is telling that the depictions of subjective crises in the doppelgänger fic- tions of Akutagawa—and for that matter, in much of the existing stories of the doppelgänger, more generally—take on an unmistakably gendered character.[75]

In both "Two Letters" and "The Shadow," the appearance of the dop- pelgänger is linked to its male protagonists' obsessive suspicion of their wives' supposed infidelity. These suspicions are not unconnected with the historical shifts in practices of visuality, for what underpins these male anxieties are transformations in the urban form and domestic space tak- ing place in early twentieth-century Japan that arguably parallel—if not prefigure—the trajectories seen in the emergence of the cinematic spec- tator. New configurations of mass consumer culture in interwar Japan facilitated an increase in the bourgeois woman's mobility that allowed her to be in public spaces unchaperoned without being reduced to a car- nal commodity, to an object of visual pleasure.[76] It is arguably the tensions provoked by the emergence of this new configuration in the gendering of spatial and visual relations that motivates the male protagonists' obses- sion with fidelity in the two stories by Akutagawa and triggers the dop- pelgänger's manifestation.

Given this underlying motivation, it is not surprising that the posi- tioning of the spectator vis-à-vis the object of vision is conventionally gendered with the male viewer as the active subject of vision and the woman as the passive object of his gaze in Akutagawa's "The Shadow." In large part, Fusako's appearances in the story place her as the object of the gaze, be it in the opening sequence with Chen Cai watching her in the restaurant, or subsequent scenes where she muses about the feeling of being watched by an unseen presence. This pattern of representation brings to mind the well-documented tendency in visual culture to render the female body as the locus of visual pleasure, generating an over-presence of the image of the woman, with the consequence of denying her the voyeuristic position of visual mastery. In its place, her spectator-ship takes on a form that can be understood as a kind of narcissism.

Yet is this not precisely the kind of spectatorial narcissism that the encounter with the doppelgänger in the cinematic apparatus entails? If so, then the specular positioning of the female spectator renders her as a subject who is effectively already a kind of doppelgänger, at once both the subject and object of vision. It would therefore be more accurate to assert that it is the crisis of a specifically masculine stance of visual mastery that the figure of the doppelgänger marks. Insofar as the doppelgänger works to take apart any illusion of visual mastery or a coherent unitary subjectivity, then one must presuppose the very possibility of identifying with such a subject position in the first place. That in Akutagawa's "The Shadow" the response to this crisis provoked by the encounter with one's double is an act of the violence the protagonist directs toward his wife further underscores the point that the appearance of the doppelgänger is intimately bound up with the visual logic of sexual difference. As if unable to find a means of recuperating his loss of visual mastery and illusion of a unified subjectivity, the protagonist of "The Shadow" falls back to committing violence directed against the female body, whose psychical threat is precisely what the doppelgänger's mani-festation within the cinematic apparatus appears to disclose. In the end, it is perhaps this foundational violence that is at the core of the histori-cal unconscious that the visual logic of the figure of the doppelgänger brings to light.

4

Rampo's Repetitions
Confession, Adaptation, and the Historical Unconscious

Repetitions and Resignifications

In the preceding chapters, I identified two historical processes that were formative of the fantasy of the doppelgänger in the context of interwar Japan. First, the expansion of the Japanese empire led to the intense negotiation of racial discourses of identity and difference vis-à-vis its new colonial subjects. Second, the modernization process entailed transformations in the regime of visuality marked by the industrial mass production of images, which facilitated the imagination of all manner of doublings and repetitions. Importantly, these were not merely parallel processes, but instead intersected and mutually reinforced one another. On the one hand, the circulation of photographic and cinematic images was instrumental in facilitating the transformation of the narratives of modernization and civilization into consumer spectacles. This had the effect of transforming imperialism itself into a value-productive image-commodity, thus extending colonial encounters from their specific contact zones in the periphery, bringing them into the imperial metropoles as spectacles for mass consumption. On the other hand, the industrialization of vision in the cinematic apparatus led to the mass penetration of image culture into the social fabric, enacting a parallel form of colonization that extends not outward geographically but inward into human subjectivities. This industrial production of images in the cinematic apparatus extended the logics of capitalism and colonialism, effecting first a systematic production of the imaginary for the subject, and then subsequently making the imaginary in itself productive for capital.

To recapitulate an earlier discussion, in the context of interwar Japan, a sense of crisis was induced by rapid urbanization and the emergence of a burgeoning consumer culture facilitated by the increasing commodification of all aspects of social life coupled with colonial expansion. This expansion left vast swaths of unevenness in its wake, which meant the turning of cities into contact zones. Against this backdrop of rapid social and material transformations, taking place within a milieu of newly circulating images, commodities, and bodies marked by a sense of dislocation and alienation, parallel discourses that rendered legible these anxieties and tensions, among which modernism, detective fiction, psychoanalysis, nativist ethnographies, and nationalist mythmaking make their appearance, and out of which the figure of the doppelgänger appears as an excess. But the story of the doppelgänger does not end there. Fittingly, in its role as an embodiment of doubling and repetition, once again a renewed interest in the motif in contemporary films and fictions appears, alongside a renewed critical interest in the figure against the backdrop of several historical developments—the increasing financialization of capital and the rise of transnational corporations, decolonization and the emergence of a new global division of labor, new forms of media relations and the circulation of spectacles and image-commodities—whose foundations can be traced back to the aftermath of the 1973 oil crisis and the collapse of the Bretton Woods system.

Several examples can be named here. Abe Kōbō (1924–1993) frequently made use of the motif of a mirroring of identity as a part of his existential meditations in such metaphysical detective stories as *Moetsukita chizu* (*The Ruined Map*, 1967) or *Hakootoko* (*The Box Man*, 1973). In line with his tendency to tell stories organized around a division between this world and another world, twins, alter-egos, and doppelgängers also populate many of the writings of Murakami Haruki (1948–), from the twins of *1973-nen no pinbōru* (*Pinball 1973*, 1980), the visions of other selves in *Nejimakidori kuronikuru* (*The Wind-up Bird Chronicle*, 1994–95) and *Supūtoniku no koibito* (*Sputnik Sweetheart*, 1999), to the doubled narrative structure of *Sekai no owari to hādoboirudo wandārando* (*Hard-boiled Wonderland and the End of the World*, 1984). Horror filmmakers like

Kurosawa Kiyoshi (1955–) have employed the doppelgänger both in its more conventional version as a figure of horror as well as in its subversion. Kon Satoshi repeatedly featured scenes of encounters with one's alter-ego as a part of his metacinematic explorations of the dreamlike worlds of film and animation in such titles as *Pāfekuto burū* (*Perfect Blue*, 1997) and *Papurika* (*Paprika*, 2006).

I must therefore disagree with Watanabe Masahiko's suggestion that Japanese literary interest in the doppelgänger motif has died down since its heyday during the Taisho and early Showa period.[1] In fact, even if one were to provisionally accept this claim, it should be noted, though, that Watanabe premises this observation on a narrowly construed conception of *the literary*, which specifically excludes popular genres such as detective fiction, horror, or science fiction, not to mention other cultural forms like comic books, film, television, or animation. Even if one were to concur with Watanabe's suggestion of an end to the literary doppelgänger, it is telling that one of the possible reasons he gives for this supposed decline of interest is precisely the saturation of doppelgängers and other related motifs like disguises, multiple personalities, clones, virtual avatars, and cyborgs in Japanese popular culture, and especially in visual culture, hence rendering it too much of a cliché or predictable plot twist to be the subject of proper literary interest.[2] However, given that the origins of the doppelgänger are already rooted in the development of a media ecology constituted out of the historical process of visual modernization, any move to isolate the figure as purely a literary motif strikes me as misguided. After all, given the preceding discussion of the underpinnings of the formation of doppelgänger fictions as a coherent category of texts in the development of mass cultural forms like detective fiction in conjunction with the rise of cinematic technologies and new regimes of visuality that such technologies engendered, it seems only apt that it is in the form of visual and popular culture that the doppelgänger continues its life. For this reason, I believe that the prevalence of images of the doppelgänger in contemporary Japanese popular culture—and especially in visual culture—is in fact more significant than Watanabe makes it out to be.

Perhaps the texts with the most potential to open up the discussion of another historical site of doubling are precisely films, specifically, the film adaptations of earlier doppelgänger fictions, in that they highlight precisely the problem of repetition as a relation between these two historical conjunctures. To begin with, inasmuch as one of the central features of the figure of the doppelgänger is the staging of the relationship between the original and copy (and the confusion of these positions by virtue of being rendered indistinguishable), might it not be productive to take up the issue of film adaptation as a form of intertextual doubling with all its attendant issues of negotiating questions of identity and difference? More to the point, the intertextual doppelgängers generated by the process of adaptation raise questions about the relationship between filmic practice and textual practice in the imagination of the unconscious. Following the discussion in the preceding chapter, if the doppelgänger's constitution as a concept emerges out of the technical and economic apparatus of cinema itself, then it would appear that the film adaptations of doppelgänger fictions can be understood not merely as a derivative copy of a fixed original, but as implicitly staging the return of a cinematic repressed that underwrites the psychoanalytic conception of the double in the first place. Consequently, it seems only apt to pose the problem of what ramifications might be drawn from the examination of texts that are not only a performance of doubling, but also take the form of cinema, the very technical and social apparatus that is arguably formative of the imagination of the doppelgänger.

But what becomes of the doppelgänger motif when it travels beyond the material and social conditions formative of its popularization as a concept to this new set of historical circumstances? If in interwar Japan the doppelgänger's emergence can be situated in the point of intersection of the historical processes of colonialism and modern visuality, how then might one account for the figure's historical repetition in the form of film adaptations in the contemporary conjuncture? Or to put it another way, how might the doppelgänger's return and repetition in the passage to late capitalism and the ensuing material and sociocultural transformations entailed therein be properly historicized? Approaching the problem of adaptations as a form of intertextual doubling makes for an effective prism through which to view precisely these questions. First, it compels the recognition of the historicity of these adaptations, whose recent appearances take place concurrently with a broader historical turn in the guise of a retro-boom of interest in the prewar period in Japanese cultural discourse. This manifests in a number of different forms, perhaps most notably in the revival of interest in such topics as Japanese detective fictions, the erotic-grotesque, as well as modernism and colonial history. The renewed interest in the figure of the doppelgänger is but another facet of this. But because it foregrounds the very logic of returns and repetitions even as it performs it, the figure of the doppelgänger also makes for a critical vehicle to interrogate the politics of the historiographic unconscious beneath not only this return in Japan specifically, but a range of other historical questions structured around issues of difference and repetition, be it the relationship between cinema and new media or between older modes of empire and the various historical developments subsumed under the name of "globalization."

Re-viewing Rampo

It is with this historical context in mind that I wish to revisit the writings of Edogawa Rampo, whose work makes for a particularly illustrative case study of the possibilities of apprehending film adaptations as intertextual doppelgängers for several reasons. First, the persistence of Rampo's deployment of the doppelgänger motif in his fiction means that film adaptations of his work also feature the figure in their narratives, in effect offering a metacinematic foregrounding of the very problem of doubling at the level of their narratives. Viewed in the light of the media-allegorical function of the doppelgänger discussed in the previous chapter, this gives the doppelgängers in these films a self-referential component that potentially serves as a commentary on the process of doubling involved in film adaptation as they perform this very act of intertextual doubling. Second, an interesting facet of Rampo's writing is that many of his literary works featured stories and styles of narration that exhibited characteristics drawn from cinematic aesthetics, which in part reflects the concurrent rise of cinema as a medium of popular entertainment and the beginnings of the penetration of image culture into all aspects of everyday life during the formative years of his literary career. As Mark Driscoll has noted, one important way this manifested was through a writing style that appeared intended to facilitate the adaptation of his works to the screen, often featuring long sequences marked by an excess of vivid visual detail as well as extended action sequences inspired by the aesthetics of popular foreign films such as *Zigomar* (1911) and others.[3]

Such an observation about the importance of the visual register in Rampo's fiction is by no means a novel claim. In fact, in the critical commentary on his work, it has almost become de rigueur to note his seemingly obsessive attention to not only cinema but all manner of optical devices—lenses, films, panoramas, and especially mirrors—as one unmistakable feature that permeates much of his writing. As a case in point, Matsuyama Iwao's influential attempt to situate Rampo's work within the transformations in the configuration of urban space in Tokyo of the 1920s underscores precisely this visual aspect of Rampo's writing. Pointing out the richly evocative representations of sensory experiences in his work, Matsuyama highlights how Rampo's fiction is illustrative of the significant impact of the rapid transformation of the space of the city on the human body and modes of perceiving, with the sense of vision increasingly becoming hegemonic in the public realm.[4] In Matsuyama's view, Rampo's work is inseparable from the autonomization and privileging of vision and its impact on the production of knowledge and configuration of bodies in space under regimes of observation; in effect, the social conditions these works attempt to capture are precisely those associated with the historical process of visual modernization discussed in the previous chapter.

Matsuyama is not the only critic to discover this interest in issues of visuality within Rampo's work. Others who have done so include Yoshikuni Igarashi, who argues that the question of the body's place within the scopic regime of modernity is a central concern in much of Rampo's fiction.[5] Another is Hirano Yoshihiko, who argues that Rampo's detective fictions articulate the limits of visuality by foregrounding exactly what exceeds its capacity to capture.[6] Rampo's deep engagement with technologies of vision in his writing is not all that unusual when considered in the context of the genre of fiction in which he established his literary career. In light of the parallels in the formal structure of their respective narrative techniques and practices, it is not a coincidence that like psychoanalysis, the formation of detective fiction as a genre is conditioned by the coming into being of a scopic regime characterized by a confluence of advanced capitalism and industrialized image-making. Like psychoanalysis, detection is premised on the principle of rendering visible what is normally invisible to the naked eye. Whereas psychoanalysis addresses the psychical anxieties of dislocation through the revelation of the invisible workings of the unconscious from the observation of exterior symptoms, detective stories offer fictionalized accounts of the desire to place the body under observation, turning it into a surface of visible clues for the identification of criminals within the new modes of mobility and circulation of urban spaces. In this task, it was dependent on the development of optical technologies that would serve as prosthetic devices allowing for the abstraction of the human body into a visible and readable surface. Put differently, a crucial condition of possibility for the development of practices of detection is the placement of visuality in a hegemonic position in the realm of knowledge production.

Throughout the period of Edogawa Rampo's career as an author of detective fiction, several of his writings from his large and varied body of work occasionally found themselves adapted for the screen. The earliest of such adaptations appeared not long after Rampo's literary debut in 1923, with the first film version of *Issun boshi* (*The Dwarf*, 1927) appearing only four years after the beginning of his career as a professional writer. Subsequently, numerous other works—*Kurotokage* (*The Black Lizard*, 1934), *Mojū* (*The Blind Beast*, 1931), *Panorama-tō kidan* (*The Strange Tale of Panorama Island*, 1926), not to mention his long-running young adult series *Shōnen tantei dan* (*Young Detective's Gang*, 1936–62) featuring the detective Akechi Kogorō and his wildly popular villain known as "The Mystery Man of Twenty Faces"—were produced throughout the postwar period, by directors that included the likes of Fukusaku Kinji, Masumura Yasuzō, and Ishii Teruo.[7] However, it was not until after his death, and especially since the 1990s, that a veritable explosion of films based on Rampo's fiction becomes particularly visible. This Rampo boom was especially marked by the appearance in 1994 of four films that adapt his fiction.[8] This boom in film adaptations was by no means a one-off event. Subsequent years witnessed a continuation of this pattern, with the appearance of multiple film adaptations of Rampo's fiction, thus raising the question of what precisely provoked this resurgence of interest in his writing.[9] After all, if a cinematic sensibility was already present in Rampo's fiction from the beginning, then the obvious question is why his work has seen this level of cinematic interest only since the 1990s.

A brief examination of the structure of doubling in the film *Ranpo* (*The Mystery of Rampo*, 1994) offers some potential answers. Produced in celebration of the centenary of Rampo's birth, the film is part adaptation, part biopic, and part blockbuster spectacle. It opens with a straightforward animated adaptation of Rampo's "Osei tōjō" (The appearance of Osei, 1927), a short story about a married woman who commits a perfect crime, murdering her wealthy husband by locking him in a trunk upon finding him trapped there after he had played hide-and-seek with the children. The film then cuts from this animated sequence to the live-action film proper with a scene of government censors banning the publication of the story for its lurid content, which they find to be "detrimental to public morale." Rampo decides to give up writing, but then he discovers a newspaper article about a woman named Shizuko with a remarkably similar story. Obsessively delving further into this matter, he begins stalking her, only to end up with his imagination running wild as his detective alter-ego Akechi Kogorō takes over the story, who then follows Shizuko to the seaside abode of a duke with whom Shizuko is having an affair. There, he witnesses various strange happenings, from the duke's seeming vampirism, to his cross-dressing sadomasochistic sexual encounters with Shizuko, to a dinner party featuring a recitation of a Poe text as images of war are projected onto the background. In the end, Shizuko conspires to kill the duke by making it look like an equestrian accident. Rampo finally returns to the scene following this incident, rushing into the castle just as Shizuko poisons herself.

Structures of doubling feature prominently at both the level of narrative and visual aesthetic in *The Mystery of Rampo*. On the one hand, the film following the animated sequence is organized around two distinct sections that map onto the doubled characters of Rampo himself and his fictional alter-ego/author stand-in Akechi, with the latter's story largely functioning as a fictionalized restaging—a doubling—of the former's. This is made explicit in a few scenes, such as one that intercuts between Rampo writing in his study and Akechi performing the actions and speaking the dialogue that Rampo writes for him, or another wherein Akechi walks before a mirror and Rampo appears as his reflection. More notably, this narrative doubling is further reinforced by a distinct shift in visual styles. While the Rampo narrative makes use of a slightly drabber, more muted color grading along with a relatively slower pace of edits, the Akechi narrative employs a bolder, more expressionistic color palette of bright reds and purples, with a more frenetic pacing. These two parts of the film are sufficiently distinct that upon seeing them juxtaposed to one another, it would not be at all unusual to suspect that these two sections came from two separate films that have been interlaced into each other, for that is, in fact, the case. After the original director assigned to the film, Mayuzumi Rintarō, completed an initial cut of the film that the studio Shōchiku found unsatisfactory, producer Okuyama Kazu-yoshi took over, ordering extensive reshoots of some 70 percent of the film, which allowed him to create a more bombastic faster-paced visual spectacle.[10]

Although it may not have initially been planned, and came about only because of the troubled production history of *The Mystery of Rampo*, the end result is still a film with an aesthetic marked by a pastiche of multiple visual styles. Instead of trying to merge the two versions of the film into a seamless, integrated whole, the producer instead accentuated their disjoint quality by adding even more film styles, from the aforementioned animated opening sequence, to interspersed newsreel footage, to clips from older films. Coupled with the fragmentary narrative, this juxtaposition of various visual styles makes the film double back onto itself,

Detective Akechi Kogorō walks in front of a mirror in the duke's manor, but Edogawa Rampo appears as his reflection. From *The Mystery of Rampo*.

calling attention to another structure of doubling that the film stages, namely, the doubling effect of adaptation itself, by highlighting the different ways a given narrative might be visualized. Indeed, the primary source text and point of departure of the film—Rampo's "The Appearance of Osei"—sees three distinct interlinked interpretations in the film, each with its own distinct visual style. First to appear is the brief animated sequence that opens the film, followed by the reinterpretation of the story as Rampo's own investigation into Shizuko, followed by a more fantastical, self-consciously fictionalized rendition of it in the form Shizuko's life in the duke's castle. One might go so far as to say that the film is less about adapting the story per se as it is about the act of adaptation itself.

One scene in *The Mystery of Rampo* makes its metacinematic interest in adaptation explicit. Early in the film, Rampo and his editor attend a party with the cast and crew of a recently completed adaptation of his popular *Kaijin nijūmensō* (*The Fiend with Twenty Faces*, 1936).[11] Later, they are treated to a private screening of the film, after one of its producers tells Rampo that it's "better to see it now than to complain about it later." Despite the producer's attempts to sing the praises of the adaptation, Rampo appears bored and uninterested, if not even disgusted by the wooden acting and clumsy dialogue that he witnesses on the screen.[12] Rather than paying attention to the scenes before them, Rampo and his editor instead engage in conversation about a recent encounter with the woman Shizuko. Here, by poking fun at this older adaptation of Rampo's work, the film stakes out a position of differentiating itself from these earlier attempts, especially ones organized around the simple, direct translation of a text from one medium to another, an approach that that has long been fraught with problems, not the least of which is the temptation to frame the conversation (whether done so consciously or not) on notions of fidelity versus originality.[13] Instead, *The Mystery of Rampo* calls attention to what Linda Hutcheon has called "the audience's 'palimpsestuous' intertextuality," activating the memory of past adaptations even as it presents multiple interpretations at various degrees of divergence from its original source text, thus raising the question of how one might apprehend the relation between original and copy.[14] As each new version of the story is introduced, it takes over the narrative, turning things increasingly fantastical, until in the end, the simple story that served as the film's initial point of departure is fully overwhelmed by the visual spectacle such that even Rampo himself can no longer dictate the actions of his alter-ego Akechi.

It is in this sense that the film structures the doubling of adaptation as a kind of intertextual doppelgänger. Rather than treating two texts (original and adaptation) as closed systems whose relation can be grasped only with tired notions of convergence and divergence, it presents each version of the text as having the potential to retroactively reframe one's understanding of the source text, analogous to the way the doppelgänger is a copy that challenges the very stability of its original. In other words, treating adaptations as intertextual doppelgängers of their source texts opens a space to articulate not just the question of difference *from* the original, but also the question of *difference* that is already in the very origins itself. While much critical work on adaptation today rightly challenges approaches that seek to privilege some form of fidelity with the original and will make allowances for transformation in every iteration of its "copies," the closure of the "original" is nevertheless often still locked in place. But this closure or completeness of a given text cannot but be a fiction. Indeed, if the doppelgänger's staging of repetition is understood as embodying a return of the repressed, then by implication there is an

Edogawa Rampo and his editor view a film adaptation of one of his novels. From *The Mystery of Rampo.*

excess that is not quite contained by the boundaries of the source text, an excess that manifests itself in the adaptation's act of doubling.

Crucial to consider here, however, is more than just the question of how adaptations configure the relations between texts themselves. In taking apart and reconstructing a source text, implicated in the process of adaptation is not only the transformations in the respective stories but also how these changes are inevitably mediated by the difference in discursive and critical contexts, not to mention the historically specific situations that each version of a given text occupies. Inherent in any adaptation or other form of intertextual transmission across history is the necessary transformation in the context of a given adaptation's reception at different moments of history, each with its own particular sets of concerns, circumstances, categories of analyses, and structures of feeling. As Eric Cazdyn put the point succinctly, "There is much to be gained by tracking how a particular scene has transformed . . . as each version, made at a different moment, will necessarily spread its historical concern over the representation of the narrative."[15] Every text, in effect, necessarily bears within it its own historical unconscious, and consequently, every adaptation—even if it somehow managed to achieve a hypothetical perfect fidelity with its original source material—would necessarily produce a difference because of the changes in the context of its reception.

Less often accounted for, though, is the historicity of the very concept of adaptation itself. The way historically specific understandings of adaptation constitute different forms of relations to their "origins"—that is, their source texts—often remains unexamined and unhistoricized. Put differently, the challenge at the heart of thinking about adaptation is something that goes beyond simply the examination of the historical unconscious underpinning the specific texts in question. We need also to historicize how these texts speak to the broader aesthetics of adaptation as such, how these texts articulate an attendant *historiographic* unconscious underlying how the very relation between past and present has come to be conceived. This takes on real significance because, for Cazdyn, there is an emerging cultural logic that characterizes adaptations since the 1990s, one he calls "transformative" adaptations. Pointing to *The Mystery of Rampo* as one of his examples, he highlights how the film gestures toward the recognition of how adaptations transform the ostensible "original" text. It challenges the usual linear temporal trajectory ascribed to the process of adaptation through its various moments wherein the film intercuts between scenes of Rampo writing his fiction and the cinematic representation of his writing.[16] These moments move back and forth from the literary to the cinematic, and refuse to grant primacy to one or the other, instead presenting them in a dynamic relation to one another. Yet at the same time, the film does not quite go far enough. By centering the narrative on Rampo himself (as a biopic must do), the film effectively fixes him as the author of these texts, as the point of origin for these narratives, undercutting its own potential to stage a more radical critique of the relation of the present to the past.

Confession and Repression

A fuller exploration of the possibilities of intertextual doubling would have to wait for another film adaptation of one of Rampo's doppelgänger fictions, namely Tsukamoto Shin'ya's *Sōseiji: Gemini* (*Gemini*, 1999). *Gemini* occupies an interesting place within the oeuvre of Tsukamoto, who rose to international cult prominence after winning best film accolades at the FantaFestival in Rome in 1989 with his extremely graphic, low-budget cyberpunk film about a man who gradually transforms into a metal mechanical being *Tetsuo* (*Tetsuo: The Iron Man*, 1989). However, unlike *Tetsuo* and much of his work since then, *Gemini* was a rare commissioned project. The originator of the project was former teen idol Motoki Masahiro, who also stars in the film in the leading roles of the titular twin brothers. Motoki took the initiative to produce and star in *Gemini* after his co-starring role as Rampo's famous detective and fictional alter-ego Akechi Kogorō in the aforementioned *The Mystery of Rampo*. Had it not been for the initial boom in Rampo-related productions, the film might have never come into being in the first place.[17]

Gemini is based on Rampo's short story "Sōseiji: Aru shikeishū ga kyōkaishi ni uchiaketa hanashi" ("The Twins: A Condemned Criminal's Confession to a Priest," 1924). At first glance, this story seems like an odd choice for adaptation, given that its highly interiorized narrative performance does not necessarily lend itself well to visualization. However, as I will show, what is interesting about the adaptation of the story is

Motoki Masahiro playing Akechi Kogorō. From *The Mystery of Rampo.*

precisely how it breaks open this seemingly closed-off narrative, bringing to the surface its historical unconscious. As its title suggests, the story of "The Twins" centers on a pair of identical twin brothers. Its opening lines quickly establish the context of narration. They read: "Father, today is the day that I've resolved to tell you my story. . . . I can no longer put up with the fear of the vengeance of the man I killed. No, not the man I killed when I stole the money. I have already confessed to that crime and nothing more needs to be said about it, but before that, there was another man, another murder that I committed."[18] The ensuing confession soon reveals that the narrator, the younger of a set of twins, had murdered his older brother to steal his identity. He accomplishes this act by first pretending to travel to Korea to look for work there, only to secretly return. Catching his brother off guard in the garden of his house, he jumps him and strangles him to death, then dumps his body in a dried-up well that he promptly seals. After taking over his identity (and along with it, his older brother's larger share of the inheritance and his wife), he begins spending his brother's money to the point that he accumulates large debts, leading him to commit further crimes to support his extravagant lifestyle. Having earlier found what he believes to be his dead brother's fingerprint, he thinks that he has found a foolproof method for committing perfect crimes: by planting his dead brother's fingerprint at the crime scenes, he can easily redirect attention away from him. But his plan backfires when the fingerprint he leaves ends up in fact being his own, appearing unrecognizable to him only because it was a negative image of it.

There are two crimes that form the premise of the story of "The Twins": the fratricidal murder and identity theft. Despite the almost fantastical extreme to which Rampo takes the story he concocts, by no means were these outlandish occurrences in his time. While not specified in the story, twins were often viewed with some superstition, and acts of abandonment or even violence sometimes followed their birth. Often, one or both twins were dumped in a box and sent down a river.[19] As for identity theft, Takeda Nobuaki has discussed the existence of sensationalistic journalistic coverage of a wave in crimes wherein individuals who accumulated debts or swindled money would take on the pseudonyms of famous writers—literally becoming their doppelgängers—to avoid having the crimes pinned on them. Not coincidentally, these crimes took place right about the time when the use of pen-names among literary authors had begun to decline in popularity, indicating a shift in the system of valuation of names, wherein its function as a signifier of "authenticity" led to the increased value attached to a writer's use of his or her real name.[20]

What these two crimes share is their grounding in the perception that a multiplicity of bodies and identities threatens the social order. I have already discussed how the challenge of attaching names to individual bodies—the fixing of identities—was the central problem in the history of crime and its detection and policing in the early twentieth century, leading to the development of all manner of optical devices to aid in this task. At both the level of its story and its narrative performance, Rampo's "The Twins" makes use of the motif of mirroring or doubling to interrogate the limits of these optical technologies of individuation. As one half of a set of twin brothers who are virtually indistinguishable from each other (with the sole exception of a mole on the younger brother's leg), neither photographic nor anthropometric techniques were capable of establishing the singular and individual identity of the story's narrator, and with that, his guilt in any crime. Certainly, he is eventually captured, but it is exactly what gives him away—his fingerprint—that is noteworthy here. As if to punctuate this motif of mirroring further, it is telling that when he is caught, the fingerprint that finally lays bare his crime is no ordinary fingerprint but *the negative image* of his fingerprint that he misrecognizes as his brother's.

But a more fundamental way that Rampo's story foregrounds the limits of techniques of individuation is through the staging of a mirroring or reversal not only in thematic terms, but also on the level of its narrative performance. Unlike many other works that Rampo produced at this stage in his writing career, the character of the detective plays only a minor role in "The Twins." Not only does he remain completely nameless, he appears only at the very end of the story for the singular purpose of apprehending the narrator following the second crime, even as he completely overlooks the first (the murder and identity theft of his twin brother). The existence of this first crime, which would have remained undetected if not for the narrator's confession, indicates that the condition of possibility for the narrative's performance is the limit of the techniques of detection and apprehension represented in detective fiction. The narrative comes into being in response to an implied detective story that fails to apprehend his earlier perfect crime of murder and identity theft. The effect of this is that although on one level the text still exhibits an attention to new scientific methods in the apprehension of crime and the intellectual tricks for which the detective genre is famous, its narrative performance appears to place less emphasis on this in contrast to its focus on the motivations and psychology of the criminal. Put another way, "The Twins" parallels the doubling of the twin brothers on a structural level as well by presenting a narrative that works as an inverted mirror image of the classical form of detective fiction. In doing so, it effectively recenters the focalizer of the narrative from the subject of surveillance (the detective) to its object (the criminal).

Reading Rampo's story against Michel Foucault's discussion of the relationship between surveillance and modern subjectivity can illuminate the significance of this structural reversal. In *Discipline and Punish* (*Surveiller et punir*, 1975; trans. 1977), Foucault interrogates the historical passage of penal systems from one based on the public display and torture of convicts to one based on prison as the dominant form of punishment. Arguing against accounts of this change that would explain it in terms of

simple humanitarian reform, Foucault suggests that the move toward in-
carceration is more productively understood as a development symptomatic of a broader historical transition to a principle of discipline within
modern industrial political-economic structures. In Foucault's conceptualization, discipline was a political technology of the body based on
refinement, individuation, and segmentation whose primary function
was to produce subjects that can more effectively fit within the regimen-
tation of the school, factory, or the military. In this respect, the problem
of discipline goes beyond the walls of prison per se. Rather, the prison is
simply one node in a nexus of disciplinary institutions in which docile
bodies are produced. For Foucault, the key mechanism shared by these
various disciplinary institutions is visual, operating through a system of
persistent surveillance. By creating the *perception* that one is constantly
and persistently observed, it became possible to not only produce the
desired docility, but to facilitate the subject's internalization of the disciplinary gaze without the need for overt force or violence.[21]

Surveillance and observation play central roles in Rampo's "The Twins."
However, unlike Foucault's model, the subject and object of the gaze
merge into a single body in Rampo's story. In the narrator's account, he
explains that in order to take over his brother's life without arousing suspicion, he had to undertake a careful month-long study of every detail
of his older twin's mannerisms, down to the level of whether "when his
brother wrung his washcloth, he would twist with his right hand or left
hand."[22] In fact, even after he had completed the deed of killing his twin
brother and taking over his life, his study continued with such details as
copying his brother's handwriting and cutting off the mole in his leg that
distinguished one from the other. Put simply, he continued his obsessive
disciplining of his own body, seeking to become his older brother to a
point beyond mere imitation. Indeed, his mimicry was so complete that
not a single person—neither the detective who later apprehends him nor
even his brother's wife (or so he claims, at least)—suspected the theft of
identity. Instead of an external gaze producing a disciplinary effect, the
narrator enacts a gaze that is reflected from his observations of his twin
brother's bodily gestures and mannerisms back onto his own body, in
effect literalizing the internalization of the surveillance that Foucault
argues to be the key operation of disciplinary power.

Of course, had his crime and mimicry in fact been perfect, he would never have been apprehended and consequently there would be no story to tell. There is an excess that cannot be contained, that threatens to return and break apart the seeming completeness and perfection of the crime. In "The Twins," it takes the form of the doppelgänger; the narrator's murdered dead twin returns, this time in the form of a persistent haunting, or alternatively, a psychic disturbance that manifests as an aversion to mirrors and other reflective surfaces, as his own reflected image has taken on the appearance of something monstrous and other. In his account, the narrator explains that when he looks at a mirror, what he sees is not his own reflection, but instead the misrecognized image of his twin brother. In his words, "[Since the day after I killed him, I developed a fear of all mirrors. . . . Within these mirrors and windows, the face of the man I killed—of course, the truth is that it was my own face— stared back at me with eyes full of hatred."[23] So thoroughly does he internalize the disciplinary gaze that he effectively switches positions with his brother. Whereas previously, it was the narrator who constantly watched his brother to learn his habits and mannerisms, this time it is the dead brother who performs the surveillance. Whereas it was the narrator who murdered his brother, in his dreams it is the other way around. Indeed, his reference to his mirror image is itself significant. It suggests that in taking his brother's place, that is, taking on his brother's body to the last detail, the effect is a repression of his former identity such that the image of his own past identity appears alien to him; he cannot help but misrecognize it as his brother's image. In fact, it is precisely this misrecognition that turns out to be his downfall, as he confuses the negative of his own fingerprint for his twin brother's. While his surveillance and self-disciplining serves to repress his own body to substitute his brother's, it is the return of this very body from the repressed that undoes his scheme.

Recalling Sigmund Freud's seminal discussion of the doppelgänger in "The Uncanny" (1919), one point that is worth underscoring is that the experience of the uncanny is an effect that comes not because something is alien or unfamiliar per se, but from the encounter with something "which is familiar and old-established in the mind and which has become alienated from it only through the process of repression" that subsequently returns to disturb the present.[24] In this sense, the figure of the doppelgänger embodies a manifestation of the return or recurrence of the traumatic constitution of subjectivity that, when it repeats in the present, appears alienated not despite of but precisely because of its similitude. Although, in "The Twins," the repressed that returns as an uncanny haunting that disturbs the stability of the present is not the primary narcissism of childhood, as Freud would have it, it is nevertheless a past image of the ego that has been surmounted. In this case, it is a product of the narrator's disciplining and transforming his own body into his brother's.

I would contend that Rampo's "The Twins" presents substantial overlaps with the psychoanalytic understanding of doubling. Indeed, it is no accident that the text closely mirrors the template for the uncanny worked out by Freud and the standard tropes and plot patterns of doppelgänger fictions elsewhere. Its narrative rehearses what Andrew J. Webber identifies as the doppelgänger story's most common plot patterns: "compulsive repetitions, hysterical crises, and the obsessive terror of persecution fantasies."[25] The narrator is persistently haunted and perceives himself to be stalked everywhere by his double; he expresses terror at the fantasy of his twin brother's vengeance; he acts out the compulsion to repeat the same actions and events by committing a second murder, then claiming that: "My second act of murder, the discovery of my crime despite all my careful planning—all these deeds may very well have been brought about by my brother's desire for revenge."[26]

It is this context that provides the narrator of "The Twins" his underlying motivation for his desire to confess his crimes. Strictly speaking the context of the narrative performance of confession encoded in "The Twins" is explicitly set up in religious terms. After all, the subtitle "a condemned criminal's confession to a priest" [*aru shikeishū ga kyōkaishi ni uchiaketa hanashi*] makes the identity of the addressee clear. That said, the narrator's articulation of the motivations behind his act of confession reveals another dimension to his performance. Along with the desire for forgiveness or absolution prior to his execution, he also expresses the desire "to rid myself of the restlessness in my heart" [*kokoro no fuan o nozokitai*], hinting at an interest in his own psychical and not simply moral integrity.[27] As such, his confession could be said to serve the function of not only laying out the facts of his crime or seeking penance, but also as a kind of "working through"—in the sense that Freud has articulated as functioning "to fill in gaps in memory" and to "overcome resistances due to repression"—of the psychical crisis stemming from the repression of his ego necessary to take his twin brother's place.[28] His confession, in this sense, takes on a performative function of reversing the repression of his body and identity. It does not simply tell a story *about* his murder of his brother and subsequent doubling of his body and life. More importantly, it is a mirror image in a discursive register—a form of interiorized self-surveillance—of his earlier surveillance and corporeal disciplining of his body that made possible this act of doubling in the first place. If it is a corporeal performance that allows him to transform his body into his brother's, it is this discursive performance that enables him to take on the identity of the younger twin again.

At the heart of this attempt to disentangle his identity from his twin brother's is an assertion of a position of visual mastery at the level of narrative time. Relevant here is Mark Currie's observation that confession, like any narrative performance, is predicated on the production of a temporal schism. Telling a reliable story is necessarily based on a splitting between the narrated past and the narrator's present, standing apart from the past to "objectively" reconstitute its events.[29] As such, acts of narration, in effect, produce conceptions of both past and present as discrete and autonomous positions. The implications of this illusory temporal schism are even more significant when dealing with first-person narrations such as confession. With acts of self-narration, involved is not only a schism between temporal positions, but also a schism between the present narrating self and the past narrated self. What this demarcation and fixing of temporal positions allows for is the appearance of a reliable narration about unreliability; that is, in Currie's words, it "constructs a contrast between 'I' of the time of the narration and the 'I' of narrated time along the lines of the former is truthful and the latter dishonest . . . confession contrasts the moral personality of the narrator with that of the narrated as the reliable narration of a former unreliability, or the truth about lies."[30]

But is there any basis for believing that the narrator's confession is truthful? Seeing as how the story he tells is based on multiple acts of deception and mistaken identities, it does not strike me as farfetched to question whether his confession is not simply a continuation of this deception in another form. Moreover, given that the twins are visually indistinguishable from one another, there is no way to objectively determine which of them is in fact speaking other than their own assertions. One cannot rule out the possibility that the narrator is not who he claims to be, that he is not the younger but the older of the twins, falsely confessing for some unarticulated motivation. Or, in light of the performative mirroring between the surveillance that allows him to take over his brother's body and the confession that allows him to return to his own, the possibility exists that the obsessive attempts to exorcise the doppelgänger through confession are themselves manifestations of the compulsion to repeat what Freud identifies as a key symptom associated with the doppelgänger's appearance. Were the narrator not scheduled to be executed shortly, might the story not have ended here? Might his attempts to demarcate past from present through his act of narration only lead to another return of a repressed version of himself from the past? Might there have been another return of the doppelgänger? While these questions are perhaps undecidable, they do open the analysis to other potentialities, other possible stories concealed behind the story told.

Flashbacks

Seventy-five years after "The Twins" was first published, the doppelgänger does indeed return from the repressed anew, this time in the intertextual form of a film adaptation. What makes Tsukamoto's *Gemini* particularly interesting as an adaptation of "The Twins" is how it enacts the return of what has been repressed through the narrative performance of Rampo's story and in doing so disrupts the usual relation typically ascribed to "original" and "copy," thus making it an illustrative example of an adaptation that generates an intertextual doppelgänger. Specifically, the schema of temporalization that structures the understanding of adaptations as simply derivative of their source texts is precisely what Tsukamoto Shin'ya's *Gemini* renders visible and arguably calls into question. Although Rampo's story is presumably set contemporary to its time of writing, Tsukamoto's film, given its much later production, can be seen as almost a period film. Although *Gemini* does not quite make the historical period in which it is set explicit, references to a recent war nonetheless hint that it takes place sometime after the Russo-Japanese war (1904–5). This is established

early in the film. Following a set of rather gruesome opening shots showing rats feeding on the carcass of another animal, *Gemini* shows a series
of patients being attended by the protagonist of the film, Daitokuji Yukio,
a doctor and veteran of the war. These scenes foreshadow several key
plot elements that play a bigger role later in the story. First, his conversation with an injured soldier makes note of medals he has received in
the line of duty and sets up his social standing in the community as a
kind of local war hero. Second, a child to whom he tends comments on
being attacked by other children from the nearby slums, establishing the
tensions existing between the social classes.

By its first few scenes, already made evident is the extent to which
Gemini takes the bare skeleton of Rampo's story and considerably fleshes
out its narrative. The unnamed characters of Rampo's story are given
names (the principal ones being the two twins—the elder Yukio and
the younger Sutekichi introduced later—as well as the wife Rin), occupa-
tions, and notably more detailed backstories. But perhaps the most significant alteration in the film is in the reversal of the relationship between
the twins. Unlike in Rampo's short story, wherein the younger twin is at
the center as the text's narrator, in *Gemini*, he does not make an on-screen
appearance until much later in the film. Indeed, in Tsukamoto's version,
the twins are initially not even aware of each other's existence. The only
hint of his brother's existence Yukio receives is when his mother suggests
that there may be problems with his inheritance just before she dies.[31] In
the beginning, Sutekichi's presence manifests only as an undercurrent
of tension as he stalks in the shadows studying his brother Yukio. Yukio's
parents initially direct their apprehensions toward Yukio's wife Rin, who
claims to have lost her memory after escaping from a fire. These tensions
are only exacerbated when strange odors begin emanating from the
house, and soon after, Yukio's father falls dead with soil in his mouth. His
mother soon follows, and Yukio's life is quickly turned upside down. It is
only in the morning after a stormy night and an argument with Rin re-
garding the preferential treatment he gives to financially well-off patients
that Yukio finally encounters Sutekichi, who promptly pushes him into a
dried-up well in the garden and begins impersonating him.

Much more noteworthy at this point, though, is the film's distinct
visual style. In contrast to the formalized illusion of representational

truth-telling deployed as the narrative strategy in "The Twins," *Gemini* takes on a more overtly presentational mode: it makes use of a distinct color palette in its lighting, and furthermore all of the characters wear deliberately overdone and almost theatrical makeup and move in an oddly affected fashion, giving their appearances a defamiliarizing quality that makes them appear almost doll-like or oddly alien. Indeed, the film's visual style could very well be called appropriately uncanny. This is especially emphasized when the film moves to a scene shot with a heavy yellow hue of a seemingly idyllic late afternoon in the Daitokuji manor that introduces Yukio, his wife Rin, and his parents, wherein a line that Yukio utters, "what a horrible color," calls attention to the film's lighting, and with that, *Gemini*'s distinct visual style that flaunts its fictionality, that foregrounds the artifice of its images rather than repressing it.

This visual style foreshadows many of the subsequent issues that take center stage in the narrative of the film. Most notably, the question of hidden secrets and their revelation becomes an important point of focus. Unlike in Rampo's short story, when Yukio falls to the bottom of the well, he does not simply die. Rather, Sutekichi proceeds to torment him by revealing the past that had been concealed from him. This past includes the knowledge that his wife Rin is only feigning her amnesia to conceal her origins in the slums, thus allowing her to marry into Yukio's wealthy

Yukio and Rin sit together in their house as the sun sets. From *Gemini*.

family. Apparently, Rin was Sutekichi's former lover during their shared life in the nearby slums. At one point in their past, Sutekichi and Rin are separated when the former is expelled from his adopted home and exiled from the town following a murder he commits. It is at this point that Rin first meets the older twin Yukio by accident. She initially thinks it is Sutekichi himself, but upon realizing that it isn't, she uses amnesia as an excuse to conceal her past from him. More importantly, because Sutekichi's very existence was concealed from Yukio, the younger twin is himself an embodiment of the violent return of this repressed past. When Yukio and Sutekichi were born, the younger Sutekichi, because of the strange snake-shaped scar on his thigh, was left to drift down a river where he was picked up by a troupe of theater actors in a slum downstream. It is only until after he comes face to face with his twin and is taunted with the knowledge of this violent past that all this is revealed to Yukio.[32]

Of interest in this return embodied by Sutekichi—particularly when considered vis-à-vis the deployment of the confessional mode in Rampo's story—is the visual style employed in Sutekichi's revelation of the twins' shared past. It is through Sutekichi's words to Yukio that the knowledge of the past comes to be revealed. But when these stories are given visual representation in a series of flashback sequences, the oversaturated light and stiff gestures that characterized the first part of the film explodes in a frenzy of colors and movement. A jittery hand-held camera replaces the sweeping picturesque pans of the earlier scenes; vibrant primary colors replace the oppressive monotone of characters' costumes seen in the film's scenes in the Daitokuji manor. The effect is to further aggravate the already foregrounded artifice of the film. For example, one such scene involves the origins of a scar on Rin's leg, previously mentioned as something she received after escaping from a fire. It is revealed in this flashback, however, that the scar is in fact self-inflicted. Rin scarred herself to mirror Sutekichi's own snake-shaped scar on his leg. Tellingly, the scene following Rin's scarring looks less like sexual intercourse and more like a highly choreographed interpretative dance between the two.

Given the centrality of depictions of class divisions in the narrative of *Gemini*, the distinct visual styles used in the film can be easily read as

A flashback to Sutekichi and Rin when they lived in the slums. From *Gemini*.

a device to distinguish members of different socioeconomic backgrounds. At the same time, though, every one of the scenes of the slums in *Gemini* is a flashback, and when that is taken into account, this reading can be further complicated. What is involved is not merely a distinguishing of members of distinct socioeconomic classes, but also a differentiation of temporal positions. As the film already foregrounds the artifice of its historical representation through its distinctive visual style, it is no surprise then that this is further emphasized when characters delve into and narrate from memory. Put simply, in contrast to the formalized truth-telling enacted through literary confession in "The Twins," wherein a concealment of its own performativity is presented, what takes place in Sutekichi's revelation of the past in *Gemini* is a foregrounding of precisely this performativity. Emphasis thus slips from the events that he narrates per se and instead moves toward the question of how the relationship between past and present is formed through this act of narration. The explosion of color and camera movement in these flashbacks suggests that the scenes represented therein refuse to be assimilated into the rest of the film's scheme of representation.

Andrew J. Webber has suggested that "[the doppelgänger] embodies a dislocation in time, always coming after its proper event. . . . It is at once a historical figure, re-presenting past times, and a profoundly anti-historical phenomenon, resisting temporal change by stepping out of time and then stepping back in as a revenant."[33] In its rehearsal of the return of the repressed, the doppelgänger does not merely bring about a return of a past that can then be assimilated into a familiar continuity, but a radical temporal alterity that resists easy temporalization, In *Gemini*, Sutekichi's appearance and disruption of Daitokuji life foreshadows a broader interruption in the form of a breakdown of the teleology of linear narrative. Near the end of the film, Yukio finally succeeds in escaping from the bottom of the well where Sutekichi keeps him prisoner. Upon his escape, he attacks his younger twin and strangles him to death. When he subsequently locates Rin, it initially appears that the disruption Sutekichi initiated has ended; the status quo has been restored.

But this is not where the film ends, and the denouement that follows complicates this picture. First to appear on screen is a scene of childbirth, followed by a shot of a pair of twin babies, one of whom bears a snake-shaped scar. This is then succeeded by a scene of an infant drifting down a river, only to be picked up by someone downstream. The next scene then returns to the Daitokuji manor, with Rin carrying her newborn child on her shoulder. On the one hand, this sequence could very well be viewed as a flashback showing Yukio and Sutekichi's repressed history. On the other hand, as a consequence of having it tacked onto the end of the film, particularly when juxtaposed with the shot of Rin and her child (whose own parentage may very well be in question, given her affair with Sutekichi while Yukio was trapped in the well), there is the suggestion that this may not be a flashback at all but rather a repetition of events, leaving open the possibility of another return of the doppelgänger. Either way, narrative beginnings and endings collapse into one another.[34]

What makes these reversals and disruptive returns of the repressed in *Gemini* especially significant is how they also extend to an intertextual level as well. Not only does the film stage the revelation of a concealed past within its own narrative, but in its capacity as an adaptation of "The Twins," it moreover retroactively exposes what has been repressed from the narrative performance of Rampo's short story. The difference in the treatment of the character of Rin in the film presents one particularly illustrative example. In contrast to the relatively pivotal role she plays

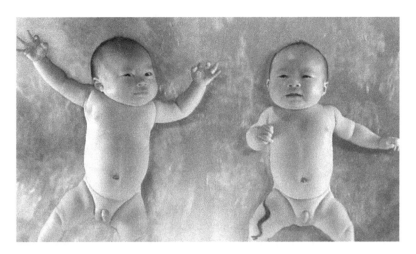

The twins Yukio and Sutekichi as newborn infants. From *Gemini*.

in *Gemini*, her unnamed counterpart in "The Twins" appears at first glance to be a largely a peripheral character. She does not even make an appearance outside of the secondhand account of the narrator himself. Yet she nonetheless plays a critical role in the story on a number of levels. In the first place, she effectively structures the interplay of desire in the dyadic relationship between the twins in her role as the mediating third term in their male homosocial triangle.[35] While the narrator points to all manner of motivations behind his murder of his brother—from the unequal inheritance to simple hatred of his very existence—the fact that his brother's wife had formerly been his lover appears to have been decisive. Moreover, her positioning in the narrative performance of the story itself as a kind of second-order narratee speaks to her significance in motivating the act of confession, and thus the very existence of the story at hand.

In "The Twins," the narrator mentions his wife relatively early in his confession, when he asks his direct interlocutor to communicate to her what he reveals. In effect, while the narrator's utterances appear to be directed to a priest, he is merely a mediator, and the ultimate narratee is the wife. He says: "Should I die without confessing this other crime of mine as well, I cannot help but feel much pity for my wife."[36] On its own, this seems like an innocuous enough line, but it oddly calls attention to itself when it is later reinforced at the end of the narrative with the words "Please, I ask you to fulfill this promise to make my story known to the courts, as well as to my wife," effectively bookending his narration with this expressed desire to tell his wife the story.[37] However, this raises a curious question. The story does not make it clear why the narrator feels the desire to reveal his "other crime" of murdering and replacing his own twin brother to his wife specifically, considering that, as the narrator himself suggests, she has no inkling whatsoever of what has taken place. Her lack of knowledge should make no difference to her life. A clue to a possible answer manifests in what initially appears to be a throwaway line the narrator utters. At one point, he notes that although he had closely observed his brother's mannerisms prior to murdering him with the goal of taking his place, he also admits that he did not observe him and his wife engaging in physical intimacy.

But what if the narrator's "wife" did in fact realize that he had replaced his twin brother in the marital bed? This question is precisely what Tsukamoto's *Gemini* seems to address when it considerably fleshes out this scene. In the film, as soon as Sutekichi has sexual intercourse with Rin, she is immediately aware that it is no longer Yukio with her and demands that Sutekichi tell her everything. Curiously, Sutekichi refuses to admit anything to her, instead asserting his new role as Yukio and accusing Rin of having gone mad. With this scene, what *Gemini* emphasizes more so than Rampo's source text is the force of rivalry between the two twins that mediates their respective relationships with Rin. As noted above, unlike in Rampo's "The Twins," in *Gemini*, the older twin Yukio is not merely murdered and his corpse hidden, but instead he is kept alive at the bottom of the well. Periodic visits by Sutekichi keep him up to date about the unfolding of the takeover of his life. Because the rivalry between the twins is as powerful a motivation as his desire for Rin, Sutekichi cannot simply remove Yukio from the picture and take back Rin. Rather, it is the taking over of Yukio's life *as Yukio* that motivates his actions.

With these scenes, *Gemini* expands a part of the narrative that is largely untold in Rampo's "The Twins," glossed over simply with words that summed up the passage of time: "And then, the year that followed was one of continued good fortune in my life. More money than I could

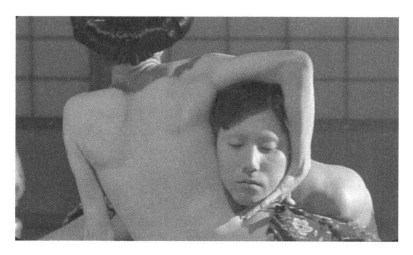

Sutekichi impersonates his twin brother Yukio. From *Gemini*.

ever use up, the woman I once loved, indeed not one of my voracious
desires went unfed during this year."[38] The bulk of the events depicted in
Tsukamoto's film take place during this elided period. But in doing so, it
does not merely fill in a gap, but more importantly, it also reveals sites
of slippage in the narrative of Rampo's original short story. Because of
the questions about the narrator's reliability built into the very form of
the story—specifically, the fact that the confession is uncorroborated
and that the twin brothers are indistinguishable from one another, and
thus making the determination of the identity of the narrator effectively
impossible—none of these scenes necessarily contradicts Rampo's story.
Even as it pursues the logical conclusion of the premise of murdering
and then subsequently taking the place of his brother set up by the narrator of "The Twins," *Gemini* ends up in a completely different place. By
the end of the film, instead of the younger twin killing the older, the
outcome is reversed; it is Yukio who has killed Sutekichi after escaping
from his imprisonment at the bottom of the well. Thus, the film enacts
the compulsion to repeat once more. The film's restaging of Rampo's
story reveals the unreliability of its narrative. It is impossible to tell which
twin in fact survives in the end, which twin is in fact performing the
confession. As an adaptation of Rampo's fiction, the film does not merely
replace one version of the narrative with another. Beyond this, just as the

film foregrounds the visual artifice of its own flashback sequences, it analogously unearths the performative contradictions of the utterances of the narrator of "The Twins," in effect rendering visible the artifice of his statements. Fittingly, for a story about the disruption of the line of inheritance through doubling, the film adaptation's repetition also has the effect of inverting its own inheritance to its source text.

Yet there is another dimension to the repetition and resignification of Rampo's "The Twins" that *Gemini* undertakes. In taking apart its source text, implicated in the adaptation of Rampo's story into film are not only matters of the transformations in the respective stories at hand but also how these changes are inevitably mediated by the broader shifts in the historical moments of production in which each text is situated. Indeed, even though Rampo's story makes few overt references to its historical context, certain details nonetheless signal toward them. Of these, the central technique of detection featured in the story—fingerprinting—is particularly noteworthy. Fingerprinting first saw use as an administrative tool in the 1860s in British India as a means of verifying the identity of contractors and pensioners and was quickly adopted as a forensic tool by the turn of the century.[39] It was introduced into Japanese policing in 1908. Fingerprinting, by virtue of the discovery that no two fingerprints are identical, became a key technology in the biopolitical management of populations, first in the colonial peripheries and subsequently in the imperial metropolitan capitals.

But a less well known fact is that the science of fingerprinting was not restricted to matters of forensic identification or population management. Often, it was studied as a means of unlocking a biological truth, typically tied to the racial classifications of colonial subjects, with an attempt to identify racially tied behavioral patterns in fingerprints.[40] In fact, one of the pioneers and major figures in early fingerprinting studies—Francis Galton—was one of the founders of the eugenics movement. This connection is significant because, although it may not be obvious from the bare text itself, in fact, the history of eugenics was an important backdrop to the Rampo's "The Twins." As Miri Nakamura points out in her detailed discussion of the story, Rampo takes as his point of departure the eugenic thinking on twins that typically portrayed them as aberrant bodies, as "deviant creatures with criminal tendencies."[41] From here,

Nakamura develops a compelling reading that highlights the text's colonial underpinnings, noting the way the multiple references to Korea in the text—as "the imaginary site where the 'other brother' (himself) resides" and "the 'otherized' place where criminals and the socially degenerate (*rakuhakushita*) roam"—draws a parallel between the relationship between the twins as "blood relations with the same face" and colonial rhetoric that drew racial and ethnic links between Japan and its colonies using the language of "brotherhood."[42]

If the histories of eugenicist discourse and colonial violence form the implicit historical backdrop in Rampo's "The Twins," they are made explicit when the narrative is retold in Tsukamoto's *Gemini*. Several scenes in the film show Yukio expressing disdain for providing medical treatment to those from the slums by suggesting that violence and disease is something in their very nature, in their very blood. At one point, he tells Rin: "The slums are breeding grounds of infection. And it's not just disease. Robberies and break-ins and numerous other crimes. . . . They're just like that, those people. From birth. The whole place should be razed to the ground." Given that the issue of genetic inheritance is central to the discourse of eugenics, and that twins often served as controls for all manner of scientific experiments for mapping out the boundaries between nature and nurture in both Europe and Japan, this attention probably should not come as a surprise.[43] Nevertheless, to bring up eugenics here cannot help but call to mind its concrete manifestation in such historical developments as the emergence of "racial sciences," and of course the material foundation thereof, colonialism. In bringing this to the surface, what *Gemini* performs then is the making manifest of the latent, the excavation of the repressed historical unconscious buried in between the lines of the deployment of the doppelgänger motif in Rampo's "The Twins," with the implication that these issues continue to be relevant to the present.

In this regard, these recent adaptations of Rampo's work seemingly respond to the much-repeated slogan "Always historicize!" that opens the preface to Fredric Jameson's *The Political Unconscious* (1981). It should be noted, though, that this imperative, in Jameson's analysis, means not just the historical situating of the texts in themselves, be it in terms of the manifest content or the formal strategies they deploy, the genres in which they participate, or the motifs they reproduce. Beyond this, he takes as the central task the historicizing of the very interpretative codes through which these texts are apprehended.[44] For Jameson, every act of interpretation is necessarily also an act of rewriting, and as such, is at once an act of narrativization. But even as the historical functions as the horizon of all signification, because "history is not a text, not a narrative," it is only accessible through a process of mediation, as the constitutive excess of the act of organizing it into a narrative form, a process that is necessarily shaped by the ideological constraints of its historical moment.[45] This has considerable ramifications for the examination of the doppelgänger, for it suggests that involved in the attention to the figure is not merely the historical circumstances that shaped its appearances in the past, but also the very act of looking historically at the figure of the doppelgänger from the position of the present. It suggests that the task at hand is to pose the problem of the historicity of the desire to historicize, that is, to apprehend the latent historiographic unconscious beneath these film adaptations of Rampo's writing.

Historical Unconscious

True to its form as an adaptation—as a doppelgänger—of its source text, *Gemini* stages a repetition. But what is enacted is not simply a repetition of a fixed original, but rather a repetition that retroactively breaks open the stability of the original text; it is not merely a repetition that generates a difference *from* an original, but is instead a repetition that reveals a difference that was already present at its origins. Here, Freud's characterization of the doppelgänger as an emblematic figure of his notion of the uncanny is worth recalling, for a crucial aspect of Freud's analysis is his linkage with the notion of the repetition-compulsion. "Whatever reminds us of this inner 'compulsion to repeat,'" Freud writes, "is perceived as uncanny."[46] An important facet of Freud's argument is the understanding that the sense of the uncanny cannot be reduced to a specific repressed content that returns and repeats. It is not *what* repeats that provokes the uncanny effect; it is instead the very fact of repetition itself, the very operation of the repetition-compulsion itself that produces it. Tsukamoto's film can be read as an illustration of what Freud has described as a structure of deferral in the process of repression, wherein a traumatic event earlier in life remains incomprehensible at the time it is experienced, and therefore is repressed without properly being assimilated. Only when another event later in life provokes its return does it come to be recognized as traumatic, and thus producing an uncanny sense as it is encountered as at once both familiar and unfamiliar.

With this in mind, I believe that the significance of the figure of the doppelgänger can be found in how it offers a critical prism to view a range of different narratives of historical repetition. After all, while the doppelgänger's embodiment of doubling and repetition puts this issue into stark relief, its enactment of historical repetition is arguably a symptomatic marker of a constellation of similar patterns of repetition also visible in other sites of discourse. Indeed, in *History and Repetition* (2004), Karatani Kōjin has gone so far as to suggest that there can be detected in the 1990s a generalized sense of an uncanny historical repetition of the 1930s in alignment with the cyclical long wave patterns first identified by Nikolai Kondratiev.[47] In part a critical response to the developing economic malaise coupled with the rise of nationalist sentiment in Japan at the time of its writing in the aftermath of the 1990s, Karatani's discussion was occasioned by the publication of a new Japanese translation of Karl Marx's *The Eighteenth Brumaire of Louis Bonaparte* (1852), a text that famously opens with the lines "Hegel remarks somewhere that all the events and personalities of great importance in world history occur, as it were, twice. He forgot to add: the first time as tragedy, the second as farce."[48] Karatani proceeds to revisit Marx's analysis of the political-economy in texts like *The Eighteenth Brumaire* along with *Capital* (1867), arguing that it is the principle of repetition-compulsion that animates the interlinked historical movements of capitalism and the state. But in claiming that the 1990s repeats the 1930s, Karatani is careful to emphasize in his argument that what repeats are not events per se, but rather the structural logic that underpins the unfolding of historical events. In Karatani's words, "To speak of historical repetition is not to mean that the same events repeat. What can repeat are not the events (content), but the forms (structures) immanent to them."[49] Specifically, for Karatani, it is the materialization of the structural tendency toward crisis—in the political, the economic, and the cultural—that sees repetition between the early twentieth century and its end.

All manner of strategies for recuperation—or what David Harvey has identified as spatio-temporal fixes—follow in the wake of the periodic crises of overaccumulation structurally embedded within the logic of capitalist expansion.[50] For example, a strategy that often comes into play is what Harvey has termed a temporal displacement, involving such fixes as a speedup in production to absorb excess capacity, or a spatial displacement involving the production of new spaces of accumulation through colonial expansion.[51] However, in Harvey's view, these processes "so revolutionize the objective qualities of space and time that we are forced to alter, sometimes in quite radical ways, how we represent the world to ourselves."[52] As such, these political-economic changes also often incorporate a cultural-aesthetic dimension. Indeed, as the previous chapters have touched upon, the development of technologies such as the telephone, railways, or cinema, not to mention the advent of imperial conquest, vastly expanded the spatial and temporal dimensions of lived experience. This compelled the development of new ways of grasping with one's social conditions, leading to cultural responses that sought to find a fixed ground in the field of representation from which the experience of time-space compression could be grasped and indeed commanded. It was against this backdrop that various forms of detective fictions, psychoanalytic theories, modernisms, or the narrative systematization of cinema—the technologies and discourses formative of the emergence of the doppelgänger—made their appearance.

For Karatani, it is the confluence of these various crises of representation—in the political, the economic, and the cultural—that sees repetition between the interwar period and the end of the twentieth century. The techniques of industrial and imperial production that emerged out of the early twentieth century had increasingly become unworkable by the 1970s. Their mechanisms for controlling the structural tendency of capitalism toward crisis had been overwhelmed by the conjoined processes of debt accumulation and decolonization that made further temporal as well as geographic displacement under the same logic difficult. This ushered in a passage into a new regime of accumulation, which Harvey terms "flexible accumulation," characterized by a new round of intensified time-space compression in the form of the acceleration of production processes through such techniques as small-batch production and improvements in media communication and information technologies as well as the transnational dissemination of sites of production and consumption.[53] Through the subsequent decades and into the present, these developments brought about a constellation of political, economic, and cultural transformations that have since been referred to with such terms as neoliberalism, late capitalism, postmodernity, or globalization. As Jameson has observed, on the levels of both "infrastructure and superstructures—the economic system and the cultural 'structure of feeling'—somehow crystallized in the great shock of the crises of 1973 . . . which, now that the dust clouds of have rolled away, disclose the existence, already in place, of a strange new landscape."[54]

Japan occupies an important position within these historical shifts. The collapse of the Bretton Woods system coupled with the oil shocks of 1973 deeply impacted the Japanese economy and prompted a range of technical and organizational innovations from the off-shoring of factories and the rationalization of labor practices, to the increasing financialization of the economy. These innovations began a shift toward informational and communicative capitalism, culminating in the subsumption of the social order into a corporate structure that has since been described as an "enterprise society" [kigyō shakai]. But just as the reconfigurations of capitalism along imperialist lines in past moments of crisis had the effect of generating new sites of contradiction and crisis, the transformations in the Japanese economic order during the 1970s created the conditions that would lead to Japan's "Lost Decade" of the 1990s. In the wake of the end of the Cold War and the death of the Showa emperor, Japan found itself in a long recessionary period that led to a generalized breakdown of the postwar Japanese social and economic system marked especially by the double blow of the Kobe earthquake and the Tokyo sarin gas attacks in 1995.[55]

These developments provide an important critical context for articulating the significance of Gemini's adaptation of the "The Twins," and with that, the broader historical repetition of the doppelgänger's proliferation in contemporary Japan. The structure of repetition that the figure embodies speaks to the question of how to apprehend the very relationship between these two historical moments in which its appearances become most visible. Consider, for instance, the way questions of continuity versus rupture often dominate the discussions of these seeming historical doublings and repetitions. On the one hand, to emphasize continuities at the expense of an attention to breaks and ruptures runs the risk of denying historical difference, indeed denying the very possibility of history altogether. On the other hand, to emphasize the difference of the present from the past often sets up the past as a fixed point of origin, treating it as something closed off and essentialized. But if there is one thing the figure of the doppelgänger calls into question, it is precisely the stability of perceived origins, breaking open the possibility of articulating a narrativization of history without having to anchor it to a vision of the past that is fixed, to a retroactively constituted origin from which to derive its coherence. After all, there are forms of repetition and there are forms of repetition.

Take the case of the contemporary transformations in the two historical conditions formative of the doppelgänger's popularization, namely visual modernization and colonial expansion, which see a historical repetition in the rise of new media technologies and the passage from colonial to postcolonial modernity. In the former case, new media presents not only another set of narratives to be populated by the doppelgänger and other related motifs like dolls and automata, but itself stages a confrontation between cinema and new media, that is, a doubling of cinema by new media. While much of the discussion surrounding new media tends to focus on identifying precisely how it differs from cinema, it is perhaps more effective not to take cinema as a fixed point of origin, but as a potential site of difference.[56] Just as the doppelgänger does not merely enact the repetition of the same, but instead breaks open the presumed fixity of the original through the process of its repetition, this doubling of cinema during the 1980s provoked what may very well be called a crisis of identity. The emergence of new modes of production and consumption that new media has prompted a rethinking of precisely what defines "cinema" in the first place. This rethinking of cinema proved to be significant in providing the impetus for a subsequent historical turn in film studies, allowing for the rediscovery of early cinema as anticipating new media. Furthermore, the nonlinear engagement with the film image enabled by the same technologies also compelled the recognition

of cinema's historicity, and with that, the calling into question of the teleology of film history itself.[57]

Similar patterns of discourse permeate the debates on "globalization"
that engage with the political-economic structures and conditions of the
contemporary moment. For example, a key point in Michael Hardt and
Antonio Negri's contribution to these debates in their book *Empire*
(2000) is their distinguishing of the current global order, which they
term simply as "Empire"—"a new logic and structure of rule"—from preceding forms of modern imperialism. Whereas imperialism was predicated on the system of nation-states, with the borders of the nation-state
marking off the centers of power from the external colonies in the
periphery they rule over (and as such functioned as an expansion of the
sovereignty of European nation-states into their colonial territories),
Empire is a fundamentally new form of global sovereignty and not
merely the extension of historical imperialisms. Empire, for Hardt and
Negri, operates under a networked structure, under the logic of a "*decen-
tered* and *deterritorialized* apparatus of rule*" marked by the increasing
hegemony of immaterial labor and biopolitical production.[58] Yet while
there is much that is compelling in their analysis, one criticism that has
been leveled against Hardt and Negri's conception of "Empire" focuses
on their insistence on the radical novelty of the contemporary moment,
in that their vision of the present is arguably underwritten by a contrast
with an oversimplified image of past historical imperialisms, painting a
picture of it that is all too monolithic in order to emphasize its difference
from the present.[59] Might their historical claims be more productively
reframed as emergent categories of analysis that enable a retroactive
rethinking of the structures of capitalism and imperialism? Might it
be possible to conceive of the historical changes in the contemporary
moment without making untenable claims about the past, without rele-
gating the past to something completed and now since overcome?

It is in this sense that the structure of repetition that the doppelgänger
embodies speaks to the question of how to apprehend the very relationship between these two historical moments in which its appearances
become most visible. It suggests that it is precisely its repetition in the
present that opens the possibility of apprehending the past historical

conditions that facilitated its emergence as a concept. Grasped in these terms, these repetitions enacted through the figure of the doppelgänger can be compared with Mieke Bal's use of the motif of the mirror in her conception of history as literally "preposterous," as at once inscribing a coeval "pre" and "post." "History," Bal writes, "as a mirroring of the past within the present, is itself, in my preposterous version of it, wed to the act of mirroring, without which we cannot live, yet for which we must not fall."[60] Bal's vision of a "preposterous" history is one wherein the past is inevitably mirrored and interiorized in the present, one that emphasizes a destabilizing entanglement rather than the severance and closure of different temporal positions. Like Bal's conception of the mirror, the figure of the doppelgänger is "a tool of semiotic theorizing" that allows one to grasp—but not fix—the contemporaneity and entanglement of temporalities.[61] As such, it is a figure that opens a space of possibility for recognizing and grappling with history without resorting to a repression of its potentialities. Thus, if the doppelgänger is indeed to be understood as positing a form of repetition without a fixed origin, then the task of historicizing it must address not only issues of historical repetition in the relationship between Japan's colonial past and its place within the contemporary conjuncture of globalization. Moreover, it must also historicize the very categories of analysis one uses in performing cultural criticism in the present vis-à-vis the object of one's intellectual inquiry.

5

Compulsions to Repeat

The Doppelgänger at the End of History

Kurosawa Kiyoshi's Compulsion to Repeat

For the spectator familiar with his work, Kurosawa Kiyoshi's film *Sakebi* (*Retribution*, 2006) immediately provokes moments of spectatorial déjà vu. Many of its plot points and narrative turns recall scenes from previous films in Kurosawa's extensive body of work. *Retribution* begins by calling upon its spectators to witness a scene of violence. Immediately after the titles appear and then vanish off the screen is a sequence of only three cuts, all shot from a distance, accentuating the sense that one is secretly witnessing the scene. A man in a black jacket drags a woman in a red dress across the barren landscape of the landfills along Tokyo's waterfront and pushes her face into a puddle of saltwater. When this is then revealed to be only the first in a series of murders, all of which are linked together by a common modus operandi—the drowning of the victim in (specifically) saltwater—police investigators, led by the film's protagonist Yoshioka Noboru, initially believe they have a serial killer on the loose. Yet when clues collected at the crime scenes seemingly point to Yoshioka himself (or possibly, his doppelgänger) as the perpetrator, suspicions arise over the possibility that he is involved in the series of murders. This is only exacerbated when the narrative takes a turn toward the supernatural with the appearance of what at first seems to be the ghost of the first victim—a woman in a striking red dress—who persistently accuses Yoshioka of murdering her. But even when a suspect is finally apprehended and confesses to the murder of the woman in red, the ghost nevertheless continues to haunt Yoshioka. It is only at this point that he realizes that despite their resemblance, the ghost who haunts him is not the murdered woman from the opening scene, but rather someone else altogether: a woman Yoshioka once glimpsed through the windows of the abandoned mental institution during a ferry ride along Tokyo's waterfront. The film ends with Yoshioka retrieving the skeletal remains of a woman in the red dress from the ruins of the mental institution. He walks down a Tokyo avenue that is eerily devoid of any of its usual crowds or any sign of human life whatsoever aside from an abandoned newspaper rustling in the wind. Everyone in the city is apparently dead, except for Yoshioka, whose life has been spared by the vengeful ghost of the woman in a red dress. Over this scene, the woman repeatedly chants a curse that is seemingly addressed not only to characters in the film, but also the film's spectators: "I died, so everyone else should die too" [*watashi wa shinda, dakara minna mo shinde kudasai*].

Echoes of Kurosawa's earlier work should already be audible from just this summary of *Retribution*. For example, the film's use of a serial killer narrative rehashes an earlier primary plot framework in his film *Kyua* (*Cure*, 1997). The suggestion that Yoshioka himself may be the killer also hints at the presence of a doppelgänger, which revisits a motif that appeared in Kurosawa's previous films *Dopperugengā* (*Doppelgänger*, 2003) and *Kōrei* (*Séance*, 2000). But perhaps the most noteworthy of these repetitions is the film's closing scene. *Retribution* is by no means the first film in Kurosawa's body of work to feature such an apocalyptic finale. To be more specific, Kurosawa's earlier film *Kairo* (*Pulse*, 2001) famously ends with similar scenes of the end of world, which is itself prefigured by the closing scene of a burning city in the distance in the 1999 Kurosawa film *Karisuma* (*Charisma*). In *Pulse*, the plot centers on ghosts who haunt the electronic networks of the world. They manifest as videos and images in secret websites, which trigger deadening ennui and a sense of social isolation in all who see them, eventually leading the viewers to commit suicide, leaving only an odd black stain on the concrete walls where they last stood. Foreshadowing the conclusion of *Retribution*, by the end of *Charisma*, a similar rapid depopulation of the city has taken place, until eventually, only one of the characters in its ensemble cast remains alive.

Yoshioka wanders the empty streets of Tokyo as a ghost enacts her vengeance. From *Retribution*.

In this respect, the closing shots of *Retribution* are haunted not only by the voice of the woman in red chanting her curse, but also by the specters of similar apocalyptic finales from earlier films.

While it would be easy to find fault in Kurosawa's repetitions in *Retribution*, to suggest that they are indicative of the exhaustion of Kurosawa's imagination, I believe that to do so would be to miss the point. Tellingly, what repeat in this film are motifs that foreground precisely the very problem of repetition itself. What is the ghost that haunts the protagonist of *Retribution* if not a revenant, a return from out of time? What is a serial killer narrative that initially structures the plot of the film if not precisely the dramatization of repetition (of murder)? That these two motifs furthermore coalesce around vague hints of a doppelgänger (the repetition of the subject) of the film's protagonist Yoshioka lurking in the background only punctuates the point. As for the persistent repetitions of apocalyptic conclusions in his films, my contention is that these provide an entry point for understanding the critical context in which to articulate the politics of the doppelgänger—of the staging of difference and repetition—in the present conjuncture, in that what is perhaps most significant about this enactment of a repetition in Kurosawa's films, especially the repeated stagings of fantasies of the end of the world, is its seeming mirroring of some of the major tropes of the discourses on the nation emerging in the aftermath of the so-called "end of history."

Indeed, Kurosawa's persistent repetition of representations of the end of the world is noteworthy for several reasons, the most obvious of which is the fact that his films are not isolated cases as far as apocalyptic scenarios go. On the contrary, these films participate in (and call attention to) a broader proliferation of end-of-the-world fantasies in Japan and beyond.[1] Predictably, much of the commentary surrounding this recurrence of representations of the apocalypse in recent Japanese texts link this trope to the dropping of the atomic bombs on Hiroshima and Nagasaki in 1945. Given this historical backdrop, it would be easy to reduce these repeated stagings of apocalyptic scenarios simply to expressions of a national-cultural sentiment. However, it is important to recognize that this recent recurrence of images of the end of the world is not restricted to Japan. On the contrary, it is arguably part of a larger global phenomenon that several thinkers, not the least of whom Fredric Jameson, have characterized as symptomatic of the political impasse of the contemporary situation. In the aftermath of Francis Fukuyama's infamous declaration of "the end of history," Jameson once famously noted that "it is easier to imagine the end of the world than the end of capitalism."[2] Raising a similar contention, Slavoj Žižek elaborates upon the point further, asserting that "nobody seriously considers possible alternatives to capitalism any longer, whereas popular imagination is persecuted by the visions of the forthcoming 'breakdown of nature,' of the stoppage of all life on Earth—it seems easier to imagine the 'end of the world' than a far more modest change in the mode of production."[3]

In contemporary Japan, this sentiment of an "end of history" takes on a particular resonance in the wake of, on the one hand, the long recession and lost decades from the 1990s that have since led to the appearance of new neoliberal conditions of precarity and a loss of a sense of futurity, and on the other hand, the Aum Shinrikyō's 1995 horrific sarin gas attack on Tokyo's subway system, which can very well be understood as a staging of a millennial apocalyptic fantasy par excellence.[4] These are not unconnected events. On the contrary, the fantasies of war and world's end that proliferate at this moment cannot be separated from the economic transformations and geopolitical realignments that brought about the deferred ending of what has been called Japan's "long postwar" that the close of the Cold War alongside the ending of the Showa period with the death of the emperor punctuated.[5] Much has already been said about how neoliberal reforms to the Japanese economy cultivated the social conditions ripe for disaffected young technocrats to become members of the Aum Shinrikyō. In more general terms, Ghassan Hage has suggested that it is becoming increasingly apparent that the escalating subsumption of everyday life into the logic of the neoliberal order—and its consequent production of material and psychic precarities and insecurities—engender the rise of what he terms "paranoid nationalism."[6] The attack on the Tokyo subway system coincided with a resurgence of nationalist discourse (revolving around the twinned centers of historical revisions of Japan's wartime past and the revision of Japan's postwar pacifist constitution) since the 1990s and continuing on into the post–9/11 present.[7]

Marilyn Ivy has also argued that there is a close structural linkage between Aum Shinrikyō's literal staging of an apocalyptic scenario and nationalist discourses. In Ivy's analysis, these discourses operate under the logic of a traumatic acting-out, specifically in response to the trauma of Japan's defeat in the Second World War and what the Japanese perceived to be the abnormal postwar nation-state that this event produced. Just as on the scale of the individual, a traumatic event is constituted only in repetition—that is, an event is recognized as traumatic only after it is first repressed and then subsequently returns to disturb the psyche—it is a compulsion to repeat war, to produce the conditions that make another war possible (through the revision of the articles prohibiting military buildup in the constitution) as a means of resolving and recuperating from the abject state produced by the defeat in its previous war (the Second World War) that animates Japanese neonationalists.[8] For Ivy, Aum's staging of a "final war" [saishū sensō] against the Japanese state on the fiftieth anniversary of the end of the Second World War is another expression of the repetition-compulsion at the heart of the same traumatic drive; it was "performed as precisely a redemptive reprisal of World War II in the mode of Armageddon, the definitive final and total war if ever there was one."[9]

The problem of history and repetition has been at the very heart of the examination of the concept of the doppelgänger in this book. Not only is the uncanny, of which the figure of the doppelgänger is emblematic, closely linked to the concept of the repetition-compulsion, but also, from a longer view, the pervasive appearances of the doppelgänger in literary, cinematic, and critical discourses in first the interwar period and then the contemporary conjuncture enact a logic of repetition on a historical register as well. In the spirit of the doppelgänger's performances of repetition, therefore, I bring the discussion of the doppelgänger here to a chiastic return. In its examination of the deployment of the motif in the films of Kurosawa Kiyoshi, the task of this chapter is twofold: first, it will revisit and recapitulate the key issues at hand made visible through the examination of the figure of the doppelgänger that I have discussed thus far; second, it will attempt to articulate the stakes of thinking about the doppelgänger and the politics of repetition, not merely as a literary or cinematic motif, but as a critical concept that appears in response to the most salient issues and concerns in the contemporary conjuncture.

I began this discussion of the doppelgänger in this book with the assertion that it names a historically specific cultural formation. Another way of putting this is to treat the doppelgänger as an informally constituted genre, at least in the sense that Ralph Cohen uses the term to refer to "open systems . . . groupings of texts by critics to fulfill certain ends."[10] Key to Cohen's understanding of genres is the recognition that they are discursive *processes* that function to govern the limits and possibilities of meaning production in texts. They are, in this sense, not natural systems but social institutions that are in history, and as such, are constantly under negotiation not only as texts identified as members in a given genre accrue, but moreover, through the very performance of definition and classification. In other words, genres are entities that are not reducible to an origin or essence but are instead discourses whose emergence is shaped by a historically specific assemblage of institutions and practices that determine its horizons of signification. But what is important about the figure of the doppelgänger specifically is that if indeed genres function on the basis of organizing texts around a tension between producing something that is recognizably familiar on the one hand and yet on the other hand offering a variation on this familiarity—or as Stephen

Neale once put it, "genres are instances of repetition and difference"—then in its play on difference and repetition, the doppelgänger can also be understood as an enactment of the very logic of genre.[11] In other words, the doppelgänger is a figure with the capacity to make visible the very limits of genre. It presents an embodiment of that which exceeds and interrupts genre's operations.

At stake in the doppelgänger's foregrounding of the work of difference and repetition in the mechanisms of genre are more than mere matters of conventions in literary or cinematic classification. In its capacity to mediate the horizons of the possibilities for meaning production in a given text—or to put it in the language of Jameson, its function to "specify the proper use of a particular cultural artifact"—systems of genres make for a paradigmatic example of other codified interpretative schemes of classification, demarcation, and regulation in other social domains and institutions.[12] As Charles Bazerman has argued: "Genres are not just forms. Genres are forms of life, ways of being. They are frames for social action. They are environments for learning. They are locations within which meaning is constructed."[13] The task of apprehending the structural mechanisms of generic iteration and permutation thus also gestures toward broader questions of the concepts and categories of analysis through which knowledge is produced, history is narrated, and social life is grasped. If genres are frames for social action—setting the limits of what can be thought and unthought, what narratives can be told and not told—then it is imperative to recognize that they are not only shaped by ideological currents but also themselves perform the work of ideology. Consequently, in the staging of their interruption, perhaps flashes of possibilities for critical intervention, even if only momentary, can become visible. If one function of genre is to facilitate the rendering familiar of what is unfamiliar, then what the doppelgänger's interruptions may very well perform is the reversal of this process through the making unfamiliar of the familiar, in other words, the generation of the uncanny.

This work of the doppelgänger only becomes more significant when situated against the backdrop of post-Aum, neoliberal Japan marked by the intersections of nationalist acting-out, proliferating apocalyptic fantasies, and what Miyadai Shinji has characterized as a sense of an "endless everyday" [*owaranaki nichijō*].[14] What the doppelgänger's interrogation of generic mechanisms of variation-in-iteration brings to attention are the structural limits of the imagination, the insufficiency of existing frames of knowledge for not only apprehending the realities of the current conjuncture, but more importantly, articulating a way out of it. Put simply, the doppelgänger discloses the desire for difference within the structure of repetition that organizes social life in the contemporary moment.

Breaking Down Genres

Kurosawa's films make for an effective test case because the staging of the interplay of difference and repetition in his work often directly addresses questions of violence and the nation. Famously, *Cure*—the film that catapulted him to international visibility—has been widely read as a critical engagement with the discourse vis-à-vis the Aum Shinrikyō in the wake of the 1995 sarin gas attacks.[15] The story of *Cure* revolves around a series of murders that share similar characteristics but are committed by seemingly unrelated individuals. All that connects them is an encounter with an amnesiac hypnotist who seemingly unearths murderous desires in those he meets. Because of his ability to lead others to commit acts of violence as if they were utterly casual and banal acts, critics have likened the amnesiac hypnotist to Aum leader Asahara Shōkō.[16] With *Retribution*, Kurosawa ups the ante by combining the plot of *Cure* with motifs of repetition and the apocalypse. As Kurosawa explains it, he was asked specifically to remake "*Cure*, but with ghosts" [*yūrei ga detekuru Kyua*].[17] True to these directions (to a practically literal extent), *Retribution* does indeed revisit the serial killer plot of *Cure*. Not only that, the film mines the imagery and plot devices of the most familiar films from the corpus of contemporary Japanese horror cinema. Readily recognizable is the haunting by a vengeful female ghost, typically coupled with images of water and drowning, made infamous by such films as Nakata Hideo's *Ringu* (*Ring*, 1997) and Shimizu Takashi's *Juon* (*The Grudge*, 2000) and further repeated in countless other so-called "J-Horror" films in the last few years.

This return to *Cure* and the familiar motifs from the J-Horror in Kurosawa's film raises the issue of difference and repetition, and with that, his approach to the question of generic repetition, specifically the simultaneous articulation and subversion of genre, which has been central to his film-making reputation. Since he initially gained wide international recognition, Kurosawa Kiyoshi has typically been positioned as a genre film auteur—a so-called "outlaw master" who at once distils and exceeds genre film-making—in film journalistic discourse.[18] In particular, much of the critical commentary on Kurosawa's films highlights his engagement with the discourse surrounding the Japanese horror genre. Given the fact that his rise to international fame took place during a milieu marked by the emerging cult popularity of Japanese horror cinema in the aftermath of the release of the films of Nakata and Shimizu, it is perhaps not at all surprising that it was to the horror genre that Kurosawa's name came to be closely attached.[19] But there is more to this than just mere historical coincidence. What is particularly noteworthy about the horror genre is that it foregrounds the generic imperative to repeat familiar and formulaic elements in that a repetition—both in intratextual terms in the form of the persistent return of a ghost or monster, and intertextual terms in the never-ending sequels and remakes for which the genre is known—is arguably the prototypical narrative structure taken by much horror cinema. Contemporary Japanese horror cinema is certainly no exception to this. As Aaron Gerow has keenly observed, many recent Japanese horror films seem to dwell upon motifs of circularity and repetition. However, while they exhibit similar tropes and techniques to other J-Horror films, Gerow also suggests that what makes Kurosawa's films exceptional is the extent to which they make use of repetition precisely to rework the genre, in effect "foregrounding what many horror films can only express unconsciously."[20] One strategy of Kurosawa's that Gerow identifies is the collapsing of the distinction between self and other. While the relationship between self and other—the human and the monster—forms the narrative foundation of much horror cinema, Kurosawa goes beyond merely rehearsing or even reversing this relation. Rather, he renders this very division fundamentally impossible. In *Cure*, Kurosawa presents an amnesiac hypnotist killer: "a monster without a self" who compels the recognition of this same emptiness in others. In *Retribution* and several other films, the doubled subjectivity of the doppelgänger provides this interruption.

Given the pervasive repetition of tropes from not only his oeuvre, but also the most familiar motifs from Japanese horror cinema, it probably does not come as a surprise either that *Retribution* is not the first film in

Kurosawa's body of work to feature the figure of the doppelgänger. Its first appearance has to be credited to a brief scene in the made-for-television movie *Séance*, when the sound engineer protagonist of the film, who is wracked by guilt after accidentally killing a child who without his knowledge sneaked into his equipment case and was locked in there, encounters (and subsequently douses in flame) his silent double staring back at him.[21] A more extensive treatment takes place in the appropriately titled *Doppelgänger*. The story of *Doppelgänger* follows the research scientist Hayasaki in his attempts to develop an "artificial body" [*jinkō jintai*]: a mentally operated wheelchair to serve as an extension of the human body for disabled individuals. Initially running into difficulties in both technical terms of the complexity of translating mental inputs into machinic responses, and financial terms as his employers and manager threaten to pull the plug on his funding, things take a turn when he encounters his doppelgänger. To assist Hayasaki in completing his project, his double subsequently sets into motion a series of events such as the illicit acquisition of funds or research data from other institutions or access to an assistant and a scrap warehouse that allows Hayasaki to work independently after he is removed from his position of employment.

Setting its story aside, what is most interesting about *Doppelgänger* is its treatment of generic categories. Its first few scenes make it appear like a horror film, especially marked by its use of atmospheric music along with shots of empty spaces and wind-blown curtains that are the staples of the genre. Although the film initially sets up a story centered on Hayasaki's difficulties in the development of the "artificial body" and a consequent psychical breakdown that triggers the appearance of his double, there is a considerable tonal shift in the film's second half. Following the completion of the "artificial body" and a violent confrontation between Hayasaki and his doppelgänger, the narrative shifts into something akin to a road movie, with various comedic set pieces as the protagonists attempt to transport the machine to a place where they can offer it up for sale.

The impact of this shift is to subvert the generic expectations often associated with the doppelgänger motif as well as Kurosawa's own reputation for horror filmmaking. This is especially the case in scenes wherein moments of undecidability in the setting up of spectatorial expectations

Hayasaki encounters his doppelgänger waiting for him in his home. From *Doppelgänger.*

is heightened, such as one sequence wherein Hayasaki's double commits a pair of murders. In the first, he brutally and repeatedly strikes a man's skull with a hammer, albeit against the aural backdrop of rather cartoonish sound effects for the hammer strikes and the doppelgänger's cheerful whistling, only to be followed by a subsequent scene of murder in which the music (now nondiegetic) takes on an appropriately dramatic tenor, but again incongruently matched up with an act of killing that takes on an almost slapstick character.

This should not be taken to mean that Kurosawa's film is better classified as comedy rather than horror; instead, *Doppelgänger* renders visible the sociohistorical constructedness of the generic categories of horror and comedy (and by implication the system of genres as such), laying bare the technical devices through which spectatorial desires are manipulated and regulated. If there is something that the genres of horror and comedy share, it is how their functioning as aesthetic objects is dependent upon the provocation of an interruption—an involuntary affective response—in the spectatorial experience, be it the eruption of terror or laughter. However, when these two genres are juxtaposed with one another as is the case with Kurosawa's *Doppelgänger*, one consequence is the provocation of conflicting affective responses in the spectator; instead of either terror or laughter, the response provoked becomes the terror at one's own laughter (or vice versa). Considered in conjunction with the very fore-grounding of the apparatus of cinema and its spectatorship effected by *Doppelgänger*'s extensive deployment of split screens—through the rep-lication and multiplication of the same images, the cutting up of the mise-en-scène, or the simultaneous presentation of multiple spaces in which the two Hayasakis act—what this performance of genre subver-sion does can thus perhaps be understood as compelling a second-guessing, a doubling—of the spectator's own affective responses; it makes doppelgängers out of its spectators, foregrounding his or her implication in the circuit of images, with the consequence of blocking any drive toward the assumption of an illusory position of visual mastery.[22]

In contrast, with *Retribution*, Kurosawa is seemingly playing the horror genre straight for the first time in several years. When juxtaposed to the two films that preceded it, *Retribution* appears almost like a throwback for Kurosawa. Up to a point, such a conclusion would not be completely off the mark. After all, *Retribution* was made specifically for the "J-Horror Theater" line-up produced by Ichise Takashige (who was also the pro-ducer of the major Japanese horror cinema titles *Ring* and *The Grudge*). That said, a few points complicate a simple reading of *Retribution* as little

Hayasaki continues working on his robotic wheelchair as his doppelgänger gathers the resources he needs. From *Doppelgänger*.

more than a straight horror film, not the least of which is the fact that *Retribution* simply fails as a horror film. Indeed, I would suggest here that *Retribution* is perhaps not so different from Kurosawa's preceding two films, *Doppelgänger* and *Loft* (*Rofuto*, 2005), in their subversion of generic classifications and conventions. Of course, the specific techniques they employ differ. While the earlier films make use of juxtapositions with other genres, *Retribution* pushes the very logical limits of a given genre through a staging of repetition that borders on a parodic excessiveness. Nonetheless, it is more productively understood not merely as a film that can be classified under the genre of horror, but instead as something that is a film that makes use of the technique of repetition to foreground the very boundaries and limits of the horror genre, and for that matter the problem of genre as such.

An illustration of how Kurosawa's *Retribution* makes use of the technique of repetition in order to rework and subvert genre can be found in its deployment of the serial killer plot. On one level, the figure of the serial killer is of course closely associated with the genre of detective or crime fiction and film. On another level, though, it is also arguably a figure that bears within it the potential to articulate the limits of detective narrative in two distinct, but nevertheless related senses: first, as the epitome of the logic of the form of the detective narrative and, second, as the point of its breakdown. In the first case, because the serial killer often lacks a motive beyond the act of murder itself, an important facet to the figure is how it shifts the object of attention from the *acts* of crime themselves to the *bodies* of individual criminals. In other words, the figure of the serial killer effectively embodies the personification of criminality itself in that, as Steffan Hantke has put it, "The serial killer is more fantastic than the murderer in conventional detective fiction; one is ostracized for what he did, the other for what he is."[23] Yet in the second case, the figure of the serial killer—precisely as an effect of the repetition of murder he or she performs—also subverts the conventional narrative logic of the detective story, at least in its most classic and orthodox forms. Recalling Tzvetan Todorov's characterization of detective fiction as structured around two distinct stories (crime and investigation), serial killer narratives differ from cases wherein there is a single event of crime to investigate in that they render these two movements, crime and investigation, not as neatly demarcated narratives with the story of the investigation beginning after the story of the crime ends, but as overlapping and proceeding effectively simultaneous to one another.[24] The story (of the crime) does not merely end followed by and demarcated from its telling (the investigation), but rather persists into the narrative present as something that is not static, there to be interpreted, but something into which one must intervene.

A key effect of this complication in the temporal ordering of crime and investigation is to raise the stakes by in effect implicating the detective in the continuation of the killings. Every subsequent repetition of murder becomes a consequence of the absence of closure in the investigation (in the construction of narrative). Moreover, in a move that literally rehearses Hantke's argument that serial killer narratives already implicitly structure the relationship between the detective and the criminal as "those of two doubles" in that the detective is compelled to mirror the criminal's every action, the deployment of the doppelgänger motif in *Retribution* only highlights this point further.[25] As the investigation proceeds, hints are dropped that the film's protagonist Yoshioka (or his doppelgänger) may himself be the killer they are tracking down. Clues recovered from the first crime scene all seemingly point to him. Not only are his fingerprints found on the dead body of the woman in red, but also, the button from a trench coat found floating in one of the puddles of saltwater at the scene coincidentally happens to match a black coat with a missing button that he owns.

In both cases, the possibility of Yoshioka's guilt is quickly dismissed. The crime lab ascribes the presence of Yoshioka's fingerprints to a simple mishandling of evidence, and the trench coat matching the button found at the scene is revealed to be a readily available mass-produced commodity. That said, it is nevertheless telling that although he strenuously denies any connection to the murders, his very defensiveness itself suggests something more is at hand. He reacts with vehemence to even the slightest hint that he might be involved, indeed even when no real accusation has been made. Moreover, this is coupled with several halfhearted attempts at concealing evidence. When he finds the coat button in the very first scene of the investigation, for instance, Yoshioka first examines the black coat in his closet and attempts to (unsuccessfully) verify that it is not his own before surrendering the evidence to the crime lab.

Although Yoshioka appears to have no conscious memory of committing these crimes, his actions nevertheless suggest that there may very well be grounds to doubt his claims of innocence, as if there is something that has been repressed—his doppelgänger perhaps—on which basis he nevertheless acts. That in the course of his investigations, he is persistently haunted by the ghost of a woman in a red dress accusing him of killing her only further raises suspicions. Every encounter between them triggers a return of the repressed in the form of a sequence of momentary mixed-up flashbacks that show Yoshioka drowning the woman in red, followed by a shot of what is later revealed to be the ruins of a prewar mental institution visible from a bayside ferry that Yoshioka regularly used in his commutes in the past.

Suggested in the serial killer plot is the implication of the detective in the crimes he investigates not only because each subsequent killing is a marker of the detective's failure to apprehend the criminal, but also because the detective must follow the killer's movements and motivations. He must, in other words, get into the criminal's mind and become his double. In this sense, the doppelgänger's confusion of self and other can be understood as a motif that literalizes this logic of the serial killer plot. But while the suggestion that Yoshioka has a secret double life is the

Yoshioka has a momentary recollection of killing the woman in red. From *Retribution*.

most obvious manifestation of the doppelgänger motif in Kurosawa's film, it is by no means the motif's only manifestation. Whereas Yoshioka's doppelgänger hints at the confusion of the positions of detective and criminal, another set of doublings collapses the distinction between victim and murderer. Following from his previous film *Cure*, Kurosawa makes use of not only a serial killer plot in *Retribution*, but more precisely, a nearly identical story of a series of killings without an obvious agent, without an immediately identifiable singular serial killer. *Cure* follows the story of a police detective in his investigation of a series of murders that on the surface appear to be perpetrated by unrelated individuals yet nevertheless oddly share similar characteristics, specifically an identical x-shaped pattern of wounding. It is then subsequently revealed that each one of the murders took place in the wake of an encounter with an amnesiac hypnotist who seemingly unearths murderous desires in those he meets. Similarly, in *Retribution*, seemingly unrelated individuals commit each of the murders that take place. The murder of the woman in red is followed by the death of the delinquent son of a doctor at the hands of his father, and then a young man by his lover after he informs her of his intention to leave his wife and marry her. What links this series of murders together is only one thing: the common act of drowning the victim in saltwater, a point that is dramatized when the third killer goes so far as to collect a large amount of saltwater for the purpose of drowning her victim in a bathtub.

What these two films share is their engagement with how the notion of crime is articulated—what crimes are representable and unrepresentable—in detective narratives. In connection with this, Hasumi Shigehiko has noted that within the milieu of Kurosawa's films (and particularly in the case of *Cure*), there is nothing out of the ordinary in the act of murder. In Hasumi's words: "No one bothers to make any effort to prove their innocence. Most gestures lack motive, and this is because not even murder is conceived of as a crime . . . indeed, with Kurosawa Kiyoshi, murder is an everyday occurrence."[26] The point here is not that murderers are able to act without being apprehended in Kurosawa's films. In fact, in both *Cure* and *Retribution*, apprehending them happens all too easily. Nevertheless, even when they are caught, their crimes remain illegible precisely they are unable to ascribe credible motives to their actions. In effect,

Kurosawa locates the problem of crime not in the individual killings, but elsewhere, in the larger social relations constitutive of them. I have discussed previously Franco Moretti's argument that individuation—that is, the fixing of a singular *individual* identity to the criminal, so as to absolve the social body at large of guilt—is one of the key social functions that underpins the narrative conventions of the detective genre.[27] Through the various forms of doublings that collapse distinctions between self and other—be it in terms of detective/criminal or victim/murderer— Kurosawa effectively refuses to individuate his killers and render them as embodiments of a monstrous otherness to be ostracized. Doubling and repetition appear as the excess to the ideological imperative in the detective genre to produce a singular scapegoat, to perform the othering of guilt so as to produce a fantasy of absolution for the larger social body. Instead, Kurosawa recognizes that the capability to murder is in everyone (albeit possibly repressed). In this sense, Kurosawa's films attempt to articulate that which exceeds representability within the detective genre. In so doing, they speak to the "the featureless, deindividualized crime that anyone could have committed because at this point everyone is the same," the perfect crime of capitalism that is unrepresentable in detective fiction wherein violence is not the exception but is instead built right into its very order.[28]

In this respect, Kurosawa's films perform a critique that is parallel to Žižek's emphasis on the distinction between "subjective violence" and "objective violence." Whereas subjective violence refers to the forms of visible violence with easily identifiable agents, objective violence names the violence that structurally underpins the proper functioning of the socioeconomic order. Both forms are of course crucial to address. But, Žižek rightly criticizes the inordinate amount of discursive attention that subjective violence receives. The tendency to focus on the subjective mode of violence is problematic because it is presupposed on reading acts of violence as exceptions, in effect positing a nonviolent baseline in which these acts take place. In Žižek's words: "Subjective violence is experienced as such against the background of a non-violent zero level. It is seen as a perturbation of the 'normal,' peaceful state of things. However, objective violence is invisible since it sustains the very zero-level standard against which we perceive something as subjectively violent."[29]

In alignment with Žižek's argument, both *Cure* and *Retribution* highlight how even the everyday—indeed even the simple act of viewing these films themselves—is very much embedded within a structure of violence. The closing scene of *Cure*—with the film's detective protagonist sitting alone inside a cafe—offers a powerful evocation of this idea. Taken on its own, this closing sequence appears to be nothing out of the ordinary. Yet, as Abe observes, the film's closing scene takes on a more ominous quality when it is juxtaposed to the preceding scenes, which consist of the protagonist killing the amnesiac hypnotist who has been at the heart of the various murders throughout the film. There are hints (a brief shot of his wife's body, or a shot of a waitress in the cafe picking up a knife) that through this act, the protagonist has acquired the ability to mesmerize others himself and activate whatever murderous tendencies are in them, with the consequence of turning what on its face is a seemingly innocent scene of everyday life into something with undertones of horror.[30]

Moreover, this horror is made to exceed the boundaries of the film itself, for in *Cure*, the mesmerism that provokes the return of the repressed and their attendant acts of murder is performed by the hypnotist through the flickering of the flame of his cigarette lighter in the darkness or the reflection of light on dripping water. In other words, it is through a play on lights and reflections—the very same interplay at work in the cinematography of the film itself—that murderous desires are activated, with the consequence that the spectator is compelled to wonder if he or she too has been the victim of the same mesmerism. In this sense, for Abe, "beyond merely making horror the subject of representation, Kurosawa renders film itself into an object of horror."[31] A similar observation can certainly be made of *Retribution*. Tellingly, scenes throughout the film are shot with an eye toward placing figures in a dark, shadowy foreground against a brightly lit background, with the effect of drawing attention and significance not to the characters in the center of the frame but to the surrounding structure that envelops them. This is given further emphasis by a key scene midway through the film, namely the interrogation of the second suspect, the doctor who killed his son. In this scene, while the doctor confesses to his son's murder readily, the interrogation continues as Yoshioka attempts to press him—without any success—to admit involvement in the earlier killing of the woman in red. Midway through the interrogation, however, the doctor begins to wander about the room, finally cowering in fear at something he and only he is apparently seeing. Most interesting in this scene is not the haunting itself, though. Rather, it is the direction of the man's gaze at this unseen presence. His eyes are turned outward, toward a space just outside the mise-en-scène, toward the frame of the shot itself; it is the film's very form itself that causes him distress.

Considering the substantial overlaps in the plot points and narrative techniques of *Cure* and *Retribution*, it would appear apt to read the latter film as an intertextual continuation of the former's staging of repetition as the engine for its narrative and critical drive. In fact, in certain respects, plot points from *Retribution* make it appear an informal sequel to *Cure*. Not only are their respective protagonists both homicide detectives played by Kurosawa's frequent lead Yakusho Kōji, but also, while *Cure* ends with the protagonist taking on the powers of mesmerism and killing his mentally ill wife, *Retribution* begins by implying that its protagonist is the serial killer they seek (although this is proved to be a red herring later on). That said, there is an important point of difference between the two films in terms of the affective responses they generate. Whereas

As Yoshioka interrogates a suspect *(right)*, he trembles in fear at an unseen presence beyond the frame of the film. From *Retribution*.

the scenes of violence and the hypnotist's repeated utterance of the question "Who are you?" to his victims in *Cure* generate genuine terror, the analogous scenes in *Retribution* border on the ridiculous; whereas *Cure* plays things straight, *Retribution* almost appears like a subtle parody of its predecessor.

There are several instances in the film when this performance of parodic excess becomes particularly salient. One example is Yoshioka's own actions within the story. Seemingly anticipating the possibility of a jaded spectator's response upon seeing the same familiar plot devices replayed, even Yoshioka himself seems to lose interest in the initial driving force of the narrative—the investigation of the murders, with the consequence of derailing the initial trajectory of the film's narrative and generic setup. As hints of his doppelgänger begin to manifest, his attention is focused less on attending to the evidence or following up leads and more on the dilemmas of his unconscious. When he does happen to locate suspects, it is largely by accident. The doctor who murdered his son is coincidentally found loitering around the Tokyo waterfront, and a rather contrived random encounter on the street is what leads Yoshioka to the young woman who killed her lover. In the latter case, Yoshioka is not even present at the crime scene when it is first investigated, further aggravating any suspicions about him.

This derailment of the narrative of the film only becomes worse with the appearance of the ghost of the woman in red. A defining characteristic of the ghost in *Retribution* is that she is not all that frightening. Rather, as the story unfolds, her appearances become increasingly more absurd, culminating in a ridiculous—if not outright comedic—moment when she takes flight and hops over the city streets. Even the responses to her by other characters within the film are not reducible to fear. In Yoshioka's case, despite his initial terror when she first appears, subsequent encounters between them might be better described as annoyance or frustration as he tries to argue with her and attempt in vain to convince her that he had nothing to do with her murder. Put simply, it is difficult to see the woman in red as anything else but a parody of the figure of the vengeful ghost. One way to understand her comedic character is to consider her appearances in the film in terms of the problem of visibility. To clarify, it is worth turning to Nakano Yasushi's analysis of the early discourse surrounding J-Horror. At the time when J-Horror began to be articulated as a coherent genre in the 1990s, one of the important points of discussion in its early days was the issue of the ghost-figure's visibility. In the commentary surrounding Nakata Hideo's film *Joyūrei* (*Ghost Actress*, 1996), there was much criticism of how the overvisibility [*misesugi*] of the ghost rendered her less frightening. In response, a technique that emerged in subsequent J-Horror films—Nakata's film *Ring* is a case in point—was to present the ghost-figure only obliquely, typically by obscuring their faces or restricting their actual appearance to momentary scenes and sequences.[32] In contrast, not only does the ghost appear constantly through the duration of the *Retribution*, but also, in her appearances, her face is made quite visible to spectators. For instance, her first appearance on-screen has her approaching the camera in silence, eventually ending with a close-up shot of her face. More fundamentally, she also embodies an overvisibility to the ghost on an intertextual level as well. Because of the motif's ubiquity and regular repetition in countless J-Horror titles, it has effectively become a stale and discredited plot device.

In sum, the central figure that identifies it with the horror genre—the stereotypical avenging ghost (of the woman in red)—is ultimately not all that frightening but is instead rather absurd or ridiculous. But if the ghost of the woman in red does not provoke terror, then it strikes me as

The ghost of the woman in red, her face in clear view. From *Retribution*.

more productive to work out what function she otherwise serves. My contention is that she paradoxically embodies the critical potential of the horror genre precisely because she is an absurd figure, precisely because she is not frightening.

Time Out of Joint

Kurosawa has written that what distinguishes horror cinema from other genres that deploy images of ghosts, monsters, or other supernatural beings is that the terror horror provokes cannot easily be dismissed or overcome through the mere closure of the narrative; nor is it something that can easily be made coherent through explanation. Rather, horror deals with an experience of fear that persists, that produces an interruption that radically transforms one's life from that moment on. Yet, as Kurosawa points out, because all cinema bears within it precisely this transformative potential, then the logical conclusion to be drawn is that all cinema is horror cinema. In an interesting performative move, Kurosawa effectively makes the point that if horror is based on the production of fear or affect that exceeds interpretation and narration, then the very act of attempting to draw boundaries around the genre of horror and reduce fear to something that can be categorized and demarcated itself inevitably meets its own constitutive excesses and immanent contradictions.[33]

It is precisely this sense of persistence and excessiveness that characterizes the ghost of the woman in red in *Retribution*, both at the level of the film's story as well as that of the discursive formation of the horror genre itself. One impact of the ghost's turn toward the absurd in *Retribution* is to produce contradictory responses in the spectator. Throughout the film, there is a persistent tension between the provocation of shock and the production of laughter. Whether or not she is meant to be taken seriously is left ambiguous and ultimately undecidable; consequently, she undermines any attempt to view her as something legible through the lens of predetermined generic categories. If indeed the critical potential of the ghost lies in resistance to exorcism by simple categorical explanation (as Kurosawa defines the horror genre), then even as she fails to be frightening at the level of the story, the woman in red nonetheless functions as a specter on a metacinematic level by virtue of her refusal to be rendered docile by the disabling and homogenizing of horror's affective possibility through the mechanisms of generic familiarity. Put another way, the ghost of the woman in red is more horrific precisely because she is not horrific.

In this respect, the ghost of the woman in red plays a role that is comparable to the doppelgänger's in that she foregrounds the boundaries of a given set of generic structures by pushing against the limits of its narrative logic. Indeed, one might go so far as to assert, as Kume Yoriko does, that the ghost of the woman in red is not just a kind of doppelgänger, but the embodiment of the doppelgänger as such. In Kume's argument, taking into account the fact that the ghost is figured as a woman, and moreover, a "madwoman," such that she is made to embody that which must be repressed to produce the subject of modernity—the feminine and the irrational—"it is possible to regard her as the doppelgänger of 'humanity' as a whole" [*"jinrui" zentai no dopperugengā toshite minasu koto ga kanō*].[34] Or as I would prefer to put it, insofar as she returns from out of time and refuses to be domesticated, she might be understood as embodying a doppelgänger of history as such. She is, to put it differently, the modern history's other personified, incorporated into the constitution of its logic precisely through her exclusion and her repression.

Indeed, at the heart of her demand for justice is not merely the response to a violence that took place in the past that has since been repressed, but the violence of the structure of repression itself, or alternatively, the condition that structurally makes the production of repression necessary. In other words, the ghost does more than just embody a reminder of the traces of remnants of the past in the present; she moreover renders visible the violence in the very demarcation of past and present. This is revealed in the film when her haunting of Yoshioka proves to be more persistent than expected. Even when suspects for each of the murders are apprehended, she refuses to be quieted and the story does not end, thus challenging attempts to ascribe a causal narrative logic to her haunting. The early hints that Yoshioka himself or his double is the perpetrator of the killings in fact turns out to be a red herring. When the Tokyo police are finally able to identify the first victim as a woman named Shibata Reiko, they are quickly able to apprehend a suspect (her ex-boyfriend), who is not only found with incriminating evidence, but also immediately confesses to the crime. Yet despite this arrest and seeming closure of the mystery, the result is not, as one might expect, to absolve Yoshioka of guilt. On the contrary, he is only further implicated in a larger crime. Yoshioka eventually realizes that the ghost is someone else altogether, someone from a memory long since repressed: a woman he once glimpsed behind the window of an abandoned mental institution by the Tokyo waterfront, who subsequently reveals to Yoshioka her fate since that moment of their first encounter: "I stayed there for years and years, waiting and waiting, forgotten by everyone. Then I died," she tells him.

Yoshioka's repeated encounters with the woman in red make it evident that the crime for which she seeks retribution is not the first murder from the opening scenes of the film. She haunts Yoshioka because he too looked and saw her silhouette through the windows of the abandoned mental institution in which she was imprisoned yet turned away and did nothing. Not surprisingly then, it is not only Yoshioka whom the woman in red haunts. Rather it is everyone who has managed to catch a glimpse of her through the windows of the abandoned mental institution, including (but apparently not limited to) each one of the perpetrators of the individual murders. It is her appearance that provokes the return of the repressed, the activation of a murderous impulse, in those she haunts, entangling their desires with her own and consequently provoking them to murder.

It is precisely in terms of this resistance to being temporally domesticated, to being rendered as dead and completed, that Jacques Derrida articulates his conception of the specter. Writing at the same moment of Japan's so-called "horror boom" in the aftermath of the end of the Cold War, following the collapse of the Soviet bloc, Derrida evokes the temporality of the specter against the pronouncements of "the end of history" made by such individuals as Fukuyama, which in essence declare the victory of capitalist modernity over any other social or material arrangement. Derrida's conception of the specter is particularly relevant in the case of *Retribution* in part because for Derrida, the specter's primary preoccupation is precisely repetition: "A question of repetition: a specter is always a *revenant*. One cannot control its comings and goings because it *begins by coming back*."[35] In placing emphasis on this point, Derrida ties the ontology of the specter to the problem of the temporal (and by implication, the historical). Just as the specter oscillates between (and in effect, deconstructs) such categories as presence and absence, life and death, and so forth, so too does it relate to temporal positions. To put it another way, the specter's appearance marks not merely a return of a past that can then be assimilated into a familiar continuity, but a radical alterity that resists easy temporalization, with the effect of calling into question the presumed stability of the present. This ultimately produces a sense that, in Derrida's quotation from Shakespeare's *Hamlet*, "time is out of joint": "A spectral moment, a moment that no longer belongs to time, if one understands by these words the linking of modalized presents (past present, actual present: 'now,' future present). We are questioning in this instant, we are asking ourselves about this instant that is not docile to time, at least to what we call time."[36]

No doubt, time is out of joint in *Retribution*. Formally, this is given particular emphasis through the ragged temporality produced by the sudden and jarring cuts that break apart the often long takes of the film's scenes, with the effect of baring the mechanism of film's illusory transparency constructed through its editing together into a continuous movement of shots that were in all likelihood taken at disparate places and times. Notably, an early scene in the film foreshadows this question of disjointed time even before the ghost makes her appearance in what might at first be dismissed as a throwaway line in a conversation between the protagonist and a woman named Harue who appears to be his intimate partner. Referencing an earthquake from an earlier scene—which itself hints at the tenuous stability of the foundations of the filmic spacetime—they discuss recent construction at the waterfront visible from the window of Yoshioka's apartment. Both note how they are no longer able to recall what stood on the land prior to the new construction, with Yoshioka further adding the comment that as a consequence of all the land reclamation, construction, and tearing down of structures, he would probably no longer know where any of the locations he used to see when he was still commuting by waterfront ferry from the nearby city of Kawasaki to Tokyo were. This constant (re)construction taking place at the waterfront is not, however, viewed as a sign of progress or development. On the contrary, to the characters in the film, it is seen as more indicative of the failure of progress, suggesting a sense of a lack of future, with the two declaring the future "a big disappointment." Their world can be characterized by, in other words, the compulsion to repeat the constant sameness produced by endless differentiation that is arguably the prime feature of the lived experience of capitalist modernization. Consequently, when the ghost of the woman in red emerges out of a crack in the walls of Yoshioka's apartment in one of the scenes of their encounters, the film literalizes her appearance from out of time, from out of the history of modernization itself.

Taking up Derrida's notion of the specter, Bliss Cua Lim reads ghost films in the postcolonial milieu as historical allegories that "make incongruous use of the vocabulary of the supernatural to articulate historical injustice, referring to 'social reality' by recourse to the undead."[37] In Lim's analysis, the temporality of colonial modernity rests on the underlying logic of a foundational or constitutive schism located on a temporal axis. The condition of possibility for modern historical time itself is a structure of exclusion; the "premodern" (or the "precapitalist") had to be overcome and repressed and rendered docile by locating it as chronologically prior to "the modern" or "the capitalist." The ghost then represents an interruption in the order of linear time imposed by the regime of modernity, such that the historical injustice at stake in its appearance is not

The ghost of the woman in red crawls through the cracks of Yoshioka's apartment. From *Retribution*.

only a matter of violence that took place in the historical past, but the violence (symbolic or otherwise) of modern historicism, of the temporality of capitalist modernity itself.

Up to a point, aspects of Lim's analysis certainly find resonance in Kurosawa's *Retribution*. I already noted above how the appearance of the ghost of the woman in red interrupts the normal and expected unfolding of narrative within the strictures of its genre in a move that can be understood as a gesture toward a disruption in the normal operation of modern historical time. However, reading the figure of the ghost (or for that matter, the doppelgänger) in terms of historical allegory presents a number of problems. Unlike the Hong Kong and Philippine contexts of the films Lim takes up, Japan was not formally colonized but was itself a colonial empire. I note this not simply to assert exceptional status to Japan. Rather, my point is that accounting for the historical specificity of Japan here is illustrative of potential pitfalls in reading the figure of the ghost as a historical allegory. If one ascribes to the figure of the ghost a role of appearing *from out of time* to disturb the historical present, then how does this differ from a naïve valorization of national allegories that set up a polarity between colonial history on the one hand and an ahistorical conception of a national culture, as if the latter were not already worked over and retroactively constituted in capitalism and colonialism?[38] This is a danger that is particularly salient when considering the context of Japan because such an appeal to an authentic cultural base outside of history was not only a key rhetorical gesture in the ideological articulation of Japanese fascism in the 1930s, but also a move seen in recent nationalist discourse in Japan that seeks precisely to disavow its history as a colonial empire.

Any mention of issues of historical repetition and return in the context of contemporary Japan cannot help but at once invoke the resurgence of nationalism in Japan since the end of the Cold War. The striking thing about this return of reactionary nationalisms is how these discourses often make use of the language of postcoloniality to return to the site of the postwar occupation as a means of representing Japan as a culturally colonized nation. Japan's defeat in the Second World War and the subsequent American occupation become alibis to assert a lack of an authentic ground upon which a national subjectivity may be constituted. However, as Harry Harootunian correctly points out, not only does this rhetoric reinscribe a victim logic that functions to disavow the history of Japan's history as colonizer, but ironically, it is a discourse underpinned by a problematic dichotomy between a notion of native culture and foreign capitalist modernity that in fact repeats the tropes of earlier prewar nationalisms.[39] This nationalist discourse therefore tends to misrecognize a uniquely Japanese cultural crisis in place of what is properly a broader structural crisis, with "the West" becoming a stand-in for capitalism, hence enabling its exteriorization from an essentialized conception of culture to which it is placed into opposition.[40]

Yet, all too often, the critical commentary vis-à-vis J-Horror rehearses precisely these premises. Consider for example the work of Jay McRoy on contemporary Japanese horror cinema. McRoy's stated objective in his study of Japanese horror titled *Nightmare Japan* is to read and situate Japanese horror within an "expansive socio-cultural analysis" of contemporary Japan.[41] However, the socio-cultural picture of Japan he paints is far too overly expansive and sweeping. Much of what he highlights in his analysis—fears of social change or critiques of the patriarchal structures— are not new themes in much of the existing commentary and discourse surrounding Japanese culture through the decades. His analysis tends to rely on a tired West/Japan binary as its starting point with the effect of implicitly reifying an ahistorical notion of "Japan" or "Japanese culture." For example, in itself McRoy's reading of ghost films such as Nakata Hideo's *Ring* as or Shimizu Takashi's *The Grudge* as "key texts for mapping crucial socio-cultural anxieties" in terms of the impact of late capitalism on the formation of the Japanese family seems fair enough.[42] But his analysis of the transformations of familial configurations in Japan reduces them to a simple question of Western (and specifically American) impact and influence, without much articulation of the social reproductive function within capitalism. Not only does this move uncritically repeat discredited narratives of modernization; moreover, it unwittingly reproduces a problematic cultural politics that conflates capitalism with the West. In this respect, even if the manifest politics they espouse differ, it seems nonetheless that the latent premises of McRoy's analysis shares much with the desire to demarcate the domain of the political-economic and the cultural—and with it, reenacts the same elision of history in the Japanese nationalist discourse of recent years.

This is not unconnected to another problem in McRoy's examination of Japanese horror cinema: the lack of specificity in the treatment of the genre named "Japanese horror cinema." If it is indeed the case that the horror genre occupies a vital place in Japanese cinema, then why is it only since the 1990s that it has become an object of fascinated attention in film discourse both globally and within Japan? Recent scholarly work on contemporary Japanese horror correctly emphasize how regimes of flexible accumulation and processes of globalization operate as key conditions that have determined the emergence of the genre that has come to be called "J-Horror" since the 1990s. For example, Mitsuyo Wada-Marciano rightly points out that the very naming of "Japanese horror cinema" or "J-horror" as a genre with any semblance of coherence has a historical specificity predicated upon shifts in the transnational flows of capital and culture. Thematically, new media technologies—for example, the unlabeled videotape of Nakata's *Ring*, the cameras and other technologies of surveillance and archiving in Shimizu's *Marebito* (2004), or the haunted websites of Kurosawa's *Pulse*—are objects productive of terror in much contemporary Japanese horror. More importantly, it is a genre whose explosion onto the global film market is underpinned by these same technologies—in particular the DVD and other forms of digital distribution—and the practices of production and circulation they facilitate.[43] Thus, contrary to any claims as to their supposed cultural particularity, the genre of "J-Horror" from the outset already imbricates the production and commodification of nationality through the circulation of images.

The global impact of Japanese horror cinema is difficult to overstate. For one thing, it led to the development of similar booms in horror filmmaking elsewhere in East Asia. For another, it also called forth a wave of Hollywood remakes of horror films from Japan and the rest of East Asia, with remakes of Nakata's and Shimizu's respective films *Ring* and *The Grudge* perhaps the most prominent examples. However, an interesting consequence of these twinned developments is the emergence of a tendency to read horror films from Japan or the rest of East Asia largely in terms of national or cultural specificity. On the one hand, transnational fan cultures began forming around horror cinema specifically from East Asia under the premise that it offered a counterpoint to the stale offerings from Hollywood. These cinephilic communities thus organized themselves around cultural objects valued precisely for their perceived aesthetic and cultural difference vis-à-vis the commercial hegemony of Hollywood cinema. The subsequent appearance of various Hollywood remakes of these films only fueled the fetishizing drive. Cult commentary and critical discourse typically viewed Hollywood's remakes with suspicion, seeing them largely as commercial attempts to cash in on the cultural phenomenon while at once effacing the perceived cultural authenticity that made the original films desirable in the first place. What these discourses perform is the effective racialization of the horror genre that effectively renders a specifically Asian horror (or, as the case may be, Japanese horror) a separate genre onto its own.

Indeed, McRoy's elision of historical specificity is made most evident when he repeatedly references a national "cinematic tradition" as if "Japanese horror" (with a distinct emphasis on *Japanese*) is a coherent and stable genre that can be distilled into a transhistorical essence. Telling, for instance, is his attempt to draw an unbroken line of continuity between the appearance of the figure of the "avenging spirit" in contemporary Japanese horror cinema and traditional "Japanese literary and dramatic arts," referencing specifically the *kaidan* and *shuramono*—the genre of supernatural plays in Kabuki theater and ghost plays in Nō theater, respectively.[44] Likewise, his coverage of films spans everything from the contemporary work of Nakata Hideo and Shimizu Takashi to pink films to even the films of Iwai Shunji. What such an expansive approach to the genre does, in Wada-Marciano's argument, is to wrench the specific films from the specific material conditions of their production and spectatorship, with the consequence that films that were not classified as horror at their moment of production retroactively come to categorized as such.[45] Indeed, considering its expansiveness, it seems to not be much of a stretch from here to grasp that, under this broad category of horror that McRoy deploys, practically any film may be considered; it is almost as if the specific genre of "Japanese horror cinema" has come to stand in for a national "Japanese cinema" as such. The consequences of this are twofold: first, it reduces all manner of different texts from different historical conjunctures into predetermined national-cultural allegories; second, viewed in conjunction with an understanding of horror as a genre that is especially attentive to alterity, the conflation of Japanese horror cinema with Japanese cinema as such hints at a positioning of "Japan" as essentially other.

This is not an isolated issue. One cannot help but recall here the criticism raised against the othering gaze employed in Jameson's assertion that "all third-world texts are necessarily . . . allegorical" that brings to attention how potentially charged the question of "national allegory" can become.[46] In the aftermath of these discussions of national allegories, the crucial consideration that needs to be taken into account is that the position of the critic performing an allegorical interpretation cannot be seen as external to the object of interpretation; rather, it is enabled precisely by the global circulation of images as commodities and the immaterial labor of their production and consumption. Shu-Mei Shih puts it well when she identifies that the problem at hand is "the politics of allegorical interpretation as value-producing labor—who has the privilege of doing it, who is forced to do it, who has the luxury not to do it."[47] Or to put it in the specific terms discussed above, it may be pertinent to pose the question: Who is compelled to produce horror, to produce ghosts for allegorical consumption? And for whom are these national-historical allegories produced?

Conclusion

Every genre film—whether enacted consciously or unconsciously—necessarily stages a repetition. Consequently, the deployment of repetition as a mode of social or political critique demands a recognition of the potential for any strategic deployment of the technique of repetition to give way to a formulaic repetition that simply rehearses these techniques but without their critical charge or potential to disturb familiar habits of thought. This raises certain questions: If one of the functions of the ghost's repetitive temporality is to call into question the understanding of history as organized around a notion of homogenous time and linear progression, then how does this square with the formulaic repetition that underpins the logic of generic reproduction? How effective can the ghost's performance of returns and repetitions be as a form of social critique if these repetitions are already inscribed in advance as the very basis of the mass-production and marketing of spectacles and image-commodities like horror cinema?

In *The Cinematic Mode of Production*, Jonathan Beller compellingly argues that cinema and the social practices and relations it constitutes are "deterritorialized factories in which spectators work, that is, in which we perform value-productive labor."[48] At the heart of Beller's claim is that especially since the inauguration of late capitalism, the logic of capitalist expansion and accumulation has been increasingly organized around the cinematic apparatus such that to look is to labor. Cinematic spectatorship effectively functions as an extension of the working day, wherein not only is value extracted from the spectator's attention, but more importantly the very logic of capitalist social relations is reproduced. Kurosawa's *Retribution* effectively places the consequences of these conditions into relief. It is worth recalling that the crime for which the woman in red seeks retribution is precisely the crime of looking, of seeing her abandoned yet doing nothing. Her haunting thus appears to hint at the complicity of the film spectator in the reproduction of the general logic of violence—the attendant exploitations and dispossessions both material and symbolic—built into capitalist social relations through the very desire to see and hence participate in the production and circulation of this violence as image-commodities.

If Beller is correct in his claim that cinema has become "the formal paradigm and structural template for social organization generally,"[49] then given that capitalism is sustained by an incessant uneven development, the problem of spectatorship compels the consideration of the unevenness of scopic regimes and the labor of looking. Indeed, as a ghost, the woman in red is the metaphor of the spectralization that characterizes the process wherein corporeal bodies are turned into image-commodities for global circulation as spectacles made literal. Further to this, in her position as the doppelgänger of history—as the disavowed revenant for the violence constitutive of the material conditions of the present—she highlights how this process of spectralization does not take place on an even terrain. Be it in terms of gender, nation, or another form of segmentation, some are more readily spectralized and subjected to becoming image-commodities for the visual pleasure of the spectator than others. More important, Kurosawa's film refuses to back away from confronting the ramifications of this. Although at the end of the film, Yoshioka is able to free himself from the wrath of the woman in red such that only he remains alive in the midst of the apocalyptic depopulation of Tokyo, this is not at all presented on a positive note. Indeed, Yoshioka expresses that he would rather not be forgiven, not be absolved of responsibility. This gestures toward a refusal of a politics of individual absolution from one's complicity in structural violence. It suggests that an individual struggle to absolve oneself of participation in processes of image-commodification at the expense of those already spectralized is insufficient. Rather, what is called for is a collective strategy of refusal that must be accountable to those who are already ghosts and as such must struggle as images. The woman in red's repeated utterance of the words "I died, so everyone else should die, too," which may very well be understood as an invocation to become ghosts addressed not only to the characters in the film, but also to the film's spectators, certainly points in this direction.[50]

Beyond this, the act of spectatorship constitutes desires, affects, and subjectivities in the service of the social relations necessary for the reproduction of capitalist modernity. The industrial production of images in the cinematic apparatus extends the logics of capitalism and colonialism, effecting first a systematic production of the imaginary for the subject, and then subsequently making the imaginary in itself productive for capital. In other words, through the labor of looking, there is also a structuring and ordering of the imaginary—what Neferti Tadiar calls "fantasy-production"—that operates.[51] It is thus also critical to recognize that "globalization" names not only a set of material and technological transformations but also an ideological force that governs the horizon of politics in the present conjuncture. Eric Cazdyn and Imre Szeman succinctly make this point with the words "globalization rested on a more fundamental ideological project, one unrecognized at the time of its constitution, even though it was essential to its effective operation. Globalization involves a certain configuration of time—one that cannot imagine an 'after.'"[52] Globalization thus marks a historical conjuncture wherein capitalism has functionally become the absolute limit to thought itself such that the very term "globalization" rendered capitalism invisible or natural, in effect precluding discussions of its own end. For Cazdyn and Szeman then, the critical challenge in the task of apprehending globalization is to go beyond its description and instead attempt to push against the limits of existing frames of knowledge through which one under-stands the problems of the present conjuncture. This returns my discus-sion to Jameson's observation of repeated fantasies of the apocalypse as symptomatic of an "increasing inability to imagine a different future," that is, a future which is a radical alternative to the structures and logics of capitalist modernity; a future that has not been colonized by (and in effect rendered docile to) the terms of the present, reduced to merely its extension.[53]

Throughout my study of the doppelgänger, a key concern has been the search for a critical practice of looking that does not simply end up in a performative contradiction that fixes the figure of the double without accounting for the contradictions it lays bare, and with this, the transfor-mative potential it might present. Insofar as the figure of the doppelgänger embodies a play on the positions of identity and difference, of subject and object, such a practice has been demanded by the object of the study itself. But if my discussion has been any indication, then this is no doubt a prob-lem that goes beyond just the analysis of the doppelgänger. While it would be overreaching to assert that it offers an answer to the problem, in its interruption of the ascribed narrative trajectories that generic categories impose, the critical force of the doppelgänger might very well be located in its potential for disclosing a desire to interrupt—to open up to critique—the limits and contradictions of the disciplinary operations and fantasy-productions that structure what can be imagined, what can be dreamed at the historically specific conjunctures. The doppelgänger's appearances in the work of various Japanese authors and filmmakers—Edogawa Rampo, Akutagawa Ryūnosuke, Tanizaki Jun'ichirō, and others—illustrate that the structuring of the imaginary is very much a crucial site of struggle.

The work of Kurosawa Kiyoshi is no exception. In this chapter, I have emphasized how the figure of the ghost in *Retribution* marks a subversion of the workings of genre. On one level, her appearance leads to the de-railment of the film's initial narrative trajectory such that the serial killer plot with which the film begins is abandoned. On another level, her fig-ure is also absurd, which has the consequence that she exceeds attempts to contain her within an interpretative frame based on the logic of horror film motifs and conventions. In this respect, the ghost of the woman in red arguably operates in tandem with Kurosawa's usual preferred formal aesthetics, which is typically dominated by long shots often obscured by screens, windows, or other obstacles, and long takes broken apart by sudden and jarring cuts that Aaron Gerow terms a "detached style." In Gerow's analysis, the impetus behind this detached style is a critical stance based on the rejection of the primacy of narrative clarity. Instead, in this style, there is a refusal to direct the spectator's gaze through edits or point-of-view shots in an effort to practice a mode of looking that can approach the image of the other without imposing a predetermined interpretation.[54] Following Gerow's suggestion that an important facet of the politics of Kurosawa's filmmaking is the representation of the other without the imposition of interpretations or a recourse to tired tropes determined in advance, I wonder if this move is something that can be extended to temporal alterities as well. Might Kurosawa's critical engagement with generic boundaries and resistance to being reduced to preformed allegorical interpretations hint at a desire to encounter the other from a future yet to be colonized by the present, yet to be imaginable or articulable in language beyond the primal, disembodied scream of the woman in red, as the film's titular *sakebi* [scream]?

In this sense, Kurosawa's films are illustrative of how the problem of genre goes beyond just textual categories. Rather, genre implicates all manner of classifications and categorizations that set the limits to the imagination and articulation of forms of knowledge production, narrative of history, or potentials for critical intervention. As Derrida has remarked, "The question of the literary genre is not a formal one: it covers the motif of the law in general, of generation in the natural and symbolic senses."[55] If it is true that on the one hand the detective does his or her work under the conditions of a temporal lag, and on the other hand detective work can be thought to parallel spectatorial work, then it seems possible to consider that it is through the mechanism of fantasy-production that this lag manifests in the latter. Just as detective work is limited by the rules and conventions of the genre in which it operates, so too is the spectator's (and critic's) imagination. Like narratives plugged into the formulaic conventions of ossified literary genres, novel phenomena tend to be understood using older concepts and categories that are insufficient to account for precisely their novelty. Indeed, the revived insistence on the category of the nation as a means of domesticating the complexity of the present moment is a symptomatic example.[56] After all, as a structuring force on the imagination, as a mechanism through which desire can be manipulated and regulated, might not "the nation," along with all manner of other categories of analysis, be understood in terms of genre?

Relevant here is my previous discussion of the historicity of the doppelgänger's conceptualization within psychoanalytic discourse. One implication that can be drawn from the doppelgänger's figuration of traumatic repetition is that if the very condition of possibility for conceiving of the traumatic constitution of subjectivity is predicated on the colonial violence that is constitutive of modernity, then implicated in the experience of trauma is also a broader "historical trauma," wherein, as Kaja Silverman has characterized it, the narratives of "dominant fictions" come to be undone. The challenge here, then, is to cultivate the doppelgänger's embodiment of excess, its enactment of traumatic repetition with the capacity to threaten to "undo our imaginary relation to the symbolic order, as well as the other elements within the social formation with which that order is imbricated."[57] Yet in suggesting this, am I not simply offering up my own allegorical imposition onto Kurosawa's films and by extension, the figure of the doppelgänger? By bringing this sustained critical attention to his films and attempting to render the images it presents coherent and legible, am I not writing a language onto the ambiguity of the woman in red's scream, against Kurosawa's critical challenge to language and interpretation itself? Insofar as any act of viewing or interpretation is necessarily mediated by established repositories of signs and metaphors that shape the horizons of meaning production within given historical conjunctures, then this is undoubtedly the case. After all, if indeed the problem of genre is about more than merely the fixing of classifications to literary or cinematic forms but are instead historically situated discursive processes that mediate how one encounters a given narrative, then by no means can I exclude my own practice of viewing from these operations.

Double Visions, Double Fictions began with the argument that the figure of the doppelgänger is not reducible to just a literary or cinematic motif. More important, it is also a conceptual practice, a prism through which one can refract views of a series of cultural formations structured around a logic of doubling and repetition, be it the relations between

East and West, literature and cinema, or imperialism and globalization, without reducing them to simple oppositions between original and imitation. The doppelgänger is at once a product of these relations, and productive of possibilities for apprehending and understanding them. It thus names a critical practice in the works of film and fiction I have examined, and as such, demands an attentiveness to this potential in my own mode of analysis. For this reason, I have endeavored to not simply offer a singular essential definition to the figure or a catalog of the motif's appearances across the history of Japanese film and fiction, but instead to articulate how the figure, through its enactment of repetition, enables these texts to become sites of critical intervention into the question of what narratives of difference are possible at the very historical conditions in which they appear.

The key approach to the examination of the figure of the doppelgänger that I have taken in this book is to reframe the concept's relationship with the language and discourse of psychoanalysis. Against the established tradition of critical commentary that would largely apprehend the doppelgänger as a rehearsal of psychoanalytic concepts or the representation of psychical schisms, I have elected to locate the conditions of possibility for the figure's imagination within a set of interlocking historical processes and discursive practices. Highlighting how the techniques of psychoanalysis are formally analogous to narrative conventions in the genre of detective fiction brings attention to the historicity of the popularization of these discourses and their concomitant treatments of the doppelgänger within the context of overlapping transformations in the material and libidinal economy marked by rapid urbanization, imperial expansion, and the restructuring of all aspects of everyday life by a burgeoning image-commodity culture in Japan during the 1920s and 1930s. Further to this, accounting for the renewed attention to the figure of the doppelgänger in literary and cinematic texts in the contemporary moment opens a space to consider a historical dimension to the figure's staging of the compulsion to repeat. If the doppelgänger is indeed to be understood as positing a repetition without a fixed origin in its embodiment of a return of the repressed, then the challenge of historicizing must address not only issues of historical repetition in the relationship between Japan's colonial empire and the contemporary conjuncture of globalization and transnationalism, but also the question of cultural criticism in the present vis-à-vis the object of intellectual inquiry, within which my own work here must of course be included.

Thus, if this analysis is to take seriously the doppelgänger's staging of repetition as a technique to undermine familiar frames for interpretation, if it is to articulate a critical practice of looking that does not simply slip into a performative contradiction that would fix an explanation to figure without accounting for the ambiguities and contradictions it foregrounds, then it would seem that the significance of doppelgänger's critical potential should not be located in the points that I have discussed here. Rather, it is precisely in what is missing, in the gaps and slippages of my arguments, in what exceeds the very categories of analysis I deploy. In the end, perhaps it is this recognition that something is missing, this desire for difference, this evocation of something beyond the horizons of our present that is at the heart of the doppelgänger's compulsion to repeat.

ACKNOWLEDGMENTS

The completion of this book would not have been possible without the support and encouragement of many individuals and institutions at various stages of its production. It began its life during my years at the University of Toronto. I am indebted to my dissertation advisor Atsuko Sakaki, whose tireless efforts in guiding me through the process of conceiving, preparing, and refining my work have been invaluable and inspirational. Her always insightful advice and suggestions, not to mention her generosity with her time and unfailing support for my endeavors, went far beyond what any student could ask for. She has truly been a mentor throughout these past years, and my gratitude for all her efforts exceeds the limits of what I can put into words.

While at the University of Toronto, I was also quite fortunate in having the opportunity to work with Eric Cazdyn, whose keen insights and incisive intellect were always generously shared, helping me open up the horizons of my own thought as he continuously encouraged me to push my ideas further, to take intellectual risks, to articulate why any of this matters at all. It is difficult to overstate the profound impact he has had on my own thinking and writing, and for that, I am immensely grateful. Ken Kawashima has also taught me much through the years, always pointing me toward other interesting directions and encouraging me to think things through. I am undoubtedly a better scholar for it. Just as invaluable were the rewarding exchanges, meanderings, and conversations with friends and colleagues in Toronto. Sean Callaghan, Joe Culpepper, Olga Fedorenko, Darcy Gauthier, Nicole Go, Monica Guu, Christina Han, Merose Hwang, Mark McConaghy, Chikako Nagayama, Sara Osenton, Erik Spigel, Wang Jing, and Martin Zeilinger have contributed all manner of ideas, moral support, and ears for some random crazed rant every so often.

Oshino Takeshi was a welcoming host and advisor during my stay in Japan. I thank him especially for his invitation to participate in his graduate seminars and for pushing me to participate in the intellectual community at Hokkaido University, all of which made my stay in Japan as productive as possible. At Hokkaido University, Han Yeonsun, Hanawa Hiroshi, Inoue Kishō, Kawasaki Kōhei, and Ōkawa Takeshi all warmly offered friendship and hospitality, for which I am grateful.

As the external reviewer of my doctoral dissertation, Seiji Lippit offered many sharp observations and comments on my work, many of which articulated the central concerns of my project better than I ever had. His contributions were invaluable for helping me understand just what exactly I was trying to say, especially as I began to seriously think about how to refine and reconceptualize my project for book publication during my postdoctoral fellowship at McGill University, with the support of the Social Sciences and Humanities Research Council of Canada. At McGill, one could not ask for a better mentor than Thomas Lamarre, who provided me with much inspiration and many opportunities. His guidance not only nudged me into articulating the necessary critical engagements with broader issues of theoretical and political concern, but also provided helpful advice for navigating the book proposal and publication process. I must also express my thanks to Ueno Toshiya, Adrienne Hurley, Brian Bergstrom, Yuriko Furuhata, Marc Steinberg, and Livia Monnet for their advice and friendship, making the few years I spent in Montreal both welcoming and stimulating.

Also deserving of immense gratitude are my colleagues at the Department of Asian Languages and Literatures at the University of Minnesota for providing an exceptionally collegial and intellectually stimulating academic home. Christine Marran, Jason McGrath, Travis Workman, Maki Isaka, Paul Rouzer, Joseph Allen, Suvadip Sinha, and Joseph Farag have all been incredible friends and supportive colleagues. Much appreciation must go to all of them for their professional guidance, their camaraderie, and their good humor during these years as I navigate starting a new life in a new city. My sincere thanks also go to Jason Weidemann at the University of Minnesota Press for his consistent support of my work. Both he and Erin Warholm-Wohlenhaus have been patient and helpful in guiding me through the publication process. I also thank the readers of my manuscript, whose comments and suggestions have been instrumental in helping me considerably refine my ideas and arguments. And thanks also go to the many others who have heard and offered feedback on portions of this project as it took shape in some form or another, especially to Michael Bourdaghs, Andrew Campana, Michelle Cho, Nathen Clerici, Aaron Gerow, Tom Keirstead, Sharalyn Orbaugh, Gavin Walker, and Tomiko Yoda.

Finally, my mother, Linda Santiago, has been ceaseless in her support of my work and the trajectory my life has taken. Without her continuing trust, which has taken so many different forms, I would not be where I am today. And my deepest appreciation, gratitude, and love go to my wife, Denise Liu. Her constant warmth and patience with me made it possible for me not only to see this project through to its end, but also to make it all worthwhile.

NOTES

1. I have reverted to the German capitalization here as it is the word itself that is under discussion. Elsewhere, when referring to the broader concept (unless in quotation), I will make use of the standard anglicized form "doppelgänger" without the capitalization. I should note though that in its earliest written appearances in the work of Jean Paul, the word was originally spelled as *Doppeltgänger*, with the "t" separating the two constitutive words (i.e., *doppel*—double and *ganger*—goer/walker). This certainly hints at the novelty of the term at the time, as the compound word had yet to be naturalized. Richter, "Siebenkäs," 242.

2. The title is in fact not Heine's own but was appended by Franz Schubert when he included the poem as one of six songs that constitute a part of his posthumous collection *Schwanengesang* (Swan song, 1829). In its original publication in Heine's *Buch der Lieder* (*Book of Songs*, 1827), the poem is presented without a title.

3. This use of *bunshin* as the conventional translation for doppelgänger is reflected in the title of the Ariuchi Yoshihiro's Japanese translation of Otto Rank's pioneering psychoanalytic work on the subject titled *Der Doppelgänger* (1925), which Ariuchi renders as *Bunshin: Dopperugengā* (1988). Similarly, Watanabe Masahiko's study of the figure, *Kindai bungaku no bunshinzō*, follows this choice of terminology. Alternatively, "doppelgänger" is also sometimes directly transliterated as either *dopperugengā* or (less frequently) *dopperugengeru*, as is the case in Yamashita Takeshi's catalogue of the appearances of the figure in Japanese literature. These terms are largely treated as interchangeable in the existing scholarship on the figure, a practice that I will also adopt in this book.

4. Mori, "Fushigi na kagami," 226.

5. For a comprehensive catalog of the dates of the publication of various fictions of the doppelgänger in Japan (both translated and original works) during this period, see Nishii, "Nihon dopperugengā shōsetsu nenpyōkō," 226–27.

6. I am far from the first to observe such a proliferation of doppelgänger fictions during this period. Existing scholarly work on the doppelgänger in Japan, namely Watanabe Masahiko's *Kindai bungaku no bunshinzō* and Yamashita Takeshi's *20-seiki nihon kai'i bungaku shi*, identify this as a distinct period in which doppelgänger stories became particularly prevalent. On this point, Mizuno Rei's and Nishii Yaeko's respective meta-analyses of the existing critical discourse on the doppelgänger motif in Japanese literature substantiate these observations. For the Meiji period 1868–1912, Mizuno lists only eight texts in contrast to the twenty-three that appear during the Taisho period (1912–26) commonly referenced as examples of doppelgänger stories. See Mizuno, "Dopperugengā shōsetsu ni miru Janru no keisei to henyō," 115–32. Likewise, Nishii's more extensive catalog of texts culled from the citations of scholarly writings on the doppelgänger that have been published in Japan—including literary work, scholarly essays, translations, and films—fills only one page for the period between 1868 to 1912 in contrast to the full nine pages that the years between 1912 and 1926 take up. See Nishii, "Nihon dopperugengā shōsetsu nenpyōkō," 224–34.

7. For example, see Suzuki, *Modan toshi no hyōgen*, 211–12; Lippit, *Topographies of Japanese Modernism*, 62–63.

8. Ivy, *Discourses of the Vanishing*, 54–56. While it has its own specific instantiations in the Japanese context, the neo-nostalgic quality of Japanese postmodernity echoes broader global patterns of culture, as touched on by the likes of Fredric Jameson, whose well-known analysis of the cultural logic of postmodernity identifies a formalized structure of nostalgia through the use of techniques of pastiche indicative of the loss of a sense of historicity as a dominant cultural mode. In Jameson's argument, nostalgic modes of narrative "restructure the whole issue of pastiche and project it onto a collective and social level, where the desperate attempt to appropriate a missing past is now refracted through the iron law of fashion and the emergent ideology of a generation." See Jameson, *Postmodernism*, 19.

9. Fonseca, "The Doppelgänger," 189.

10. Keppler, *The Literature of the Second Self*, ix.

11. Tymms, *Doubles in Literary Psychology*, 97.

12. Rogers, *A Psychoanalytic Study of the Double in Literature*, 4.

13. Herdman, *The Double in Nineteenth-Century Fiction*, 14.

14. Hallam, "The Double as Incomplete Self," 12–13.

15. Freud, "The Uncanny," 243.

16. Ibid., 236.

17. Rank's book was translated into English by Harry Tucker Jr. as *The Double: A Psychoanalytic Study* in 1971. Although the book upon which this translation was based was not published until 1925, earlier versions of its chapters saw dissemination

as early as 1914. It is worth noting here that Freud specifically cites Rank's work in his own discussion of the doppelgänger figure in "The Uncanny." For reference, an overview of the publication history of *Der Doppelgänger* appears in the preface of the English translation. Rank, *The Double*, vii–viii.

18. Ibid., 85–86.

19. Ibid., 35.

20. Ibid., 48.

21. Foucault, *The Archaeology of Knowledge and the Discourse on Language*, 49.

22. Jameson, *The Political Unconscious*, 47.

23. Todorov, *The Fantastic*, 160.

24. Webber, *The Doppelgänger*, 42.

25. Todorov, *The Fantastic*, 161–64.

26. Lawrence Grossberg defines a cultural formation as "a structured assemblage of practices . . . which already includes both discursive and nondiscursive practices." See *Cultural Studies in the Future Tense*, 25.

27. Mizuno, "Dopperugengā shōsetsu ni miru janru no keisei to henyō," 130.

28. Cohen, "History and Genre," 210.

29. Nakamura, *Monstrous Bodies*, 6–7.

30. Saitō, *Shinrigakka suru shakai.*

31. Oshino, "'Junsui shōsetsu' toshite no gendai misuteri."

32. Rosen, *Change Mummified.*

33. On this point, Karatani has discussed the repetition of "Things Taisho-esque" in the 1970s from the angle of the historical shifts in Japan's perceived relation to a putative Western modernity. Whereas both the Meiji periods and the postwar period in Japan are marked by the imperative to "catch up" with the West (in line with a Eurocentric teleology), what marks both the Taisho era and the period after 1970 is a perception that this modernizing process has been completed and a simultaneity with the West has been achieved. See Karatani, *Karatani Kōjin shū 5.*

1. Stalkers and Crime Scenes

1. The translator of the anthology was Tanizaki Seiji, the brother of writer Tanizaki Jun'ichirō. He is arguably one of the most prolific of Poe's Japanese translators. For a more detailed discussion of the dissemination and reception of Poe's work in Japan, see Miyanaga , *Pō to Nihon: Sono juyō no rekishi.*

2. Quoted in Meyers, *Edgar Allan Poe: Mournful and Never-Ending Remembrance*, 207.

3. *The Student of Prague* was released in Japan in 1914, a year after the publication of the Japanese translation of "William Wilson." See Nishii, "Nihon dopperugengā shōsetsu nenpyōkō," 226–27.

4. See Rank, *The Double*, 1–7.

5. Miyanaga, *Pō to Nihon: Sono juyō no rekishi*, 20.

6. Harootunian, *Overcome by Modernity*, xv.

7. Although his name is properly transliterated "Edogawa *Ranpo*" under revised Hepburn romanization conventions (which I otherwise follow in the rest of this book), I have opted to use "Rampo" instead to reflect how his name is typically written in English translations of his work. Also, following Japanese convention with pseudonymous authors, while the surname is "Edogawa," I refer to the author as "Rampo."

8. Edogawa Rampo, "'Watashi no pen nêmu,'" 212.

9. Igarashi, "Edogawa Rampo and the Excess of Vision," 300–303.

10. Shimizu, "Ranpo no kyōjin na nimensei," 32. Shimizu also points to a third category—Rampo's popular juvenile fiction—but considers it an attempt to synthesize the two sides and as such, can be considered derivative of the primary doubleness.

11. Ozaki, "Ranpo bungaku no zentaizō," 122.

12. See Kōga, "Baiu-ki no nōto kara," 202–6; Hirabayashi, "Tantei shōsetu-dan no shokeikō."

13. Despite the prevalence of such a perception, it is important to nonetheless recognize that taking "Western detective fiction" as a fixed point of reference cannot simply be taken for granted. On the contrary, these debates in Japan took place precisely when, in Europe and the United States, several significant shifts were taking place in the genre's construction concurrent with the debates surrounding orthodox and unorthodox detective fiction in Japan. The now familiar form of detective fiction that has subsequently come to be called the "whodunit" based on principles of rationality and deductive logic (and posited as "Western detective fiction") only consolidated its privileged status within the genre as a reaction to various mutations, to burgeoning developments of new forms of detective narratives such as the hard-boiled novel, the thriller, and the suspense story. Tellingly, it was not until 1928 that S. S. Van Dine pens the now famous "Twenty Rules for Writing Detective Stories." The other major treatise that codified the rules and conventions of the genre—Ronald Knox's "Decalogue" of ten commandments—also did not appear until 1929. Understood symptomatically, the appearance of these codes at these specific points in time suggests that the genre's "proper" boundaries needed assertion, precisely because they were still subject to debate and discursive contestation. What these developments in the literary history of the detective genre reveal is that contrary to the static standard typically imagined in the received histories of Japanese detective fiction, so-called "Western detective fiction" was itself under revision at this historical conjuncture. Its contours and boundaries were themselves often under intense discursive negotiation.

14. Edogawa, "Tantei shōsetsu ni tsuite"; Kozakai, "'Nisen dōka' o yomu."

15. Hirabayashi, "Tantei shōsetu-dan no shokeikō," 28–36.

16. Kasai, "Tantei shōsetsu no chisōgaku," 10.

17. Edogawa, *Injū*, 559.

18. Edogawa, "Sōseiji," 169.

19. Edogawa, *Ryōki no hate*, 424.

20. The earliest Japanese translation of Stevenson's novel did not appear until 1935 with the Iwanami edition translated by Iwata Ryōkichi. It is likely therefore that Rampo's readers would have only been familiar with these references by way of the classic 1920 film adaptation directed by John Robertson and starring John Barrymore in the titular role. According to Nishii Yaeko, the adaptation saw reasonably wide release in Japan in the same year, albeit with the title alternating between *Jikiru-hakase to haido-shi* and *Noroeru akuma* depending on the theater in which it was shown. Nishii, "Nihon dopperugengā shōsetsu nenpyōkō," 231.

21. Edogawa, *Injū*, 653. In the original Japanese, the titles cited are "Panorama-koku" and "Hitori futayaku."

22. Suzuki, *Narrating the Self*, 2–3.

23. Edogawa, *Injū*, 577.

24. Todorov, "The Typology of Detective Fiction," 44.

25. Sweeney, "Locked Rooms," 8.

26. Ibid., 5.

27. Inoue Yoshio is one critic (among several) who found the concluding chapter of *The Beast in the Shadows* troublesome and unnecessary. Inoue, "*Injū* ginmi," 42–47.

28. Kawana, *Murder Most Modern*, 95.

29. Silver, *Purloined Letters*, 152.

30. Saito, *Detective Fiction and the Rise of the Japanese Novel, 1880–1930*, 257.

31. Rampo discusses the development of his interest in Freudian psychoanalysis in Edogawa, "Waga Yume to Shinjitsu."

32. Oyama, Sato, and Suzuki, "Shaping of Scientific Psychology in Japan," 398–99. Early practitioners were, more often than not, oriented toward experimental psychology and behaviorism. In fact, the first laboratory of psychology that was formed at the Tokyo Imperial University was called a "psycho-physical laboratory" (*seishin butsurigaku*)

33. Taketomo, "Cultural Adaptation to Psychoanalysis in Japan, 1912–1952," 955.

34. See Blowers and Yang, "Ohtsuki Kenji and the Beginnings of Lay Analysis in Japan," 27–42.

35. Freud, "Psycho-Analysis and the Establishment of the Facts in Legal Proceedings," 108.

36. Strowick, "Comparative Epistemology of Suspicion," 657.

37. Freud, "Psycho-Analysis and the Establishment of the Facts in Legal Proceedings," 108.

38. Žižek, "The Detective and the Analyst," 39–40.

39. Moretti, *Signs Taken for Wonders*, 134–35.

40. Ibid., 135.

41. Matsuyama, *Ranpo to Tokyo: 1920 toshi no kao*, 20.

42. Deleuze and Guattari, *Anti-Oedipus*, 281.

43. Serizawa, *"Hō" kara kaihō sareru kenryoku*, 74.

44. Gunning, "Tracing the Individual Body," 19.

45. In Kobayashi, *Literature of the Lost Home*.

46. Kobayashi, *Literature of the Lost Home*, 128.

47. See Freud, "The Uncanny," 219–56.

48. Thompson, *Fiction, Crime, and Empire*, 111–12. In his analysis of the genre in the context of British imperialism, Jon Thompson links detective fiction, psychoanalysis, and Marxism with the tradition of modernism. To the extent that modernism is "organized around the desire to translate the incoherent into the coherent, the inarticulate into the articulate, the unsaid into the said," it "shares an analogous epistemological form with detective fiction." As I elaborate further below, I believe a similar discursive space is evident in the Japanese context as well.

49. Silverberg, *Erotic Grotesque Nonsense*.

50. Ibid., 39. On the relationship between modernology and detective fiction, especially in connection with the technique of tailing, see also Kawana, *Murder Most Modern*, 44–58.

51. Lippit, *Topographies of Japanese Modernism*, 17–19. Seiji Lippit suggests that a symptom of this new cultural milieu is an increasing suspicion of the institution of literature. In Lippit's view, this emerged as a consequence of two transformations in the context of cultural production. The first is the rapidity of the process of urbanization and "consolidation of a mass consumer capitalism ... and the commodification of all levels of culture" such that by the end of the decade, there was much talk of the demise of the literary novel only to be replaced by popular fiction and cinema. The second is an increasing politicization of literature, with the consequence of calling into question literature's demarcation from politics, a discourse upon which the very concept of "literature" was first constructed.

52. Bloch, "A Philosophical View of the Detective Novel," 21.

53. Harootunian, *Overcome by Modernity*, 414.

54. Karatani, *The Origins of Modern Japanese Literature*. In *The Origins of Modern Japanese Literature*, Karatani presents an analysis of modern forms of literary narrative and subjectivity in Meiji Japan. In his account, he articulates a complex process involving a radical transformation in modes of perception, indeed the total discursive and epistemological configuration through which knowledge and experience are mediated. Focusing on the emergence of a conception of an interiorized subject (*naimen*) and its differentiation from an exterior "landscape" [*fūkei*], Karatani suggests that modern modes of literary narration enable a projection of a space that exceeds the interior, that is, the exterior landscape, through the mapping out of the very boundaries of the modern subject, becomes possible.

55. Angles, "Seeking the Strange."

56. Simmel, "The Metropolis and Mental Life."

57. Edogawa, *Ryōki no hate*, 342.

58. Driscoll, *Absolute Erotic, Absolute Grotesque*, 135–39.

59. Benjamin, *Charles Baudelaire*, 43.

60. Edogawa, *Ryōki no hate*, 339.

61. Ibid., 361–62.

62. Ivy, *Discourses of the Vanishing*, 21–23.

63. Of course, such a perception presupposes that Japan is categorically outside the West, despite the fact that it is precisely through the process of "Westernization" that the very concept of "Japan" becomes legible. See Sakai, *Translation and Subjectivity*.

64. Driscoll, *Absolute Erotic, Absolute Grotesque*, ix.

65. On this point, I follow Fredric Jameson in his analysis of the cultures of imperialism in his "Modernism and Imperialism," 50–51. Raymond Williams has raised a similar argument in *The Politics of Modernism*, 44.

66. Pratt, *Imperial Eyes*, 6.

67. Further discussions of this facet of the genre can be found in Siddiqi, *Anxieties of Empire and the Fiction of Intrigue*. A similar point is also raised in Ikeda, *"Kaigai shinshutsu bungaku" ron josetsu*, 10.

68. Thomas, "Fingerprint of the Foreigner," 656.

69. Khanna, *Dark Continents*, 6.

70. Rank, *The Double*, 48.

71. Ibid., xvii–xviii.

72. Kōjin, *The Origins of Modern Japanese Literature*, 115.

73. Freud, "The Uncanny," 236.

74. Chakrabarty, "Postcoloniality and the Artifice of History; Who Speaks for 'Indian' Pasts?," 13.

2. Repressing the Colonial Unconscious

1. Edward Fowler counts Tanizaki among "the triumvirate" (along with Kawabata Yasunari and Mishima Yukio) that dominated English translations of Japanese fictions in the aftermath of the Second World War. These translations, in Fowler's argument, set the precedent for which other texts saw English translations, thus shaping perceptions of Japan in the United States for years to come. Among Tanizaki's fictions, it was *Some Prefer Nettles* (*Tade kuu mushi*, 1929; trans. 1955) and *The Makioka Sisters* (*Sasameyuki*, 1943–48; trans. 1956) to first make an appearance in English. See Fowler, "Rendering Words, Traversing Cultures," 6–9.

2. Freud, "The Uncanny."

3. Long, *This Perversion Called Love*.

4. Indeed, it would be easy to frame the analysis of the doppelgänger with the question of its cultural particularity, in effect reducing doppelgänger fictions in Japan to nothing more than a particular variation on Euro-American films and fictions of the doppelgänger that is imagined to be a baseline universal standard. Of course, such an approach would simply reproduce a central trope of the discourse

of "Western civilization," which is marked by, as Naoki Sakai has perceptively noted, a fundamentally contradictory notion wherein the location designated as "the West" claims to be at once particular in its distinction as a "civilized" locale while at once putatively representing a universality. See Sakai, "'Dislocation of the West and the Status of the Humanities,'" 75–76.

5. For an extended discussion of this subject, see also Cornyetz and Vincent, "Introduction—Japan as Screen Memory."

6. Michel Foucault, for one, has pointed out that these two disciplines occupy a privileged position in the history of the human sciences in that, in concert, they took on key roles in facilitating the emergence of a discursive regime through which the conditions of possibility for "knowledge about man in general" could be constituted, with psychoanalysis looking inward as ethnography looks outward. See Foucault, *The Order of Things*, 378.

7. Freud, "On Narcissism," 101.

8. Rank, *The Double*, 80.

9. Ibid., 83.

10. Fabian, *Time and the Other*, 31.

11. Khanna, *Dark Continents*, 6.

12. Outside of Rank's work on the doppelgänger, perhaps the most explicit expression of this analogy can be found in Freud's *Totem and Taboo* (1913), whose very subtitle—"resemblances between the mental lives of savages and neurotics"— calls attention to the fundamental presupposition underpinning the discussion in the book, which is a parallel between the respective objects of scrutiny in the disciplines of psychoanalysis and anthropology. Freud's premise reproduces the foundational contradiction at the heart of the historical emergence of a conception of the subject in psychoanalysis. On the one hand, by way of this posited analogy between the "neurotic" and the "savage," Freud is able to assert the universality of his concepts, suggesting that the Oedipus complex or the incest taboo can be traced back to the origins of the human species as such. On the other hand, paradoxically, this claim of universality is predicated on precisely the exclusion of others from the field of analysis. See Freud, *Totem and Taboo*, 1.

13. This should not be taken to suggest that racism was not nevertheless an operative force in the Japanese empire. Rather, the important point of distinction here is what Etienne Balibar has identified as a difference between "inclusive" and "exclusive" racisms. Whereas the latter operates on the principle of extermination and elimination, the former makes use of a twinned principle of assimilation and exploitation. See Balibar and Wallerstein, *Race, Nation, Class*, 39–40.

14. Bhabha, *The Location of Culture*, 85–86.

15. Oguma, "Yūshoku no shokumin teikoku," 81–102.

16. Ching, *Becoming "Japanese,"* 17. For a more expansive examination of shifting terrain of Japanese racial discourses, see Oguma, *A Genealogy of "Japanese" Self-Images*.

17. Marilyn Ivy has raised a similar point in her *Discourses of the Vanishing*, 6–8. Ivy writes: "It is no doubt Japan's (some would say presumptuous) entry into geopolitics as an entirely exotic and late-modernizing nation-state instead of as an outright colony that has made its mimicry all the more threatening. As the only predominantly nonwhite nation to have challenged western dominance on a global scale during World War II—and to have done so by becoming colonialist, imperialist, and (some would say) fascist—Japan, in its role as quasi-colonized mimic, has finally exceeded itself." More recently, Robert Tierney has developed this analysis further by conceptualizing it as "imperial mimicry—the mimicry of one imperial power by another," that has the effect of engendering a form of an ambivalence vis-à-vis Western powers as both objects of admiration and resentment. See his *Tropics of Savagery*, 16–19.

18. Tanizaki, "Tomoda to Matsunaga no hanashi," 426.

19. Anderson, *The Spectre of Comparisons*, 229. For a parallel discussion of the double life entailed by non-Western modernity in the Japanese context, see Harootunian, *History's Disquiet*, 111.

20. Fanon, *Black Skin, White Masks*, 116. It is worth noting that Fanon uses the term "epidermalization" specifically to contrast it against the notion of "internalization" in an effort to highlight how the production of a racialized subjectivity operates on the basis of a visual schema, that is, through a sense of overvisibility such that one is "overdetermined from without." Interestingly, in contrast to Fanon's conceptualization, Tanizaki's account in "The Story of Tomoda and Matsunaga" locates racialization not *on* the body but *in* the body in that the transformation from Matsunaga to Tomoda is made through the consumption of food. I do not think this is necessarily a contradiction per se. Rather, the significance of this difference may very well lie in compelling the complication of the surface/depth dialectic typically ascribed to visuality and corporeality.

21. Tanizaki, *In Praise of Shadows*, 48–49.

22. Tanizaki, "Tomoda to Matsunaga no hanashi," 472.

23. Jay Rubin argues as much when he writes that the story "turns Tanizaki's famous aesthetic of shadow on its head, negating the very core of Japan's cult of restraint and suggestion" in his *Injurious to Public Morals*, 238. Similarly, Yamashita Takashi suggests that the story serves as an intertextual foreshadowing of Tanizaki's "return to Japan" in later writings like *In Praise of Shadows* in his discussion of Tanizaki in *20-seiki nihon kai'i bungaku shi*, 386.

24. Tanizaki, *In Praise of Shadows*, 48.

25. Long, *This Perversion Called Love*, 15–18.

26. See Gilroy, *Postcolonial Melancholia*; Cheng, *The Melancholy of Race*.

27. Freud, "Mourning and Melancholia," 240–50.

28. Cheng, *The Melancholy of Race*, 10.

29. Freud, "The Ego and the Id," 34–35.

30. Tanizaki, "Tomoda to Matsunaga no hanashi," 493.

31. Ibid.

32. The source of the passage is an English travel guide from 1935 titled *All About Shanghai*. While the first part of the passage is premised on the standard West/East bifurcation, the second part also speaks to the city's spatial positioning vis-à-vis the Japanese empire. See Meng, *Shanghai and the Edges of Empires*, vii.

33. Although it is widely employed as a term to describe conditions in China at the time, as Jürgen Osterhammel has pointed out, the notion of "semicolonialism" can nonetheless also obscure precisely what concrete effects the incompleteness of Chinese colonization generated in social and material terms. See Osterhammel, "Semi-Colonialism and Informal Empire in Twentieth-Century China." The details of these debates are beyond the scope of my discussion here, but for an examination of the impacts of semicolonialism in the specific space of Shanghai, see Goodman, "Improvisations on a Semicolonial Theme."

34. Meng, *Shanghai and the Edges of Empires*, xii.

35. Pratt, *Imperial Eyes*, 4.

36. Duus, "Introduction," xi–xxix.

37. Zarrow, *China in War and Revolution, 1895–1949*, 206.

38. Tanizaki, "Tomoda to Matsunaga no hanashi," 425.

39. For a more detailed discussion of Tanizaki's various travel writings on China from this period (and its place within the history of Japanese literary discourse on China more generally), see Sakaki, *Obsessions with the Sino-Japanese Polarity in Japanese Literature*, 82–85.

40. Tanizaki, "Tomoda to Matsunaga no hanashi," 476–85.

41. Tanizaki, *Kōjin*, 82.

42. Silverberg, *Erotic Grotesque Nonsense*, 178.

43. Tanizaki, *Kōjin*, 57–58.

44. For further discussion, see Tanaka, *Japan's Orient*.

45. Tanizaki repeats a similar sentiment in his short essay, "Shina shumi to iu koto."

46. Sakaki, *Obsessions with the Sino-Japanese Polarity in Japanese Literature*, 95–102.

47. Lamarre, *Shadows on the Screen*, 13.

48. Said, *Orientalism*. Of course, the focus of Said's analysis is the so-called Middle East, more specifically, its representations in nineteenth-century European travelogues, governmental documents, and literature. He does not take up the Japanese case specifically, whether in terms of Euro-American representations of Japan, or Japanese representations of its colonial periphery. That said, this has not stopped others from extending his analysis to the Japanese case. For further discussion, see, for example, Minear, "Orientalism and the Study of Japan."

49. Oguma, *A Genealogy of "Japanese" Self-Images*, 252–253n12.

50. Kang, *Orientarizumu no kanata e*.

51. Komori, *Posutokoroniaru*, 15.

52. Webber, *The Doppelgänger*, 3.

53. Kittler, "Romanticism—Psychoanalysis—Film," 94.

54. McClintock, *Imperial Leather*, 33.

55. Kano, *Acting Like a Woman in Modern Japan*, 190.

56. Foucault, *Discipline and Punish.*

57. Foucault, *The Birth of the Clinic.*

58. Pratt, *Imperial Eyes*, 36.

59. Kano, *Acting Like a Woman in Modern Japan*, 201–2.

60. While both Tanizaki's story and the film within the story have been referred to by the same title in English, I should nevertheless point out that despite the identical translation, in Japanese, the former is titled "Jinmenso" while the latter takes on the more literal title of *Ningen no kao o motta dekimono*. See Tanizaki, "Jinmenso," 283–84.

61. Ibid., 302.

62. Deleuze, *Cinema 1*, 102.

63. Tanizaki, "Jinmenso," 283.

64. Ibid., 301.

65. Ibid., 305.

66. McClintock, *Imperial Leather*, 33–36.

3. Projections of Shadow

1. Rank, *The Double*, 4. As I noted in the introduction, although Rank's book *Der Doppelgänger* (1925) did not see publication until a decade after the film, the essays upon which it was based came out as early as 1914, just shortly after the release of Ewers and Rye's film.

2. Ibid., 7.

3. This relationship between Rank's psychoanalytic investigations and early cinema is perhaps best understood as one manifestation of the oft-noted structural link between cinema and psychoanalysis. Given the historical concurrence of their respective developments—with the parallel between the Lumière brothers' first public screening of a film in Paris and the publication of Sigmund Freud and Josef Breurer's *Studies in Hysteria*—much has already been written on this subject, and an extended discussion should no longer be necessary. That said, it should nonetheless be noted that despite this parallel history, the relationship between cinema and psychoanalysis has not always been symmetrical. On the one hand, the deployment of psychoanalytic theories of the unconscious played a crucial role in the institutionalization and consolidation of film studies as a discipline. Yet on the other hand, psychoanalytic discourse has often exhibited a resistance to a rigorous engagement with cinema, with the relation between cinema and psychoanalysis often reduced to taking up the former merely as a means of illustrating concepts in the latter. For a discussion, see Heath, "Cinema and Psychoanalysis," 25–26. This asymmetry is especially significant for approaching the doppelgänger motif, as I discuss further below.

4. For analyses of *The Student of Prague* and other German Expressionist films of the period, see Coates, *The Gorgon's Gaze*.

5. Ewers's film saw its first remake produced as early as 1926, with Henrik Galeen's similarly titled film, only to be followed yet again in 1935 by another version directed by Arthur Robison. A Czech television miniseries (*Praski Student*, 1990) and an English short film remake (*The Student of Prague*, 2004) also exist.

6. Per Nishii Yaeko, *The Student of Prague* saw limited release in the Asakusa Denkikan, the Yokohama Odeon, and other film theaters in Japan in 1914. See Nishii, "Nihon dopperugengā shōsetsu nenpyōkō," 227.

7. Watanabe, *Kindai bungaku no bunshinzō*, 70.

8. For a discussion of the commentary on cinematic technologies in "Tumor with a Human Face" and other fictions of Tanizaki, see Lamarre, *Shadows on the Screen*. On the linkages between cinema, psychoanalysis, and the double in Satō Haruo's "The Fingerprint," see Ubukata, "'Tantei shōsetsu' izen."

9. Recall that Edogawa Rampo's numerous references to Robert Louis Stevenson's *The Strange Case of Dr. Jekyll and Mr. Hyde* in several of his fictions appeared prior to Japanese translations of the novel becoming widely disseminated among the reading population, suggesting that it is the novel's film adaptation that introduced the characters to his readership. Likewise, Japanese translations of "William Wilson" did not make an appearance until 1913, only a year prior to the release in Japan of *The Student of Prague,* in the form of a collection of Poe's fiction under the title *Akaki shi no kamen*, translated by Tanizaki Seiji, brother of the novelist Tanizaki Jun'ichirō. A new translation was subsequently published in 1929, prepared by none other than Edogawa Rampo himself. For details of the publication history of these translations, see Nishii, "Nihon dopperugengā shōsetsu nenpyōkō," 227–36.

10. Watanabe, *Kindai Bungaku no bunshinzō*, 72.

11. Webber, *The Doppelgänger*, 2.

12. Rashidi, "Divided Screen," 9.

13. Benjamin, "The Work of Art in the Age of Mechanical Reproduction," 237.

14. Baudrillard, *Symbolic Exchange and Death*, 84.

15. Derrida and Steigler, *Echographies of Television*, 117.

16. Kittler, *Discourse Networks 1800/1900*, 277.

17. Kittler, "Romanticism—Psychoanalysis—Film," 94.

18. Ibid.

19. Ibid., 98.

20. Lacan, *The Four Fundamental Concepts of Psychoanalysis*, 106.

21. Karatani, *The Origins of Modern Japanese Literature*, 69.

22. The term "scopic regime," referring to a field of visual practices and institutions, is from Martin Jay. For further discussion, see his "Scopic Regimes of Modernity."

23. Karatani's discussion here can be compared with the work of Jonathan Crary. In *Techniques of the Observer* (1990), Crary provides an account of just what

the historical process of visual modernization that took place during the nineteenth century entailed. For Crary, classical visuality is associated with the principles of Cartesian perspective, with all its attendant features of decorporealization and interiorization of the subject. By the nineteenth century, however, this dominant paradigm for grasping the problem of vision went through a fundamental reorganization and this classical model of fixed vision was replaced by a discourse of subjective vision, which uprooted the truth value ascribed to classical vision, supplanting it with a more mechanistic view that placed its emphasis on locating vision not with its object but within the mechanics of the corporeal body of the observer, subjecting it to processes of abstraction, rationalization, and quantified measurement. In Crary's words, "What takes place from around 1810 to 1840 is an uprooting of vision from the stable and fixed relations . . . what occurs is a new valuation of visual experience: it is given an unprecedented mobility and exchangeability, abstracted from any founding site or referent." See Crary, *Techniques of the Observer*, 27.

24. Chow, *Primitive Passions*, 8.

25. On the mirror stage, see Lacan, "The Mirror Stage as Formative of the Function of the I as Revealed in Psychoanalytic Experience"; Lacan, *The Four Fundamental Concepts of Psychoanalysis*.

26. Chow, *Primitive Passions*, 14. Eric Cazdyn suggests a similar process is at work in the Japanese context by expanding Karatani's discussion onto the terrain of cinema. See his *The Flash of Capital*, 40–44.

27. Gerbert, "The Influence of Vision Technology on Narrative in Taishō," 28.

28. Silverberg, *Erotic Grotesque Nonsense*.

29. For example, the cultural critic Hirabayashi Hatsunosuke observed that literary texts were increasingly becoming tainted by the emphasis on their commercial value in his essay "Shōhin toshite no kindai shōsetsu." In a similar vein, Miriam Silverberg suggests that what characterized this period in the history of Japanese modernity was the proliferation of all manner of mass-cultural forms that together had the effect of constituting a kind of cinematic montage of different discourses and cultural practices. See Silverberg, *Erotic Grotesque Nonsense*, 30–35.

30. Benjamin, "The Work of Art in the Age of Mechanical Reproduction," 230–37. Several Japanese authors, Tanizaki Jun'ichirō and Edogawa Rampo among them, have expressed a similar sentiment. For example, in his "Eiga no kyōfu" (The horrors of film, 1926), Rampo compares the experience of cinematic spectatorship to something akin to looking at a concave mirror and its terrifying capability to magnify the images therein, and through that, to threaten the fragmentation of the subject. See Edogawa, "The Horrors of Film," 137.

31. Harootunian, *Overcome by Modernity*, xxv. On literary responses to these historical circumstances, see also Suzuki, *Modan toshi no hyōgen*; Takahashi, *Kankaku no modan*.

32. Akutagawa, "Kage," 142–44. In these references, the author of the letters alternates between the using the German term *Doppelgänger* as is, or transliterating

it as *dopperugengeru*. The *-geru* ending as opposed to *-gā* (as is more often seen in contemporary writings on the figure) is probably indicative of a transliteration from the German directly, as opposed to the latter's mediation through its Anglicized form. Elsewhere in the text, Akutagawa also uses *dai-ni no watashi* [second self] rather than the more common translation *bunshin* [split self]. This multiplicity of terms used by Akutagawa reflects a period when standardized translations or transliterations into Japanese have yet to be consolidated. Coupled with the extensive explanatory text about the concept embedded into the story, what is indicated is that at the time of the story's writing the doppelgänger had yet to be domesticated into the popular milieu of Japan and that its consolidation as a generic trope had yet to be completed.

33. Ibid., 155.

34. In his analysis of Akutagawa's story, Satoru Saito also offers the observation that Sasaki is familiar with the doppelgänger from secondhand accounts even prior to his first encounter, seeing as how he immediately recognizes the phenomenon. Saito reads this detail as indicative of an anxiety (and its disavowal) at the belatedness of Japanese modernization wherein the knowledge of a phenomenon precedes its experience. See Saito, *Detective Fiction and the Rise of the Japanese Novel, 1880–1930*, 214.

35. Ichiyanagi, "Samayoeru dopperugengā," 120.

36. Ibid., 119.

37. Watanabe, *Kindai bungaku no bunshinzō*, 104.

38. Jameson, "Postmodernism and Consumer Society," 119.

39. Akutagawa, "Haguruma," 119.

40. Ibid., 131–32.

41. Ibid., 133. Following the pattern established in several instances in "Two Letters," the word *Doppelgänger* appears untranslated from the German in the original Japanese text. Likewise, other references to foreign languages—*la mort* and *all right*, among others—appear as is.

42. Lippit, *Topographies of Japanese Modernism*, 59.

43. Akutagawa, "Kage," 38.

44. Ibid., 48.

45. For example, C. F. Keppler writes: "Often the conscious mind tries to deny its unconscious through the mechanism of 'projection,' attributing its own unconscious content (a murderous impulse, for example) to a real person in the world outside; at times it even creates an external hallucination in the image of this content." See Keppler, *The Literature of the Second Self*, 25.

46. Aaron Gerow raises a similar point in his analysis of Akutagawa's story. He writes: "['The Shadow'] interestingly connects this split in identity with the problematic of seeing, both in the case of the film seemingly manufactured by the two spectators at the end (who remain ignorant of their role in this process), as well as in the example of Chen Cai watching his wife from outside her window. The latter

episode is itself a spatial allegorization of the film viewing process. Chen remains immobile in the dark, his hidden desires giving life to his double through a form of projection that corresponds with his utterance of his wife's name Fusako." See Gerow, "The Self Seen As Other," 199.

47. Akutagawa, "Kage," 51.

48. Cavanaugh, "Junbungaku Goes to the Movies," 310.

49. Metz, *The Imaginary Signifier*, 49. I should note, though, that the underlying presupposition in Metz's analysis is a marked distinction between the moment of specular subject formation before the mirror that Jacques Lacan has famously articulated and the event of subject formation before the screen of cinema. In Metz's view, while a process of identification also takes place before the screen, the transcendent subjectivity of the cinematic spectator is predicated precisely upon the *absence* of the spectator from the screen, in other words, that the screen is *not* fully identical to a mirror. Hence, the appearance of the doppelgänger on the screen is a sign not of the confirmation of the production of a transcendental subjectivity in the spectator, but precisely its failure.

50. Akutagawa, "Kage," 150.

51. Ibid.

52. For a more detailed discussion of these seemingly "magical" properties ascribed to cinematic technologies, see Moore, *Savage Theory*.

53. Gunning, "The Cinema of Attractions," 56.

54. Ibid., 57.

55. Gerow, *Visions of Japanese Modernity*, 3.

56. On the subject of *misemono* spectacles, see Markus, "The Carnival of Edo."

57. Gerow, *Visions of Japanese Modernity*, 47–52.

58. Ibid., 106–17. The Pure Film movement [*jun'ei eigageki undō*] was named for a tendency in film criticism in Japan to advocate ridding film practice of so-called impurities—borrowings from theatrical practice such as the use of a live narrator or female impersonators instead of actresses—in an effort to make a properly cinematic cinema. Critics within the movement called for adopting Hollywood practices in both aesthetic terms and industrial terms, which included such developments as organizing film production around large studios to facilitate mass production, the development of a star system of actors to shift focus from the live commentators to actors and directors, and the production of coherent narratives without the need for the aid of a film commentator.

59. Baudrillard, *Symbolic Exchange and Death*, 55.

60. Debord's analysis builds upon the Marxian concept of reification to describe social conditions characterized by the fetishism of image-commodities such that they appear to have a life of their own that occludes the social relations that underpin their circulation. In Debord's words: "The spectacle is not a collection of images; rather it is a social relationship between people that is mediated by images." See Debord, *The Society of the Spectacle*, 12.

61. Beller, *The Cinematic Mode of Production*, 1.

62. Ibid., 9.

63. Harvey, *The Limits to Capital*, 119.

64. Wada-Marciano, *Nippon Modern*, 42.

65. Negri, *Marx Beyond Marx*.

66. Driscoll, *Absolute Erotic, Absolute Grotesque*, xi.

67. Ibid., xiii.

68. Akutagawa, "Kage," 139.

69. Žižek, *The Fright of Real Tears*, 31–54.

70. Ibid., 52–53.

71. Doane, *The Emergence of Cinematic Time*, 24.

72. Ibid., 5–8.

73. Beller, *The Cinematic Mode of Production*, 163.

74. Freud, "The Uncanny," 230.

75. While there are a exceptions, it is worth noting that the authors most often cited as pioneers in the deployment of the doppelgänger motif—for example, Edgar Allan Poe, E. T. A. Hoffmann, or Robert Louis Stevenson—are invariably male, as are the characters who encounter their doubles in their fiction. This characteristic of the doppelgänger arguably reflects the traditional positioning of women as a constitutive other in the psychoanalytic conception of subjectivity.

76. On this point, see Friedberg, *Window Shopping*. For a discussion of the impact of these historical changes in the specific context of Japan, see Silverberg, *Erotic Grotesque Nonsense*.

4. Rampo's Repetitions

1. Watanabe, *Kindai bungaku no bunshinzō*, 212–13.

2. Ibid., 213.

3. Driscoll, *Absolute Erotic, Absolute Grotesque*, 220.

4. Matsuyama, *Ranpo to Tokyo*, 31.

5. Igarashi, "Edogawa Rampo and the Excess of Vision."

6. Hirano, *Hofuman to 'Ranpo*.

7. The adaptations in question are as follows: *Kurotokage* (*The Black Lizard*, 1968), directed by Fukusaku Kinji; *Mōjū* (*The Blind Beast*, 1969), directed by Masumura Yasuzō; *Edogawa Ranpo zenshū: Kyōfu kikei ningen* (*The Horrors of Malformed Men*, 1969), directed by Ishii Teruo and drawing from various fictions of Rampo's. His *Young Detective's Gang* series also appeared numerous times in film and television productions during the 1950s.

8. For a brief discussion of this boom in films connected with the work of Edogawa Rampo, see Katsura, "Ranpo no eigaka ni tsuite," 70–75.

9. Alongside the two different versions of *The Mystery of Rampo* (*Rampo*, 1994) that I discuss further below, the two other films released in 1994 were *Stalker in the Attic* (*Yaneura no sanposha*) and *The Man Traveling with a Brocade Portrait*

(*Oshie to tabi suru otoko*), both distributed under the Edogawa Ranpo Gekijō (Edogawa Rampo Theater) series. Other titles that have appeared in the subsequent years include: an omnibus film, *Rampo Noir* (*Ranpo Jigoku*, 2005); the "Erotic Rampo" film series, which includes *The Human Chair* (*Ningen isu*, 2007) and yet another adaptation of *Stalker in the Attic* (*Yaneura no sanposha*, 2007); adaptations by famed pink film directors Jissōji Akio and Wakamatsu Kōji, *Murder on D-Hill* (*D-zaka no satsujin jiken*, 1998) and *Caterpillar* (*Kyatapirā*, 2010) based on Rampo's "Caterpillar" ("Imomushi," 1929); a transnational production titled *Inju, the Beast in the Shadow* (*Inju, la bête dans l'ombre*, 2008) by Franco-Swiss director Barbet Schroeder, based on the Rampo novel of the same title; and most recently, a trio of soft-core erotic films, *Lost Love Murder* (*Shitsurensatsujin*, 2010), another version of *Murder on D-Hill* (*D-zaka no satsujin jiken*, 2015), and yet another version of *Stalker in the Attic* (*Yaneura no sanposha*, 2016). Finally, there are also several television and anime appearances by (or inspired by) Rampo's trademark detective Akechi Kogorō that are too numerous to list here.

10. While the so-called "Mayuzumi version" saw a simultaneous theatrical release, it is Okuyama's revised edition that is more widely recognized and generally considered the authoritative version of the film. Only the Okuyama version saw international release.

11. Note the curious anachronism here. Aside from the fact that no such prewar adaptation of *The Fiend with Twenty Faces* is known to exist, the story depicts a film adaptation of this novel already in existence when "The Appearance of Osei" is banned, even though, in reality, it was not written until ten years after the publication of "The Appearance of Osei." In part, this anachronism was a consequence of the troubled production history of the film, as the scene of the wrap party (which features cameos by several major figures in the history of Japanese cinema such as Wakamatsu Kōji and Fukusaku Kinji) was only added in the Okuyama version of the film.

12. The snippets of the film that Rampo and his editor are shown viewing are from an early Shōchiku series featuring Detective Akechi, later released in 1954 as a single film simply titled *Kaijin nijūmensō* (*The Fiend with Twenty Faces*), directed by Yumizuri Susumu.

13. For a discussion of the discourse of fidelity in adaptation studies, see Stam, "Beyond Fidelity."

14. Hutcheon, *A Theory of Adaptation*, 21–22.

15. Cazdyn, *The Flash of Capital*, 89.

16. Ibid., 127.

17. For an overview of the background and films of Tsukamoto Shin'ya, see Mes, *Iron Man*.

18. Edogawa, "Sōseiji," 155.

19. For a comparable discussion of the cultural discourse on twins in Europe, see also Schwartz, *The Culture of the Copy*. The scenario of floating a twin down a

river is precisely what happens in a later film adaptation of Rampo's story, Tsukamoto Shin'ya's *Sōseiji: Gemini* (*Gemini*, 1999).

20. Takeda, "Yonin no Aoki Aisaburō," 272–74.

21. Foucault, *Discipline and Punish*.

22. Edogawa, "Sōseiji," 161.

23. Ibid., 156–57.

24. Freud, "The Uncanny," 243.

25. Webber, *The Doppelgänger*, 17.

26. Edogawa, "Sōseiji," 156.

27. Ibid., 158.

28. Freud, "Remembering, Repeating and Working-Through," 148.

29. Currie, *About Time*, 61. In highlighting these points, it should go without saying that my analysis is indebted to the work of Roland Barthes, especially his theorization of the preterite as necessary to the development of the novel in *Writing Degree Zero*, 29–40. While recognizing that it is not strictly speaking reducible to a past tense, Karatani Kōjin has extended Barthes's argument about the preterite to the Japanese literary context with his analysis of the use of the *-ta* verb ending as enabling the neutralization of the narrator's positionality. See Karatani, *The Origins of Modern Japanese Literature*, 72–75.

30. Currie, *About Time*, 61.

31. Considering that the film does not make itself out to be an accurate historical period piece, this may be beside the point, but nonetheless, it should be said that Tsukamoto's film exhibits a small anachronistic detail here. Seeing as how Yukio is apparently the older of the twins (Sutekichi at one point calls him *oniisan* [older brother]), why Sutekichi's appearance should cause complications about Yukio's inheritance is unclear, given that until 1945, the Japanese civil code granted the right of inheritance exclusively to the first son. In contrast, Rampo's story has the older twin receiving the full inheritance.

32. This linkage between the figure of the doppelgänger and themes of lost or accounted time or memory is well established. Karl Miller, for one, identifies it as one of the more common motifs associated with the figure, appearing in several well-recognized nineteenth-century double fictions such as James Hogg's *Confessions of a Justified Sinner* (1824) and Robert Louis Stevenson's *The Strange Case of Dr. Jekyll and Mr. Hyde* (1886). See Miller, *Doubles*, 1–38.

33. Webber, *The Doppelgänger*, 9–10.

34. In this respect, although strictly speaking there is nothing that is necessarily supernatural in the plot of *Gemini*, the combined force of its narrative and heightened visual style easily lends to a reading of the film as fantastic, especially in terms of the tendency toward a temporal critique associated with the genre that Bliss Cua Lim has articulated, or as Lim puts it, "as a form of temporal translation: narratives that represent enchanted worlds within the framework of secular homogenous time but intimate a sense of discrepant temporality." See Lim, *Translating Time*, 21.

35. On the dynamics of the homosocial triangle, see Sedgwick, *Between Men*. Sedgwick convincingly argues that the expression of heterosexual desire is more often than not organized around a sociocultural structure of homosocial male-male bonds, be it in terms of a relationship of rivalry or a displaced homosexual desire. Homosocial triangles feature prominently in doppelgänger fictions, with a woman often serving as a mediating figure for the rivalry between doubles. Rampo's "The Twins" is no exception. In the story, the narrator's desire for his brother's wife has less to do with the woman per se, and more with the mere fact that she is his brother's wife.

36. Edogawa, "Sōseiji," 155.

37. Ibid., 173.

38. Ibid., 165.

39. Cole, *Suspect Identities*, 63.

40. For an excellent discussion of literary representations of fingerprinting and its linkages with eugenics discourse, see, for example, Inoue, "'Shimon' to 'Chi.'"

41. Nakamura, *Monstrous Bodies*, 55.

42. Ibid., 56–57.

43. Francis Galton himself authored a study on twins titled "History of Twins."

44. Jameson, *The Political Unconscious*, ix.

45. Ibid., 20.

46. Freud, "The Uncanny," 240.

47. Karatani, *Karatani Kōjin shū 5*.

48. Marx, *The Eighteenth Brumaire of Louis Bonaparte*, 1.

49. Karatani, *Karatani Kōjin shū 5*, 5.

50. The problem of crisis is a much-discussed subject within Marxian thought. Crucially, the recurrence of crisis in capitalist economies is not simply the product of individual or even institutional failures. On the contrary, crisis is a necessary systemic feature of capital accumulation that arises not when it fails, but precisely when it works. What fuels the drive toward crisis is the limit set by the internal contradiction of overproduction (resulting from its constant expansion) and underconsumption (resulting from wage repression) in capital accumulation. But capital's imperative to expand the production of surplus value regardless of limits is incessant. Crisis is what happens when these limits to expansion are reached, necessitating a systemic recuperation through the restructuring of modes of accumulation in such mechanisms as monopolization, financialization, and imperialism.

51. Harvey, *The Condition of Postmodernity*, 182–84.

52. Ibid., 240.

53. Ibid., 147.

54. Jameson, *Postmodernism*, xx–xxi.

55. For a cogent discussion of this historical transition in Japan, and in particular, the cultural discourses that emerged during this period, which have subsequently set the terms of the existing debates in contemporary Japan, see Yoda, "A Roadmap to Millennial Japan."

56. See, for example, Manovich, *The Language of New Media*.

57. My understanding of the relationship between cinema and new media here is indebted to the work of Thomas Lamarre, especially in his essay "The First Time as Farce."

58. Hardt and Negri, *Empire*, xi.

59. For a critical reading of *Empire*, see, for example, the essays collected in Passavant and Dean, eds., *Empire's New Clothes*.

60. Bal, *Quoting Caravaggio*, 263.

61. Ibid.

5. Compulsions to Repeat

1. I would be far from the first to mention such a proliferation in Japanese cultural production and discourses. For example, referencing a range of texts spanning the history of postwar Japan—from the film *Gojira* (*Godzilla*, 1954) and its multiple sequels and remakes, to Komatsu Sakyo's famous science fiction novel *Nihon chinbotsu* (*Japan Sinks*, 1973) and its adaptations, to animations like *Uchū senkan yamato* (*Space Battleship Yamato*, 1974–75) and *Akira* (1988)—William Tsutsui has claimed that "there can be little doubt that, in the years since World War II, fictional apocalypse has been visited upon Tokyo more frequently (and often with much greater thoroughness) than any other location on the globe." Tsutsui, "Oh No, There Goes Tokyo," 104.

2. Jameson, *Archaeologies of the Future*, 199.

3. Žižek, "The Spectre of Ideology," 55.

4. Aum Shinrikyō was a new religious movement whose philosophy combined idiosyncratic Buddhist concepts with science-fictional tropes. Yumiko Iida provides an extended discussion of the Aum phenomenon, linking it with the emergence of groups devoted to nationalist historical revisionism as well as youth violence. See her *Rethinking Identity in Modern Japan*, 237–44.

5. Carol Gluck and Harry Harootunian have both offered discussions of this so-called "long postwar." See their respective essays "The 'End' of the Postwar"; "Japan's Long Postwar."

6. Hage, *Against Paranoid Nationalism*.

7. The controversy over constitutional revision in Japan centers on the issue of Article 9, in which belligerence and the use of military force is renounced. It should be also be noted that accompanying proposals to revise the constitution so as to allow a military buildup in Japan as well as to legally participate in American military action (under the euphemism of "collective self-defense") is also accompanied by moves to revise history textbooks in an effort to portray imperial Japanese aggression in a more favorable light.

8. Within the work of Sigmund Freud, the most well known discussion of the repetition-compulsion is in the 1920 essay "Beyond the Pleasure Principle." Laplanche and Pontalis have also provided a succinct definition of the concept in *The Language of Psycho-Analysis*, 465. They describe trauma as "an event in the subject's

life, defined by its intensity, by the subject's incapacity to respond adequately to it and by the upheaval and long-lasting effects that it brings about in the psychical organization."

9. Ivy, "Trauma's Two Times," 177.

10. Cohen, "History and Genre," 210.

11. Neale, *Genre*, 48.

12. Jameson, *The Political Unconscious*, 106.

13. Bazerman, "The Life of Genre, the Life in the Classroom," 19.

14. Miyadai, *Owaranaki nichijō o ikirō.*

15. Although Kurosawa had been directing 8mm films since the 1970s and had begun to establish his domestic reputation with his V-cinema work in the 1980s, it was primarily with his supernatural thriller *Cure* that he first received wide international regard. His reputation was further established with the screening of the aforementioned *Pulse* in the Un Certain Regard section of the 2001 Cannes Film Festival.

16. For example, Abe Kashō specifically names *Cure* a "horror film after Aum" [*Ōmu ikō no kyōfu eiga*]. See Abe, *Nihon eiga ga sonzaisuru*, 121–24.

17. "Intabyū—Kurosawa Kiyoshi."

18. The term "outlaw master" is from Chris D, who counts Kurosawa among those "genre filmmakers who made genre movies usually labeled as samurai, *yakuza*, horror, *pink*, etc., but who pushed the envelope beyond the usual conventions in some way either in style or content." D, *Outlaw Masters of Japanese Film.*

19. For a discussion of Kurosawa's critical dialogue with the discourse vis-à-vis J-Horror, see Kinoshita, "The Mummy Complex."

20. Gerow, "The Empty Return," 19–23.

21. Kurosawa's film *Séance* is itself a loose remake of the British film *Séance on a Wet Afternoon* (1964), directed by Bryan Forbes, which is itself an adaptation of the Mark McShane novel (1961) of the same title.

22. *Rofuto* (*Loft*, 2005), Kurosawa's film subsequent to *Doppelgänger*, features a similar parodic subversion of the horror genre. Its narrative—which revolves around a novelist who moves into a house in the countryside to cure her writer's block and her encounter with a troubled scientist who has recovered a thousand-year-old mummy from a nearby swamp—certainly makes use of some of the staple tropes of the horror genre. But as its story proceeds, it moves in and out of one genre or another. While one scene might play up the empty rooms of a haunted house, the next will bring overwrought professions of undying love from the protagonists more appropriate for a tired melodrama.

23. Hantke, "'The Kingdom of the Unimaginable,'" 181.

24. Todorov, "The Typology of Detective Fiction," 36.

25. Hantke, "'The Kingdom of the Unimaginable,'" 194.

26. Hasumi, *Eiga hōkai zen'ya*, 69.

27. Moretti, *Signs Taken for Wonders*, 134–35.

28. Ibid., 135.

29. Žižek, *Violence*, 2.

30. Abe, *Nihon eiga ga sonzaisuru*, 124.

31. Ibid., 123.

32. Nakano, "Joyūrei-ron," 115–18.

33. Kurosawa, "Horā eiga to wa nani ka?," 23–26.

34. Kume Yoriko, "'Bunkateki' na shutai no yamai," 134.

35. Derrida, *Specters of Marx*, 11.

36. Ibid., xx.

37. Lim, *Translating Time*, 151.

38. Harry Harootunian has criticized the postcolonial politics of Partha Chatterjee precisely on these terms, arguing that Chatterjee's desire for an indigenous alternative modernity that has not already been worked over by capitalism and colonialism repeats the same logic that facilitated fascist ideologies in 1930s Japan. See Chatterjee, *The Nation and Its Fragments*; Harootunian, "Postcoloniality's Unconscious/Area Studies' Desire."

39. Harootunian, "Japan's Long Postwar," 113–14.

40. Marilyn Ivy has noted a mutual complicity between Western and Japanese discourses in producing a narrative of Western assimilation that nonetheless leaves the national culture intact. In her words: "Disclosed in the image of assimilation with its insistence on the final imperviousness of Japanese culture is a profound categorical uneasiness, an uneasiness contained only by keeping the spheres of the economic and cultural distinct." See Ivy, *Discourses of the Vanishing*, 1–2.

41. McRoy, *Nightmare Japan*, 5.

42. Ibid., 81.

43. Wada-Marciano, "J-Horror," 25–33.

44. McRoy, *Nightmare Japan*, 75.

45. Wada-Marciano, "J-Horror," 34–35.

46. Jameson, "Third-World Literature in the Era of Multinational Capitalism," 69. The most well known critique of Jameson's essay is Aijaz Ahmad's "Jameson's Rhetoric of Otherness and the 'National Allegory.'"

47. Shih, "Global Literature and the Technologies of Recognition," 21.

48. Beller, *The Cinematic Mode of Production*, 1.

49. Ibid., 2.

50. Viewed in this light, Hasumi Shigehiko is without a doubt on the mark in his description of Kurosawa's film as an "exceptionally ethical work that compels a consciousness of looking and the responsibility thereof with every shot" [*miru koto to sono sekinin wo shotto goto ni ishiki-ka saseru kōdo ni rinriteki na sakuhin*]. Hasumi, *Eiga hōkai zen'ya*, 34.

51. Tadiar, *Fantasy-Production*, 5–6.

52. Cazdyn and Szeman, *After Globalization*, 1–2.

53. Jameson, *Archaeologies of the Future*, 232.

54. Gerow, "Recognizing 'Others' in a New Japanese Cinema," 1–6.

55. Derrida, *Acts of Literature*, 242.

56. Michael Hardt and Antonio Negri critique this as a kind of "domestic analogy" that is unable to grasp the novelty of the contemporary moment because of the reliance on older concepts and categories. See *Empire*, 7–8.

57. Silverman, *Male Subjectivity at the Margins*, 55.

BIBLIOGRAPHY

Abe Kashō. *Nihon eiga ga sonzaisuru* [Japanese film exists]. Tokyo: Seidosha, 2000.

Ahmad, Aijaz. "Jameson's Rhetoric of Otherness and the 'National Allegory.'" *Social Text* 17 (1987): 3–25.

Akutagawa Ryūnosuke. "Futatsu no tegami [Two Letters]." In *Akutagawa Ryūnosuke zenshū 2* [The complete works of Akutagawa Ryūnosuke 2]. Tokyo: Kadokawa Shoten, 1968.

———. "Haguruma [Spinning Gears]." In *Akutagawa Ryūnosuke zenshū 10* [The complete works of Akutagawa Ryūnosuke 10]. Tokyo: Kadokawa Shoten, 1968.

———. "Kage [The Shadow]." In *Akutagawa Ryūnosuke zenshū 5* [The complete works of Akutagawa Ryūnosuke 5]. Tokyo: Kadokawa Shoten, 1968.

Anderson, Benedict. *The Spectre of Comparisons: Nationalism, Southeast Asia, and the World*. London: Verso, 1998.

Angles, Jeffrey. "Seeking the Strange: Ryōki and the Navigation of Normality in Interwar Japan." *Monumenta Nipponica* 63, no. 1 (2008): 101–41.

Bal, Mieke. *Quoting Caravaggio: Contemporary Art, Preposterous History*. Chicago: University of Chicago Press, 1999.

Balibar, Etienne, and Immanuel Maurice Wallerstein. *Race, Nation, Class: Ambiguous Identities*. London: Verso, 1991.

Barthes, Roland. *Writing Degree Zero*. London: Cape, 1967.

Baudrillard, Jean. *Symbolic Exchange and Death*. London: SAGE, 1993.

Bazerman, Charles. "The Life of Genre, the Life in the Classroom." In *Genre and Writing: Issues, Arguments, Alternatives*, edited by Wendy Bishop and Hans A. Ostrom, 19–26. Portsmouth, N.H.: Boynton/Cook-Heinemann, 1997.

Beller, Jonathan. *The Cinematic Mode of Production: Attention Economy and the Society of the Spectacle*. Dover, N.H.: Dartmouth College Press, 2006.

Benjamin, Walter. *Charles Baudelaire: A Lyric Poet in the Era of High Capitalism*. London: New Left Books, 1973.

———. "The Work of Art in the Age of Mechanical Reproduction." In *Illumina-tions*, 217–51. New York: Schocken Books, 1968.

Bhabha, Homi. *The Location of Culture.* New York: Routledge, 1994.

Bloch, Ernst. "A Philosophical View of the Detective Novel." In *The Utopian Func-tion of Art and Literature: Selected Essays*, translated by Jack Zipes and Frank Mecklenburg, 245–64. Cambridge, Mass.: MIT Press, 1988.

Blowers, Geoffrey H., and Serena Hsueh Chih Yang. "Ohtsuki Kenji and the Begin-nings of Lay Analysis in Japan." *International Journal of Psychoanalysis*, no. 82 (2001): 27–42.

Cavanaugh, Carole. "Junbungaku Goes to the Movies: Akutagawa Ryūnosuke and Katsudō Shashin." *Ga/Zoku Dynamics in Japanese Literature.* Proceedings of the Midwest Association for Japanese Literary Studies, no. 3 (1997): 298–315.

Cazdyn, Eric. *The Flash of Capital: Film and Geopolitics in Japan.* Durham, N.C.: Duke University Press, 2002.

Cazdyn, Eric, and Imre Szeman. *After Globalization.* Malden, Mass.: Wiley-Blackwell, 2011.

Chakrabarty, Dipesh. "Postcoloniality and the Artifice of History; Who Speaks for 'Indian' Pasts?" *Representations* 37 (1992): 1–26.

Chatterjee, Partha. *The Nation and Its Fragments: Colonial and Postcolonial Histo-ries.* Princeton, N.J.: Princeton University Press, 1993.

Cheng, Anne Anlin. *The Melancholy of Race: Psychoanalysis, Assimilation, and Hidden Grief.* New York: Oxford University Press, 2001.

Ching, Leo T. S. *Becoming "Japanese": Colonial Taiwan and the Politics of Identity Formation.* Berkeley: University of California Press, 2001.

Chow, Rey. *Primitive Passions: Visuality, Sexuality, Ethnography, and Contempo-rary Chinese Cinema.* New York: Columbia University Press, 1995.

Coates, Paul. *The Gorgon's Gaze: German Cinema, Expressionism, and the Image of Horror.* Cambridge: Cambridge University Press, 1991.

Cohen, Ralph. "History and Genre." *New Literary History* 17, no. 2 (1986): 203–18.

Cole, Simon A. *Suspect Identities: A History of Fingerprinting and Criminal Identifi-cation.* Cambridge, Mass.: Harvard University Press, 2001.

Cornyetz, Nina, and J. Keith Vincent. "Introduction—Japan as Screen Memory: Psychoanalysis and History." In *Perversion and Modern Japan: Psychoanalysis, Literature, Culture*, 1–19. New York: Routledge, 2010.

Crary, Jonathan. *Techniques of the Observer: On Vision and Modernity in the 19th Century.* Cambridge, Mass.: MIT Press, 1990.

Currie, Mark. *About Time: Narrative, Fiction, and the Philosophy of Time.* Edin-burgh: Edinburgh University Press, 2007.

D, Chris. *Outlaw Masters of Japanese Film.* London: I.B. Tauris, 2005.

Debord, Guy. *The Society of the Spectacle.* Translated by Donald Nicholson-Smith. New York: Zone Books, 1994.

Deleuze, Gilles. *Cinema 1: The Movement-Image.* Translated by Hugh Tomlinson and Barbara Habberjam. Minneapolis: University of Minnesota Press, 1986.

Deleuze, Gilles, and Félix Guattari. *Anti-Oedipus: Capitalism and Schizophrenia.* Translated by Mark Seem and Helen R. Lane. New York: Viking Press, 1983.

Derrida, Jacques. *Acts of Literature.* Translated by Derek Attridge. New York: Routledge, 1992.

———. *Specters of Marx: The State of the Debt, the Work of Mourning, and the New International.* New York: Routledge, 1994.

Derrida, Jacques, and Bernard Steigler. *Echographies of Television: Filmed Interview.* Cambridge: Polity, 2002.

Doane, Mary Anne. *The Emergence of Cinematic Time: Modernity, Contingency, the Archive.* Cambridge, Mass.: Harvard University Press, 2002.

Driscoll, Mark. *Absolute Erotic, Absolute Grotesque: The Living, Dead, and Undead in Japan's Imperialism, 1895–1945.* Durham, N.C.: Duke University Press, 2010.

Duus, Peter. "Introduction." In *Japanese Informal Empire in China, 1895–1937,* edited by Peter Duus, Ramon H. Myers, and Mark R. Peattie, xi–xxix. Princeton, N.J.: Princeton University Press, 1989.

Edogawa Rampo. "The Horrors of Film." In *The Edogawa Rampo Reader,* translated by Seth Jacobowitz, 137–42. Tokyo: Kurodahan Press, 2008.

———. *Injū* [*The Beast in the Shadows*]. In *Edogawa Ranpo zenshū 3: Injū* [The complete works of Edogawa Rampo 3: The beast in the shadows]. Tokyo: Kōbunsha bunko, 2005.

———. *Ryōki no hate* [*Beyond the Bizarre*]. In *Edogawa Ranpo zenshū 4: Ryōki no hate* [The complete works of Edogawa Rampo 4: Beyond the bizarre]. Tokyo: Kōbunsha bunko, 2005.

———. "Sōseiji: Aru shikeishū ga kyōkaishi ni ichuaketa hanashi [The Twins: A Condemned Criminal's Confession to a Priest]." In *Edogawa Rampo zenshū 1: Yaneura no sampōsha* [The complete works of Edogawa Rampo 1: Stalker in the attic], 155–75. Tokyo: Kōbunsha bunko, 2005.

———. "Tantei shōsetsu ni tsuite [On detective fiction]." *Shinseinen,* no. 5 (1923).

———. "Waga yume to shinjitsu [My dreams and my truths]." In *Edogawa Ranpo zenshū 30: Waga yume to shinjitsu* [The complete works of Edogawa Rampo 30: My dreams and my truths]. Tokyo: Kōbunsha bunko, 2005.

———. "'Watashi no pen nêmu' [My pen name]." In *Edogawa Ranpo, shinbungei tokuhon* [Edogawa Rampo: A new literary reader]. Tokyo: Kawade Shobō shinsha, 1992.

Fabian, Johannes. *Time and the Other: How Anthropology Makes Its Object.* New York: Columbia University Press, 2002.

Fanon, Frantz. *Black Skin, White Masks.* Translated by Charles Lam Markmann. New York: Grove, 1967.

Fonseca, Tony. "The Doppelgänger." In *Icons of Horror and the Supernatural*, edited by S. T. Joshi, 187–213. Santa Barbara, Calif.: Greenwood Publishing Group, 2006.

Foucault, Michel. *The Archaeology of Knowledge and the Discourse on Language*. Translated by Alan Sheridan. New York: Pantheon Books, 1972.

———. *The Birth of the Clinic: An Archaeology of Medical Perception*. New York: Pantheon Books, 1973.

———. *Discipline and Punish: The Birth of the Prison*. New York: Vintage Books, 1977.

———. *The Order of Things: An Archaeology of the Human Sciences*. New York: Pantheon Books, 1970.

Fowler, Edward. "Rendering Words, Traversing Cultures: On the Art and Politics of Translating Modern Japanese Fiction." *Journal of Japanese Studies* 18, no. 1 (1992): 1–44.

Freud, Sigmund. "Beyond the Pleasure Principle." In *The Standard Edition of the Complete Psychological Works of Sigmund Freud, Volume XVIII*, 1–64. New York: W. W. Norton, 2000.

———. "The Ego and the Id." In *The Standard Edition of the Complete Psychological Works of Sigmund Freud, Volume XIX*, 3–66. New York: W. W. Norton, 2000.

———. "Mourning and Melancholia." In *The Standard Edition of the Complete Psychological Works of Sigmund Freud, Volume XIV*. New York: W. W. Norton, 2000.

———. "On Narcissism." In *The Standard Edition of the Complete Psychological Works of Sigmund Freud, Volume XIV*, 67–145. New York: W. W. Norton, 2000.

———. "Psycho-Analysis and the Establishment of the Facts in Legal Proceedings." In *The Standard Edition of the Complete Psychological Works of Sigmund Freud, Volume IX*. New York: W. W. Norton, 2000.

———. "Remembering, Repeating, and Working-Through." In *The Standard Edition of the Complete Psychological Works of Sigmund Freud, Volume XII*, 147–56. New York: W. W. Norton, 2000.

———. *Totem and Taboo: Some Points of Agreement Between the Mental Lives of Savages and Neurotics*. London: Routledge, 1999.

———. "The Uncanny." In *The Standard Edition of the Complete Psychological Works of Sigmund Freud, Volume XVII*, 219–56. New York: W. W. Norton, 2000.

Friedberg, Anne. *Window Shopping: Cinema and the Postmodern*. Berkeley: University of California Press, 1995.

Galton, Francis. "History of Twins." In *Inquiries into Human Faculty and Its Development*, 216–43. London: Macmillan, 1883.

Gerbert, Elaine. "The Influence of Vision Technology on Narrative in Taishō." In *New Trends and Issues in Teaching Japanese Language and Culture*, edited by Kyoko Hijirida, Haruko M. Cook, and Mildred Tahara, 15–30. Honolulu: University of Hawai'i at Mānoa, 1997.

Gerow, Aaron. "The Empty Return: Circularity and Repetition in Recent Japanese Horror Films." *Minikomi: Informationen des Akademischen Arbeitkreis Japan* 64 (2002): 19–24.

———. "Recognizing 'Others' in a New Japanese Cinema." *Japan Foundation Newsletter* 39, no. 2 (January 2002): 1–6.

———. "The Self Seen as Other: Akutagawa and Film." *Literature/Film Quarterly* 23, no. 3 (1995): 197–203.

———. *Visions of Japanese Modernity: Articulations of Cinema, Nation, and Spectatorship, 1895–1925*. Berkeley: University of California Press, 2010.

Gilroy, Paul. *Postcolonial Melancholia*. New York: Columbia University Press, 2005.

Gluck, Carol. "The 'End' of the Postwar: Japan at the Turn of the Millennium." *Public Culture* 10, no. 1 (1997): 1–23.

Goodman, Bryna. "Improvisations on a Semicolonial Theme; or, How to Read a Celebration of Transnational Urban Community." *Journal of Asian Studies* 59, no. 4 (November 2000): 889–926.

Grossberg, Lawrence. *Cultural Studies in the Future Tense*. Durham, N.C.: Duke University Press, 2010.

Gunning, Tom. "The Cinema of Attractions: Early Film, Its Spectator, and the Avant-Garde." In *Early Cinema: Space, Frame, Narrative*, edited by Thomas Elsaesser, 56–62. London: British Film Institute, 1990.

———. "Tracing the Individual Body: Photography, Detectives, and Early Cinema." In *Cinema and the Invention of Modern Life*, edited by Leo Charney and Vanessa L. Schwartz, 15–45. Berkeley: University of California Press, 1995.

Hage, Ghassan. *Against Paranoid Nationalism: Searching for Hope in a Shrinking Society*. Annandale, Vic.: Pluto Press Australia, 2003.

Hallam, Clifford. "The Double as Incomplete Self: Toward a Definition of Doppelgänger." In *Fearful Symmetry: Doubles and Doubling in Literature and Film*. Papers from the Fifth Annual Florida State University Conference on Literature and Film. Tallahassee: University Presses of Florida, 1981.

Hantke, Steffan. "'The Kingdom of the Unimaginable': The Construction of Social Space and the Fantasy of Privacy in Serial Killer Narratives." *Literature/Film Quarterly* 26, no. 3 (1998): 178–95.

Hardt, Michael, and Antonio Negri. *Empire*. Cambridge, Mass.: Harvard University Press, 2000.

Harootunian, Harry D. *History's Disquiet: Modernity, Cultural Practice, and the Question of Everyday Life*. New York: Columbia University Press, 2000.

———. "Japan's Long Postwar: The Trick of Memory and the Ruse of History." In *Japan After Japan: Social and Cultural Life from the Recessionary 1990s to the Present*, edited by Tomiko Yoda and Harry Harootunian, 98–121. Durham, N.C.: Duke University Press, 2006.

———. *Overcome by Modernity: History, Culture, and Community in Interwar Japan*. Princeton, N.J.: Princeton University Press, 2000.

———. "Postcoloniality's Unconscious/Area Studies' Desire." In *Learning Places: The Afterlives of Area Studies*, edited by Masao Miyoshi and Harry Harootunian, 150–74. Durham, N.C.: Duke University Press, 2002.

Harvey, David. *The Condition of Postmodernity: An Enquiry into the Origins of Cultural Change*. Cambridge, Mass.: Blackwell, 1989.

———. *The Limits to Capital*. London: Verso, 2006.

Hasumi Shigehiko. *Eiga hōkai zen'ya* [On the eve of the end of film]. Tokyo: Seido-sha, 2008.

Heath, Stephen. "Cinema and Psychoanalysis: Parallel Histories." In *Endless Night: Cinema and Psychoanalysis, Parallel Histories*, 25–56. Berkeley: University of California Press, 1999.

Herdman, John. *The Double in Nineteenth-Century Fiction*. Basingstoke: Macmillan, 1990.

Hirabayashi Hatsunosuke. "Shōhin toshite no kindai shōsetsu [The modern novel as commodity]." In *Bungaku riron no shomondai* [Problematics of literary theory], 149–60. Tokyo: Chikuma Shobō, 1929.

———. "Tantei shōsetu-dan no shokeikō [Directions of detective fiction circles]." In *Kyōyō to shite no satsujin* [Murder as cultivation], edited by Gonda Manji, 28–36. Tokyo: Kagyūsha, 1979.

Hirano Yoshihiko. *Hofuman to 'Ranpo: Ningyō to kōgaku kikai no eros* [Hoffmann and Rampo: The eros of dolls and optical technologies]. Tokyo: Misuzu Shobō, 2007.

Hutcheon, Linda. *A Theory of Adaptation*. New York: Routledge, 2006.

Ichiyanagi Hirotaka. "Samayoeru dopperugengā: Akutagawa Ryūnosuke 'Futatsu no tegami' to tantei shōsetsu" [Meandering doppelgänger: Akutagawa Ryūnosuke's 'Two Letters' and detective fiction]." In *Tantei shōsetsu to nihon kindai* [Detective fiction and Japanese modernity], 110–31. Tokyo: Seikyūsha, 2004.

Igarashi, Yoshikuni. "Edogawa Rampo and the Excess of Vision: An Ocular Critique of Modernity in 1920s Japan." *Positions: East Asia Cultures Critique* 13, no. 2 (2005): 299–327.

Iida, Yumiko. *Rethinking Identity in Modern Japan: Nationalism as Aesthetics*. New York: Routledge, 2002.

Ikeda Hiroshi. *"Kaigai shinshutsu bungaku" ron josetsu* [An introduction to "Literature of Overseas Advancement"]. Tokyo: Inpakuto shuppankai, 1997.

Inoue Kishō. "'Shimon' to 'Chi': Kōga Saburō 'Bōrei no shimon' o tansho ni ['Fingerprint' and 'Blood': Kōga Saburō's 'Ghostly Fingerprint' as clue]." *Sō: Eizō to hyōgen* 2 (2008): 201–21.

Inoue Yoshio. "*Injū* ginmi [Scrutinizing *The Beast in the Shadows*]." In *Edogawa Ranpo, Hyōron to Kenkyū* [Edogawa Rampo: Criticism and research]. Tokyo: Kōdansha, 1980.

"Intabyū—Kurosawa Kiyoshi: Yūrei o riarizumu de egaku kokoromi [Interview with Kurosawa Kiyoshi: Attempting a realistic portrayal of ghosts]." *Kinema Junpō*, March 2007.

Ivy, Marilyn. *Discourses of the Vanishing: Modernity, Phantasm, Japan.* Chicago: University of Chicago Press, 1995.

———. "Trauma's Two Times: Japanese Wars and Postwars." *Positions: East Asia Cultures Critique* 16, no. 8 (2008): 165–88.

Jameson, Fredric. *Archaeologies of the Future: The Desire Called Utopia and Other Science Fictions.* New York: Verso, 2005.

———. "Modernism and Imperialism." In *Nationalism, Colonialism, and Literature,* 43–68. Minneapolis: University of Minnesota Press, 1990.

———. *The Political Unconscious: Narrative as a Socially Symbolic Act.* Ithaca, N.Y.: Cornell University Press, 1981.

———. "Postmodernism and Consumer Society." In *The Anti-Aesthetic: Essays on Postmodern Culture,* edited by Hal Foster, 111–25. Seattle: Bay Press, 1983.

———. *Postmodernism; or, The Cultural Logic of Late Capitalism.* Durham, N.C.: Duke University Press, 1991.

———. "Third-World Literature in the Era of Multinational Capitalism." *Social Text* 15 (1986): 65–88.

Jay, Martin. "Scopic Regimes of Modernity." In *Vision and Visuality,* edited by Hal Foster, 3–23. Seattle: Bay Press, 1988.

Kang Sang-jung. *Orientarizumu no kanata e* [Beyond orientalism]. Tokyo: Iwanami Shoten, 1996.

Kano, Ayako. *Acting Like a Woman in Modern Japan: Theater, Gender, and Nationalism.* New York: Palgrave, 2001.

Karatani Kōjin. *Karatani Kōjin shū 5: Rekishi to hanpuku* [Collected works of Karatani Kōjin 5: History and repetition]. Tokyo: Iwanami Shoten, 2004.

———. *The Origins of Modern Japanese Literature.* Durham, N.C.: Duke University Press, 1993.

Kasai Kiyoshi. "Tantei shōsetsu no chisōgaku [Archaeology of detective fiction]." In *Honkaku misuteri no genzai* [Orthodox mystery today], 5–21. Tokyo: Kokusho Kanōkai, 1997.

Katsura Chiho. "Ranpo no eigaka ni tsuite [On film adaptations of Rampo]." *Kokubungaku: Kaishaku to Kanshō* 59, no. 12 (1994): 70–75.

Kawana, Sari. *Murder Most Modern: Detective Fiction and Japanese Culture.* Minneapolis: University of Minnesota Press, 2008.

Keppler, C. F. *The Literature of the Second Self.* Tucson: University of Arizona Press, 1972.

Khanna, Ranjanna. *Dark Continents: Psychoanalysis and Colonialism.* Durham, N.C.: Duke University Press, 2003.

Kinoshita, Chika. "The Mummy Complex: Kurosawa Kiyoshi's Loft and J-Horror." In *Horror to the Extreme: Changing Boundaries in Asian Cinema,* edited by Mitsuyo Wada-Marciano and Jinhee Choi. Hong Kong: Hong Kong University Press, 2009.

Kittler, Friedrich. *Discourse Networks 1800/1900*. Stanford, Calif.: Stanford University Press, 1990.

———. "Romanticism—Psychoanalysis—Film: A History of the Double." In *Literature, Media, Information Systems: Essays*, 85–100. New York: Routledge, 1997.

Kobayashi Hideo. *Literature of the Lost Home: Kobayashi Hideo—Literary Criticism, 1924–1939*. Stanford, Calif.: Stanford University Press, 1995.

Kōga Saburō. "Baiu-ki no nōto kara [Notes from the rainy season]." *Shinseinen*, no. 15 (1934).

Komori Yōichi. *Posutokoroniaru* [Postcolonial]. Tokyo: Iwanami Shoten, 2001.

Kozakai Fuboku. "'Nisen dōka' o yomu [Reading 'A Two-Sen Copper Coin']." *Shinseinen*, no. 5 (1923).

Kume Yoriko. "'Bunkateki' na shutai no yamai: Kurosawa Kiyoshi to Yamamoto Fumio no dopperugengā, soshite sakebi [Sickness of the 'cultural' subject: Kurosawa Kiyoshi's and Yamamoto Fumio's doppelgängers, and retribution]." In *Naitomea sōsho 4: Eiga no kyōfu* [Nightmare series 4: The horror of cinema], edited by Ichiyanagi Hirotaka and Yoshida Morio, 129–36. Tokyo: Seikyūsha, 2007.

Kurosawa Kiyoshi. "Horā eiga to wa nani ka [What is horror cinema]?" In *Eiga wa osoroshii* [Film is frightening], 23–26. Tokyo: Seidosha, 2002.

Lacan, Jacques. *The Four Fundamental Concepts of Psychoanalysis*. New York: W. W. Norton, 1981.

———. "The Mirror Stage as Formative of the Function of the I as Revealed in Psychoanalytic Experience." In *Ecrits: A Selection*, 3–9. New York: W. W. Norton, 1977.

Lamarre, Thomas. "The First Time as Farce: Digital Animation and the Repetition of Cinema." In *Cinema Anime: Critical Engagements with Japanese Animation*, edited by Steven T. Brown, 161–88. New York: Palgrave Macmillan, 2005.

———. *Shadows on the Screen: Tanizaki Jun'ichirō on Cinema and Oriental Aesthetics*. Ann Arbor: University of Michigan Center for Japanese Studies, 2005.

Laplanche, Jean, and J. B. Pontalis. *The Language of Psycho-Analysis*. New York: W. W. Norton, 1974.

Lim, Bliss Cua. *Translating Time: Cinema, the Fantastic, and Temporal Critique*. Durham, N.C.: Duke University Press, 2009.

Lippit, Seiji M. *Topographies of Japanese Modernism*. New York: Columbia University Press, 2002.

Long, Margherita. *This Perversion Called Love: Reading Tanizaki, Feminist Theory, and Freud*. Stanford, Calif.: Stanford University Press, 2009.

Manovich, Lev. *The Language of New Media*. Cambridge, Mass.: MIT Press, 2001.

Markus, Andrew L. "The Carnival of Edo: Misemono Spectacles from Contemporary Accounts." *Harvard Journal of Asiatic Studies* 45, no. 2 (December 1985): 499–541.

Marx, Karl. *The Eighteenth Brumaire of Louis Bonaparte*. New York: Mondial Books, 2005.

Matsuyama Iwao. *Ranpo to Tokyo: 1920 toshi no kao* [Rampo and Tokyo: Visage of the city, 1920]. Tokyo: Chikuma gakugei bunko, 1984.

McClintock, Anne. *Imperial Leather: Race, Gender, and Sexuality in the Colonial Contest.* New York: Routledge, 1995.

McRoy, Jay. *Nightmare Japan: Contemporary Japanese Horror Cinema.* Amsterdam: Rodopi, 2008.

Meng Yue. *Shanghai and the Edges of Empires.* Minneapolis: University of Minnesota Press, 2006.

Mes, Tom. *Iron Man: The Cinema of Shinya Tsukamoto.* Surrey, UK: FAB Press, 2005.

Metz, Christian. *The Imaginary Signifier: Psychoanalysis and the Cinema.* Bloomington: Indiana University Press, 1982.

Meyers, Jeffrey. *Edgar Allan Poe: Mournful and Never-Ending Remembrance.* New York: Cooper Square Press, 1992.

Miller, Karl. *Doubles: Studies in Literary History.* Oxford: Oxford University Press, 1985.

Minear, Richard H. "Orientalism and the Study of Japan." Edited by Edward W. Said. *Journal of Asian Studies* 39, no. 3 (1980): 507–17.

Miyadai Shinji. *Owaranaki nichijō o ikirō* [Live the endless everyday]. Tokyo: Chikuma Shobō, 1995.

Miyanaga Takashi. *Pō to Nihon: Sono juyō no rekishi* [Poe and Japan: A history of his reception]. Tokyo: Sairyūsha, 2000.

Mizuno Rei. "Dopperugengā shōsetsu ni miru janru no keisei to henyō" [Formations and transformation of genre as seen in doppelgänger fiction]." *Jōhō bunka kenkyū,* no. 15 (2002): 115–32.

Moore, Rachel O. *Savage Theory: Cinema as Modern Magic.* Durham, N.C.: Duke University Press, 2000.

Moretti, Franco. *Signs Taken for Wonders: On the Sociology of Literary Forms.* London: Verso, 2005.

Mori Ōgai. "Fushigi na kagami [A strange mirror]." In *Mori Ōgai zenshu II,* 2: 224–31. Tokyo: Chikuma Shobō, 1964.

Nakamura, Miri. *Monstrous Bodies: The Rise of the Uncanny in Modern Japan.* Cambridge, Mass.: Harvard University Asia Center, 2015.

Nakano Yasushi. "Joyūrei-ron: Arui wa, eiga no jikogenkyūsayō ni hasamu 'ma' ni tsuite [A study of ghost actress; or, on the haunting of film's self-referential operation]." In *Naitomea sōsho 1: Horā japanesuku no genzai* [Nightmare series 1: Horror japonesque in the present], edited by Ichiyanagi Hirotaka and Yoshida Morio. Tokyo: Seikyūsha, 2005.

Neale, Stephen. *Genre.* London: British Film Institute, 1980.

Negri, Antonio. *Marx Beyond Marx: Lessons on the Grundrisse.* New York: Autonomedia, 1991.

Nishii Yaeko. "Nihon dopperugengā shōsetsu nenpyōkō [Draft chronology of Japanese doppelgänger fiction]." In *Naitomea sōsho: Gensō bungaku, kindai no makai e* [Nightmare series: Fantastic literature, toward the hell of modernity], 214–46. Tokyo: Seikyūsha, 2006.

Oguma Eiji. *A Genealogy of "Japanese" Self-Images.* Translated by David Askew. Melbourne: Trans Pacific Press, 2002.

———. "Yūshoku no shokumin teikoku: 1920-nen zengo no Nikkei imin haisō to Chōsen tōjiron [A colored colonial empire: The retreat of Japanese immigration and the discourse on Korean rule in the 1920s]." In *Nashonariti no datsukōchiku* [Deconstructing nationality], 81–102. Tokyo: Shin'yōsha, 1996.

Oshino Takeshi. "'Junsui shōsetsu' toshite no gendai misuteri" [Contemporary mystery as 'pure novel']." *Shakai bungaku* 22 (2005): 21–36.

Osterhammel, Jürgen. "Semi-Colonialism and Informal Empire in Twentieth-Century China: Towards a Framework of Analysis." In *Imperialism and After: Continuities and Discontinuities,* edited by Wolfgang J. Mommsen and Jürgen Osterhammel, 290–314. Washington, D.C.: German Historical Institute, 1986.

Oyama, Tadasu, Tatsuya Sato, and Yuko Suzuki. "Shaping of Scientific Psychology in Japan." *International Journal of Psychology* 33, no. 6 (2001): 396–406.

Ozaki Hotsuki. "Ranpo bungaku no zentaizō [The image of totality in Rampo's fiction]." In *Edogawa Ranpo, hyōron to kenkyū* [Edogawa Rampo: Criticism and research], edited by Nakajima Kawatarō. Tokyo: Kōdansha, 1980.

Passavant, Paul, and Jodi Dean, eds. *Empire's New Clothes: Reading Hardt and Negri.* New York: Routledge, 2003.

Pratt, Mary Louise. *Imperial Eyes: Travel Writing and Transculturation.* New York: Routledge, 1992.

Rank, Otto. *Bunshin: Dopperugengā.* Kyoto: Shūeisha, 1988.

———. *The Double: A Psychoanalytic Study.* Chapel Hill: University of North Carolina Press, 1971.

Rashidi, Bahareh. "Divided Screen: The Doppelgänger in German Silent Film." PhD dissertation, University of Edinburgh, 2007.

Richter, Jean Paul. "Siebenkäs." In *Werke.* Munich: Carl Hansen Verlag, 1959.

Rogers, Robert. *A Psychoanalytic Study of the Double in Literature.* Detroit: Wayne State University Press, 1970.

Rosen, Philip. *Change Mummified: Cinema, Historicity, Theory.* Minneapolis: University of Minnesota Press, 2001.

Rubin, Jay. *Injurious to Public Morals: Writers and the Meiji State.* Seattle: University of Washington Press, 1984.

Said, Edward. *Orientalism.* New York: Vintage Books, 1979.

Saito, Satoru. *Detective Fiction and the Rise of the Japanese Novel, 1880–1930.* Cambridge, Mass.: Harvard University Asia Center, 2012.

Saitō Tamaki. *Shinrigakka suru shakai: Naze torauma to iyashi ga motomerareru no ka* [The psychologization of society: Accounting for the desire for trauma and healing]. Tokyo: PHP Editāzu gurūpu, 2003.

Sakai, Naoki. "'Dislocation of the West and the Status of the Humanities.'" In *Specters of the West and the Politics of Translation*, edited by Yukiko Hanawa and Naoki Sakai, 71–94. Hong Kong: Hong Kong University Press, 2001.

———. *Translation and Subjectivity: On "Japan" and Cultural Nationalism*. Minneapolis: University of Minnesota Press, 1997.

Sakaki, Atsuko. *Obsessions with the Sino-Japanese Polarity in Japanese Literature*. Honolulu: University of Hawai'i Press, 2006.

Schwartz, Hillel. *The Culture of the Copy: Striking Likenesses, Unreasonable Facsimiles*. New York: Zone Books, 1996.

Sedgwick, Eve Kosofsky. *Between Men: English Literature and Male Homosocial Desire*. New York: Columbia University Press, 1985.

Serizawa Kazuya. *"Hō" kara kaihō sareru kenryoku* [Power liberated from "law"]. Tokyo: Shinyōsha, 2001.

Shih, Shu-Mei. "Global Literature and the Technologies of Recognition." *Proceedings of the Modern Language Association* 119, no. 1 (January 2004): 16–30.

Shimizu Yoshinori. "Ranpo no kyōjin na nimensei [Rampo's tenacious two-facedness]." *Kokubungaku: Kaishaku to kanshō* 59, no. 12 (1994): 29–35.

Siddiqi, Yumna. *Anxieties of Empire and the Fiction of Intrigue*. New York: Columbia University Press, 2008.

Silver, Mark. *Purloined Letters: Cultural Borrowing and Japanese Crime Literature 1868–1937*. Honolulu: University of Hawai'i Press, 2008.

Silverberg, Miriam. *Erotic Grotesque Nonsense: The Mass Culture of Japanese Modern Times*. Berkeley: University of California Press, 2006.

Silverman, Kaja. *Male Subjectivity at the Margins*. New York: Routledge, 1992.

Simmel, Georg. "The Metropolis and Mental Life." In *The Sociology of Georg Simmel*, edited by Kurt Wolf, 409–24. New York: Free Press, 1950.

Stam, Robert. "Beyond Fidelity: The Dialogics of Adaptation." In *Film Adaptation*, edited by James Naremore, 54–76. New Brunswick, N.J.: Rutgers University Press, 2000.

Strowick, Elisabeth. "Comparative Epistemology of Suspicion: Psychoanalysis, Literature, and the Human Sciences." *Science in Context* 18, no. 4 (2005): 649–69.

Suzuki Sadami. *Modan toshi no hyōgen: Jiko, gensō, josei* [Expressions of the modern city: Self, fantasy, woman]. Kyoto: Shirojisha, 1992.

Suzuki, Tomi. *Narrating the Self: Fictions of Japanese Modernity*. Stanford, Calif.: Stanford University Press, 1997.

Sweeney, Susan Elizabeth. "Locked Rooms: Detective Fiction, Narrative Theory, and Self-Reflexivity." In *The Cunning Craft: Original Essays on Detective Fiction and Contemporary Literary Theory*, 1–14. Macomb: Western Illinois University Press, 1990.

Tadiar, Neferti Xina M. *Fantasy-Production: Sexual Economies and Other Philippine Consequences for the New World Order*. Hong Kong: Hong Kong University Press, 2004.

Takahashi Seori. *Kankaku no modan: Sakutarō, Jun'ichirō, Kenji, Ranpo* [Sensation's modernity: Sakutarō, Jun'ichirō, Kenji, Ranpo]. Tokyo: Serika Shobō, 2003.

Takeda Nobuaki. "Yonin no Aoki Aisaburō: Bunshin no 'namae' [Four Aoki Aisaburōs: 'Name' as double]." *Gunzō* 48, no. 11 (1993): 266–82.

Taketomo Yasuhiko. "Cultural Adaptation to Psychoanalysis in Japan, 1912–1952." *Social Research* 57, no. 4 (1990): 951–92.

Tanaka, Stefan. *Japan's Orient: Rendering Pasts into History*. Berkeley: University of California Press, 1993.

Tanizaki Jun'ichirō. *In Praise of Shadows* [*In'ei raisan*]. Translated by Thomas J. Harper and Edward Seidensticker. New Haven: Leete's Island Books, 1977.

———. "Jinmenso [The Tumor with a Human Face]." In *Tanizaki Jun'ichirō zenshū* 5 [The complete works of Tanizaki Jun'ichirō 5], 281–305. Tokyo: Chūō kōronsha, 1966.

———. *Kōjin* [Sirens]. In *Tanizaki Jun'ichirō zenshū* 7 [The complete works of Tanizaki Jun'ichirō 7], 27–212. Tokyo: Chūō kōronsha, 1966.

———. "Shina shumi to iu koto [On the fetish for Chinese things]." In *Tanizaki Jun'ichirō zenshū* 22 [The complete works of Tanizaki Jun'ichirō 22], 121–23. Tokyo: Chūō kōronsha, 1966.

———. "Tomoda to Matsunaga no hanashi [The story of Tomoda and Matsunaga]." In *Tanizaki Jun'ichirō zenshū* 10 [The complete works of Tanizaki Jun'ichirō 10], 409–93. Tokyo: Chūō kōronsha, 1966.

Thomas, Ronald H. "Fingerprint of the Foreigner: Colonizing the Criminal Body in 1890s Detective Fiction and Criminal Anthropology." *ELH: A Journal of English Literary History* 61, no. 3 (1994): 655–83.

Thompson, Jon. *Fiction, Crime, and Empire: Clues to Modernity and Postmodernism*. Urbana: University of Illinois Press, 1993.

Tierney, Robert Thomas. *Tropics of Savagery: The Culture of Japanese Empire in Comparative Frame*. Berkeley: University of California Press, 2010.

Todorov, Tzvetan. *The Fantastic: A Structural Approach to a Literary Genre*. Ithaca, N.Y.: Cornell University Press, 1975.

———. "The Typology of Detective Fiction." In *The Poetics of Prose*, 42–52. Ithaca, N.Y.: Cornell University Press, 1977.

Tsutsui, William M. "Oh No, There Goes Tokyo: Recreational Apocalypse and the City in Postwar Japanese Culture." In *Noir Urbanisms: Dystopic Images of the Modern City*, edited by Gyan Prakash, 104–26. Princeton, N.J.: Princeton University Press, 2010.

Tymms, Ralph. *Doubles in Literary Psychology*. Cambridge: Bowes and Bowes, 1949.

Ubukata Tomoko. "'Tantei shōsetsu' izen: Satō Haruo 'Shimon' ni okeru nazotoki no wakugumi [Before 'detective' fiction: The framework of mystery in Satō Haruo's 'The Fingerprint']." *Nihon Kindai Bungaku* 74 (May 2006): 168–81.

Wada-Marciano, Mitsuyo. "J-Horror: New Media's Impact on Contemporary Japanese Horror Cinema." In *Horror to the Extreme: Changing Boundaries in Asian*

Cinema, edited by Mitsuyo Wada-Marciano and Jinhee Choi, 15–38. Hong Kong: Hong Kong University Press, 2009.

———. *Nippon Modern: Japanese Cinema of the 1920s and 1930s*. Honolulu: University of Hawai'i Press, 2008.

Watanabe Masahiko. *Kindai bungaku no bunshinzō* [The image of the double in modern literature]. Tokyo: Kadokawa Sensho, 1999.

Webber, Andrew J. *The Doppelgänger: Double Visions in German Literature*. Oxford: Oxford University Press, 1996.

Williams, Raymond. *The Politics of Modernism*. London: Verso, 1989.

Yamashita Takeshi. *20-seiki nihon kai'i bungaku shi: Dopperugengā bungakukō* [Catalog of 20th-century Japanese uncanny literature: The literary doppelgänger]. Tokyo: Yūraku Shuppansha., 2003.

Yoda, Tomiko. "A Roadmap to Millennial Japan." In *Japan After Japan: Social and Cultural Life from the Recessionary 1990s to the Present*, edited by Tomiko Yoda and Harry Harootunian, 16–53. Durham, N.C.: Duke University Press, 2006.

Zarrow, Peter. *China in War and Revolution, 1895–1949*. London: Routledge, 2005.

Žižek, Slavoj. "The Detective and the Analyst." *Literature and Psychology* 27, no. 4 (1990): 27–46.

———. *The Fright of Real Tears: Krzysztof Kieślowski between Theory and Post-Theory*. London: BFI, 2001.

———. "The Spectre of Ideology." In *The Žižek Reader*, edited by Elizabeth Wright and Edmond Wright, 53–86. Oxford: Blackwell, 1999.

———. *Violence*. London: Profile, 2008.

INDEX

Abe Kōbō, 4, 178; *The Box Man*, 124;
The Ruined Map, 124
accumulation: capital, 116, 117, 192,
221n50; colonial, 50, 156; flexible,
156–57, 189
adaptations: of films, 19, 91–92, 126,
127–35, 143–54; as intertextual
doppelgänger, 133, 143
Akira (animation), 222n1
Akutagawa Ryūnosuke, 4; "Asakusa
Park," 93; doppelgänger in, 18–19, 41,
91, 101–12, 120, 194, 215n32, 216n41;
"San Sebastian," 93; "The Shadow,"
19, 92–93, 105–12, 113–14, 117–22,
216n34, 216n46; "Spinning Gears,"
19, 93, 103–5; "Two Letters," 19, 93,
101–3, 105, 121, 215n34, 216n41;
"Unrequited Love," 92
alienation, 14–15, 44; visual, 117–18,
120, 121
allegory: of cinematic spectatorship,
110, 120; doppelgänger, 77, 93–96,
101, 114, 127; historical, 186, 187;
national, 190–91; spatial, 216n46
alter-egos, 2, 33, 124, 125. *See also* ego,
the; ego-ideal

alterity, 1, 14, 87, 185, 191; temporal, 148,
195. *See also* other, the
Anderson, Benedict, 65
animation, 125, 130, 222n1; anime, 5,
218n9
anthropology, 59, 210n12. *See also*
ethnography
apocalypse, representations of, 164–65,
167, 168, 194, 222n1
Ariuchi Yoshihiro, 203n3
Asahara Shōkō, 168
Asakusa district (Tokyo), 75–76, 77, 116
assimilation, 61–62, 155, 210n13;
Western, 24, 65, 76, 79, 224n40
Aum Shinrikyō, 164–65, 167, 168, 222n4

Bal, Mieke, 160
Bálàzs, Béla, 111
Balibar, Etienne, 210n13
Barrymore, John, 207n20
Barthes, Roland, 220n29
Baudrillard, Jean, 93–94, 114
Bazerman, Charles, 167
Beller, Jonathan, 114–15, 120, 192
Benjamin, Walter, 48, 93, 100, 111
Bertillon system, 43

BARYON TENSOR POSADAS is assistant professor of Asian languages and literatures at the University of Minnesota.

CPSIA information can be obtained
at www.ICGtesting.com
Printed in the USA
BVHW01s2034230218
508993BV00010B/32/P